PENGUIN CLASSICS

PENSÉES

Blaise Pascal was born in Clermont in 1623, the son of a government official. During his short life he left his mark on mathematics, physics, religious controversy and literature. A convert to Jansenism, he engaged with gusto in a controversy with the Jesuits, which gave rise to his *Lettres Provinciales* on which, with the *Pensées*, his literary fame chiefly rests. A remarkable stylist, he is regarded by many as the greatest of French prose artists. He died, after a long illness, in 1662.

Dr A. J. Krailsheimer was born in 1921 and has been Tutor in French at Christ Church, Oxford, since 1957. His publications are *Studies in Self-Interest* (1963), *Rabelais and the Franciscans* (1965), *Three Conteurs of the Sixteenth Century* (1966), *Rabelais* (1967), and *A. J. de Rancé, Abbot of La Trappe* (1974). He has translated Flaubert's *Bouvard and Pécuchet* and *Salammbo* and Pascal's *Lettres Provinciales* for the Penguin Classics as well as the *Pensées* and edited one volume of the Pelican Guide to European Literature, *The Continental Renaissance 1500–1600*.

PASCAL
PENSÉES

Translated with an Introduction by
A. J. Krailsheimer

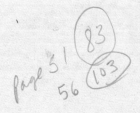

PENGUIN BOOKS

PENGUIN BOOKS

Published by the Penguin Group
27 Wrights Lane, London W8 5TZ, England
Viking Penguin Inc., 40 West 23rd Street, New York, New York 10010, USA
Penguin Books Australia Ltd, Ringwood, Victoria, Australia
Penguin Books Canada Ltd, 2801 John Street, Markham, Ontario, Canada L3R 1B4
Penguin Books (NZ) Ltd, 182–190 Wairau Road, Auckland 10, New Zealand

Penguin Books Ltd, Registered Offices: Harmondsworth, Middlesex, England

This translation first published 1966
19 20

Printed and bound in Great Britain by
Cox & Wyman Ltd, Reading
Set in Monotype Bembo

CONTENTS

Section Two: *Papers not classified by Pascal* (Translator's Titles)

NOTE: Except for the Old Testament series and XXI–XXII these titles are only a rough indication of the main contents of each series.

CONTENTS

Section Three: *Miracles*

Section Four: *Fragments not found in the Copy*

INTRODUCTION

I

Pascal's reputation today does not correspond very closely with the contents of the single volume which quite comfortably contains his collected works. In the first place, something like half the total bulk is occupied by writings on a wide range of mathematical, scientific and even technological subjects. His work on probability is still recognized as being of fundamental importance for the development of a then almost unsuspected science, and his experiments in connexion with the vacuum and atmospheric pressure, though anticipated by those of Torricelli, still represent a model of clear thinking and methodical organization. He designed and superintended the construction of a calculating machine which, whatever its faults, actually worked, and the omnibus service, the *carosses à cinq sols*, which he devised and inaugurated at the end of his short life further illustrates his extraordinary genius, combining in rare degree inventive and practical powers. It was to these activities, and to personal qualities to which numerous contemporaries bear witness, that Pascal owed such fame as he enjoyed at the time of his death in 1662. Such diverse characters as Mitton and Méré, worldly socialites, Fermat and Descartes, leading mathematicians, Arnauld, Nicole and many others at Port Royal, even Christina of Sweden and Christopher Wren, are among his friends or correspondents. Yet it is not for these things that he is now remembered three hundred years later. Modern scientists have their eyes too firmly fixed on the future to spare more than a passing thought for so notable a pioneer of scientific method, manufacturers of computers and directors of public transport services might properly regard Pascal as their patron saint, or at least founding-father, but there can be few who pay him pious homage even on anniversaries.[1] And yet today he ranks among the world's most constant best-sellers, and his recent tercentenary only stimulated interest that was already lively.

The reason for this paradox lies in the second half of his collected

1. A Paris transport undertaking is said to have commemorated him some years ago.

works, where history has played tricks even more ironic than those of whatever muse rules over that other, scientific, culture. By 1662 it was a more or less open secret, at least among the wider circle of those sympathetic to Port Royal, that the anonymous *Provincial Letters* were by Pascal. In France at any rate, and perhaps absolutely, no work of immediate polemical relevance has ever had so resounding and lasting a success, while remaining a work of literature in its own right. Interest or competence in theology and casuistry is much rarer today than in 1656–7, when the *Letters* made their initial impact, but the brilliance of the performance has excited the admiration of readers from the Cardinal de Retz and Mme de Sévigné in Pascal's own time, to Voltaire, Sainte-Beuve and even Jesuits of later ages. The *Letters* alone would guarantee Pascal an honourable place in the literary history of a century richly distinguished in prose-writers, but outside France this would not be enough to make him a best-seller. For this we must turn to the final quarter of his collected works, to the *Pensées*.

The critical problems posed by the *Pensées* may not be insuperable, though there are black days when it seems that they must be, but it is certainly premature to claim that they have all been solved. The crowning irony of the many concerning Pascal and his work is that the tercentenary edition currently being produced by M. Jean Mesnard comes closer to the author's own thoughts and intentions than any that has yet been published. A blend of piety and prudence prevented his literary executors from being completely frank and full, prejudice and polemic coloured the reception of earlier versions of the *Pensées* and inadequate critical principles impaired later editions. Only now, when much original material has gone for ever, can a reader feel reasonably confident that he has before him the documents necessary for forming his own judgement. The mere fact of survival in the face of such adverse conditions speaks for itself.

The very title invites misunderstanding: if one mentions 'Pascal the thinker', the image of some Rodin-like figure, every nerve bent to solve the agonizing riddle of an oppressive existence, may spring un-bidden to mind, or one may expect yet another purveyor of aphorisms and sententiae, telling us with elegance or pomposity what human behaviour amounts to. Worst of all, one may envisage the all too familiar Angst-ridden intellectual making a drama out of disquiet, which vigorous cabbage-planting or childlike faith, according to taste, would dispel. In a way the *Pensées* are all that, but so much more besides that no description can be a substitute for reading and re-reading them. Pascal is by no means a one-work celebrity, but the *Pensées* at once crown and illuminate the rest of his life and work. Moreover, in their extant form they tell us more about Pascal than we could ever have known if he had lived long enough to tidy up his papers.

2

Attempts are still made to 'explain' Pascal and the *Pensées* in terms of his heredity, class-background and even physiology, and, lamentably as these have failed, there are indisputably some grounds for beginning with what is objectively verifiable. Born on 19 June 1623, Pascal lost his mother when he was only three, and was brought up with his two sisters, Gilberte and Jacqueline, entirely by his father, Étienne Pascal, a legal officer of substance at Clermont (now Clermont-Ferrand). In 1631 Étienne Pascal left Auvergne and installed his family in Paris, where he directed Blaise's education himself, setting high standards and demonstrating clear principles to such effect that the twelve-year-old boy is reported to have discovered for himself the first thirty-two propositions of Euclid. The family stayed in Paris until 1640, when Étienne, reconciled with Richelieu after a bold but imprudent protest against the financial policy of the government, was appointed Commissioner for Taxes in Upper Normandy and moved to Rouen.

These early years undoubtedly left their mark on Blaise. Deprived from an early age of a mother's care, he was always of sickly constitution and, moreover, an only son between an older and a younger sister. He was inevitably given extra, perhaps excessive, consideration, and his precocious intelligence can only have increased his individualism. At the same time, this unusual family situation seems to have aroused in him an attitude to human affection which came out in later life with such reactions as his censure of Gilberte, by then married to her cousin Florin Périer, for exchanging caresses with her children. He found such visible marks of affection not only distasteful, but morally wrong; the basis for such a judgement may be surmised from certain of the *Pensées* (e.g. 396).

His education, too, could not fail to produce a marked effect on his character, lasting throughout his life. While his father's direct supervision enabled him to make rapid, even spectacular progress and encouraged the highest degree of independent judgement based on sound principles, his isolation from boys of his own age and from the society and discipline of school life may have protected him from psychological, and physical, discomfort, but allowed him to have his own way too much in formative years. To his father's enthusiasm for mathematics, and to many intellectually distinguished friends, Blaise certainly owed a great deal, and perhaps even more to the humane and enlightened methods of a widower who could so easily have become an authoritarian crank.

1640 was what may be called a seminal year in the history of French Catholicism as of the Pascal family. In that year Blaise published his first mathematical work, an essay on conic sections, and the *Augustinus* of Cornelius Jansenius, Bishop of Ypres, came out, two years after its author's death. The connexion between Pascal's mathematical début and the book which provoked the bitter struggle between Port Royal and its enemies (the Jesuits were coincidentally celebrating their own first centenary that year) must seem wholly fortuitous (or perhaps providential), and yet the *Pensées* directly link the two publications. It was through his reputation as a scientist and mathematician that Pascal's abilities became recognized, and it was the adoption of Jansenius's views by Port Royal and its friends which led Pascal into their orbit and then made him their spokesman.

The next few years saw Pascal's invention of the calculating machine and his series of experiments on the vacuum and atmospheric pressure. Meanwhile Jansenius's collaborator, Jean Duvergier de Hauranne (known as the abbé Saint-Cyran from the abbey of which he was commendatory abbot), had died in 1643, after several years in prison, the result as much of political as of religious disagreement with Richelieu, and the theologian Antoine Arnauld had come to the defence of the *Augustinus*, which had soon aroused strong opposition. It is one of the many ironies in the history of Jansenism that neither the eponymous Bishop of Ypres, as obscure in his life as he was prominent after his death, nor Saint-Cyran, who shared in the formulation of his doctrine and was almost entirely responsible for transmitting it as the driving force for a close-knit body of believers, lived to explain the obscurer implications of their teaching, let alone to see the results it had in the Church.

In 1646 the repercussions of Saint-Cyran's work at last reached the Pascal family, and henceforth their fortunes became ever more closely linked with those of Jansenism and Port Royal. As a result of a fall, Étienne Pascal made the acquaintance of two pious gentlemen, with some skill as bonesetters, who in their turn brought the family into contact with a neighbouring priest, M. Guillebert, vicar of Rouville, one of Saint-Cyran's converts. One must be careful in using the word 'conversion' not to over-emphasize the enlightenment which followed the experience at the expense of the condition which preceded it. It seems that the Pascals were good, conventional Catholics, performing their duties with regularity, if not with fervour, but keeping their daily life and their faith in separate compartments. Their introduction to Saint-Cyran's ideas, especially on grace, made them enthusiastic Christians, regarding worldly pre-occupations as irrelevant, and even inimical, to salvation. Jacqueline even more than Blaise seems permanently to have changed the whole course of her life as a consequence of this experience.

For Blaise, the immediate fruit of intensified piety was his participation in a theological dispute, in which he helped to secure the condemnation of one Jacques Forton, sieur de Saint-Ange, an ex-friar, for opinions of a rationalistic, but somewhat eccentric, nature concerning the faith. His scientific researches, however, continued unabated, and began to involve him in controversy, among others with a Jesuit, Père Noël, and with Descartes, whom he met briefly on two occasions during an illness in 1647. The family had left Rouen and settled again in Paris when Étienne died there in 1651. The following year, no longer inhibited by paternal opposition, Jacqueline entered Port Royal as a nun. The undignified financial wrangles provoked by this act are symptomatic of a particularly unhappy period of Pascal's life, when he found himself within a few months irrevocably separated from both his father and his favourite sister, and thrown for the first time on his own resources. This phase ended with what Pascal himself, and everyone since, has recognized as the most decisive event of his life.

He had become internationally famous for his scientific work, he had many friends in aristocratic society, especially the young duc de

Roannez and his sister Charlotte, and Jacqueline's religious vocation had deeply disturbed the pattern of his life. His so-called worldly period was, from all accounts, far short of profligacy, but pride, selfishness, and materialism apparently played a more prominent part in his life than was consistent with the faith renewed by the events of 1646. It must also be remembered that ill-health caused him real and frequent suffering. In this confused state he suddenly had a personal revelation which brought about what can only be called total conversion. On 23 November 1654 he saw the light that guided him for the rest of his life, setting down his account in the *Memorial* (913), a scrap of paper, later copied on to parchment, which he always thereafter carried on his person. The 'hidden God', with whom some critics have made such play, was manifested that night to Pascal in the person of Jesus Christ. Whatever his doubts may have been, they were dispelled by this direct contact with God in the only form in which he henceforth sought him, and sought to communicate him to others. The witness of the two Testaments, the Passion of Christ, and Pascal's personal obligations as a Christian are the three elements of a definitive realization of the truth, which brought him at last to certainty and joy.

A few weeks later he translated this experience into action, and made a retreat, first near and then at Port Royal des Champs, where the community of male solitaries had taken over when the nuns moved to Port Royal de Paris. It must be emphasized that neither then, nor at any other time, was Pascal one of the 'Messieurs de Port Royal', and he was never for more than a week or so at a time even resident there. It is true, of course, that his spiritual director, M. Singlin, and his sister, as well as other members of Port Royal, like Arnauld and Nicole, regarded him from now on as an active ally, rather than a mere well-wisher, but on the doctrinal plane Pascal was never wholly at one with his Jansenist friends, who were, indeed, divided amongst themselves.

Just a year after this first retreat, in January 1656, Pascal showed the world just how active an ally he had become. In the sixteen years since the publication of the *Augustinus* attitudes had hardened and ranks had closed. The enormous Arnauld family, especially Antoine and the Mères Angélique and Agnès at Port Royal, were conspicuous defenders of the teaching and way of life entrusted to them by Saint-

Cyran, while certain elements at the Sorbonne, and soon the Jesuits in a body, constituted an ever more impatient opposition. In 1649 seven propositions (reduced next year to five) were allegedly extracted from the *Augustinus* and submitted to the Sorbonne, and then to the Pope, with a request for censure, but Pope Innocent IV showed no disposition to act with undue haste, and it was only by stages that he was finally induced, in 1654, to condemn not only the Five Propositions (by now capitalized and made into a shibboleth) but to say explicitly that he was condemning Jansenius's doctrine. Arnauld continued to protest that the Propositions were, indeed, heretical, but not, as the latest papal pronouncement dogmatically asserted, either textually or implicitly in *Augustinus*. His enemies were by now anxious to put an end once and for all to resistance, and at the end of 1655 Arnauld was put on trial by the theologians of the Sorbonne, inevitably incurring the censure of a majority, of whom many had been either tricked or otherwise persuaded by the Jesuits. Behind all the technical arguments concerning grace, the crucial point was that of fact (*de fait*), whether the Five Propositions were really in Jansenius's work, not of right (*de droit*), whether the Pope had the right to condemn them as heretical, and this distinction remained the last ditch in which Arnauld and his supporters were finally overwhelmed.

It was precisely at this juncture, when all seemed lost, that Pascal was making another retreat at Port Royal des Champs, and was begged by his friends to do something. Only a few days elapsed before the first of the *Letters written to a friend in the provinces*, the *Provincial Letters*, appeared. From then until March of the following year eighteen *Letters* came out one after another, in conditions of the greatest secrecy and real danger, giving a running commentary on events and provoking fury or delight, but never indifference, in those who read them.

Things went at first very badly for the Jansenists: Arnauld was expelled from the Sorbonne (at that time the Faculty of Theology and not, as now, the whole University of Paris), the *Petites Écoles* (of which Racine was the most illustrious alumnus) were closed, and the solitaries dispersed. On 25 March the tide seemed momentarily to turn. Pascal's niece, Marguerite Périer, was suddenly cured of a fistula, which she had had in her eye for more than three years, when a relic of the Holy Thorn, kept by the nuns of Port Royal, was applied to the spot. While continuing the *Letters* (from the eleventh addressed directly to the Jesuits, and not to the provincial friend), Pascal began to collect material for a work on miracles (Section III of this translation) and, it seems, for what was later planned as the *Apology for the Christian Religion*. Unfortunately, while the miracle, authenticated by both medical and ecclesiastical authorities, encouraged the friends of Port Royal and while the Jesuits were smarting under Pascal's flagellation of their laxism and casuistry, the temper of Louis XIV and the higher clergy was not sympathetic to acts of insubordination, prompted by whatever motives. It is also relevant that the royal confessor was a Jesuit. The controversy dragged on, causing ever deeper divisions and involving ever wider circles among clergy and laity, Paris and the provinces. Even when the *Provincial Letters* came to an abrupt end (a nineteenth *Letter* breaks off after a few sentences), Pascal continued the struggle both in writings of his own and in helping to draft various declarations by bodies of the clergy. He somehow managed to combine with this intense polemical activity new work, of the most sophisticated kind, on the mathematical problem of the cycloid, in connexion with which he wrote letters to Christopher Wren and Christian Huyghens among others. Above all he composed the greater part of what we now know as the *Pensées*. By 1658 his work on the *Apology* was far enough advanced for him to give his friends at Port Royal an address (or perhaps more than one) on his proposed method and main arguments.

In 1659 his chronic ill-health, perhaps of tubercular or cancerous origin, had finally reached a state which made it virtually impossible for him to concentrate for long on any serious work. With a person of Pascal's unique gifts, idleness and inability to work are, of course, relative terms, and he continued whenever he felt strong enough to write, or dictate, what he could. Perhaps a quarter of the *Pensées* belong to this last period, as well as some *Reflections on the condition of the great* and considerable correspondence on a wide range of topics. It was, for example, only in March 1662 that his omnibus service was inaugurated, and by that time he was a very sick man indeed.

The last two years of his life were overshadowed not only by sickness but also by the final stages of the Jansenist struggle, by now directed mercilessly at the community of which his sister was one of the most intransigent members. The point at issue still remained

submission on the question of fact, but formulated in ever more un-
ambiguous terms. One expedient after another was tried to enable
the nuns to satisfy both the demands of their own consciences and
those of ecclesiastical obedience. At length no alternative was left but
unconditional surrender. Jacqueline died, it is said of a broken heart,
in October 1661, and at the end of November the community capitu-
lated, signing the latest and most explicit of the formularies succes-
sively put before them.

The death of his sister and the failure, as he saw it, of the nuns and
their advisers to defend their cause to the bitter end occasioned Pascal
the cruellest spiritual anguish. Convinced as he was that the Jesuits
were truly forces of evil, and that the simple, theologically inexpert
nuns were the remnant of the faithful few, he could not easily reconcile his duty as a Catholic to obey with his duty as a Christian to
follow the truth even unto death. While he remained implacably
hostile to his enemies, he was by now, at least for a time, estranged
from many of his friends. In June 1662 he moved in with his sister
Gilberte in a state of extreme physical and mental weakness. The last
weeks of his life were attended by Père Beurrier, the parish-priest of
St Étienne du Mont (next to the Panthéon), to whom he confided his
views on the religious conflicts in which he had been so deeply
involved. There is much debate as to the exact significance and value
of Beurrier's testimony, but the basic facts are not in dispute: realizing
that continued membership of the Catholic Church was incompatible
with disobedience to the most formal orders of the Pope and hierarchy, Pascal submitted unconditionally and recognized himself incompetent to pronounce unilaterally on matters of faith, at the same
time remaining to the end on the most friendly terms with Arnauld,
Nicole and others, whose willingness to compromise had so upset
him a year before.

The record of his last days is a melancholy and terrible one. The
gruesome attentions of doctors as ingenious in devising treatment as
they were obtuse in diagnosis, the extraordinary obstinacy of his
friends and doctors in withholding from him until it was almost too
late the consolation of the sacrament, for which he longed, the ghastly
autopsy inspired by curiosity and callousness, all makes a distressing
tale. Robbed of serenity and dignity, too sordid in its details for
a shining example of heroic martyrdom, Pascal's death agony

represents the slow corruption of the flesh, poisoning even the mind until little is left to snatch away. His spirit, however, rallied at the last, and he died on 19 August 1662, lucid and happy to be finally united with his Saviour. Two days later he was buried at St Étienne du Mont, where a tablet to his memory today looks across at one commemorating Racine.

3

His imperishable monument lives on in the *Pensées*, and every reader who finds them impressive on the printed page should try to see what the original manuscript looked like. The superb photographic reproduction issued for his tercentenary is a deeply moving document, showing the feverish haste with which fragments were written down before the thought could slip away, the alterations and erasures, the very disposition of many of the fragments in the form of poetry rather than prose, and throughout the dynamic and impetuous flow of the handwriting of a genius. It is only through a series of extraordinary, almost miraculous, chances that we have this priceless collection of autograph material, enabling us to know more about Pascal than about almost any other great writer of so long ago.

It is possible, because it has been done, to look only at those elements of the *Pensées* which were intended for the *Apology*, but apart from uncertainty as to what goes where, this method has the disadvantage of presenting in unfinished form a book Pascal never wrote. A method more widely favoured today is to take the papers as Pascal can be shown to have left them, and concentrate on his preoccupations and chains of thought rather than attempt to reconstruct fragments of conjectural works.

The non-specialist reader may well regard the whole question of edition and textual arrangement as none of his business, but the *Pensées* present an intractable problem which it would be simply fraudulent to disguise. In its essentials, what is here translated is what his literary executors found and had copied (in duplicate). It is from the master-copy that the basis for an order can be deduced, and from the original papers, mostly still surviving, but only collected into the volume of the *Recueil Original* much later, that the correct reading can be established.

Pascal worked on large sheets of paper (although, like anyone else, he sometimes jotted down notes on whatever scrap he had by him), writing down his thoughts on various subjects as they occurred to him, with each one, long or short, separated clearly by a line from the next, and sometimes using the length rather than the breadth of the paper. At some time before 1659 he began systematically to classify all the work he had so far done towards his *Apology*. To that end he cut up each sheet into its component *pensées*, arranging them under twenty-eight headings (one remained in fact unused) and fastening the fragments within each bundle (*liasse*) by threading string through them (the marks can still be seen on the original papers). He presumably had to abandon this work of classification as a result of increasing illness about 1659, and consequently only fragments 1–382 were filed. There remained fragments 383–829 in thirty-one series, some of which are homogeneous enough to suggest a partial preliminary classification, but containing a certain amount of material obviously never intended for the *Apology* (e.g. drafts for the *Provincial Letters*), and three more series of eighty-three fragments (830–912), entitled 'Miracles', but including a few on other topics. The *Copy* ended there, except that five fragments were for some reason put only into the second copy. There are in addition fifty-six original papers omitted from both copies (913–69), for the most part notes of a private nature or drafts for the *Provincial Letters* or other polemical works, and a still growing number of fragments of certain authenticity but preserved neither in the *Copy* nor in the *Recueil Original*.

What we possess, therefore, is at once a good deal more and a good deal less than the draft of the *Apology*: more, because, apart from a fair amount of extraneous matter, the *Copy* includes much raw material (e.g. Biblical texts) awaiting treatment, successive versions of many fragments, and numerous notes made by Pascal to remind himself how to proceed, all of which gives us a precious insight into the development of his thought and style; less, because a great part of what Pascal left had never been worked out, let alone written up, many of the briefer fragments are not only cryptic, but quite incomprehensible until laborious scholarship can restore them to their context, and a certain number, for linguistic reasons, just do not make sense. The twenty-eight headings of the first part certainly represent Pascal's intentions up to the moment when he had to give up the work, but the chapters of the final draft, if he had ever written it, would certainly not all have had these titles (e.g. XI, 'At Port Royal', referring to the address he gave there), or even perhaps have been twenty-eight in number, though it is likely that much the same order would have been followed. It is reasonable to suppose that such long and carefully corrected fragments as Disproportion (199) or Diversion (136) are in something like final form, and this must be equally true of such unclassified fragments as the 'Wager' (418) or the long attack on unbelievers (427), but no one can be quite sure what would have been put in or left out, or put to some other purpose, for the very good reason that Pascal himself never knew for certain. Indeed, it is not even possible to hazard a guess at how long the completed *Apology* would have been.

It is not only more sensible, but infinitely more rewarding to turn from wistful thoughts of what never was and perverse ingenuity about what might have been, to what actually is: the principal recorded and surviving thoughts of Pascal on religion and kindred subjects.

It must be remembered that events forced Pascal into writing the *Provincial Letters*, which are a consequence of his *nuit de feu* only in so far as they represent in general his uncompromising commitment to Christian truth and in particular the closer relations with Port Royal promoted by the experience. The *Pensées* are a far more direct attempt to communicate to others what had been vouchsafed to him, but they are at the same time not exempt from the theological distortions inseparable from controversy. The libertines with whose conversion Pascal was concerned might be diverted by seeing the Jesuits so discomfited, the heretics might congratulate themselves on remaining outside an institution as corrupt and divided as the Catholic Church seemed to be, but it can hardly be claimed that the wider interests of Christianity or even of the Church were served by the mutual recriminations of Jesuits and Jansenists, as Pascal himself recognized. The *Pensées* do not retract the *Provincial Letters*, and in some important ways they illuminate them, but their aim is much more positive and universal: to bring men to God, through Christ, in the Catholic Church. They are not a Jansenist tract, but, as might be expected, show unmistakable marks of the Augustinian influence common to most rigorists and reformers, inside and outside the Catholic Church.

The pattern, not only of the *Pensées*, but of all Pascal's religious writing, is the stark contrast between man in his state of fallen nature and in a state of grace. The doctrine characteristic of Augustinians in general, and of Jansenists in particular, was that human nature was so corrupted by the Fall that only the direct intervention of God's grace, mediated by the redeeming power of Christ, could enable man to do good and be saved. This grace could never be earned, and man could never put God under an obligation to save him, but man could try to remove some of the chief obstacles to grace and thus create in himself a disposition more favourable to its reception. Jansenists had a strong sense of election, and tended to dwell on the smallness of the number to be saved, at the same time seeing in worldliness presumptive evidence of grace withheld. They were also characterized by a certain austerity and puritanism, reacting against prevalent casualness by a rigid attitude to the sacraments, and laying much stress on the necessity for constant effort and vigilance lest grace should be forfeited. Their enemies accused them of being Calvinists, but neither in their views on Predestination nor, above all, on the Church can this charge be substantiated. As an ally of Port Royal, holding and practising the sort of Christianity just described, Pascal may be called a Jansenist, but such a label is not very helpful, and, in the light of the very restrictive sense subsequently acquired by the word, may be grossly misleading.

The two poles of Pascal's argument are concisely defined at the beginning: 'Wretchedness of man without God / Happiness of man with God / otherwise / Nature is corrupt, proved by nature itself / There is a Redeemer, proved by Scripture' (6). The recognizably Augustinian emphasis on the corruption of nature is here inseparable from the promised cure. There can be no doubt that the section which retains its interest today is the first, so much so, indeed, that the arguments concerning Scripture in the second part are often not only ignored but even excused. Narcissism is deep-rooted in human nature, and there is nothing strange in modern readers preferring to indulge psychological hypochondria as well rather than examine the remedy prescribed by Pascal. Biblical exegesis has now developed too far for the second part of Pascal's work to be effectively salvaged, but it can at least be claimed that the Christianity which the *Pensées* offer to the unbeliever is complete; there is no escape-clause in small print to be revealed only after the contract is signed.

In the opening sections of his argument Pascal gradually reveals to his interlocutor (for this is a dialogue, or correspondence, rather than a treatise) the truth about himself. He is addressing a person well versed in the social graces, familiar with the world of the great and its pastimes, such as hunting, gambling, dancing, and tennis, sufficiently informed about the discoveries of contemporary science to recognize references to worlds revealed by telescope and microscope, anxious for popularity and approval, a critic of style and fashion, priding himself on being a hardheaded rationalist, for whom two and two make four, and laughing at pretentions that reason cannot sustain. This is not the honest doubter (though this is what Pascal tries to make him), but nor is it the hardened sinner; by worldly standards the cultured devotee of self-interest, ruled by pride, may be offending neither the law of the land nor even social convention. Much of Pascal's initial argument is, however, designed to make him see that he is harming himself, let alone breaking the law of a God whose existence is yet to be proved. The so-called libertines were motivated not so much by hostility as by indifference with regard to religion, and only by piercing their carapace of complacency can Pascal touch the vital organ, the heart. For the whole concept of the defence of Christianity is based both on the contrast already mentioned between the state of nature and that of grace, and also on Pascal's theory of the three orders.

This concept stemmed originally from mathematics, and Pascal had made use of it in other contexts before he ever applied it to religion. Just as lines, squares and cubes (or x, x^2, and x^3) cannot be added together as being of different orders, so in the realm of human knowledge that which is proper to the body (the senses), to the mind (the reason), and to the heart are of different orders and must be carefully distinguished if error is to be avoided. The heart, in Pascal's scheme, is the appropriate channel for intuitive knowledge, for apprehending pre-rational first principles and assenting to supra-rational propositions, as well as for emotional and aesthetic experiences. A text indispensable to an understanding of what Pascal meant is 110. In the sphere of religion the heart is the seat and recipient of charity, and only in this connexion is it correct to speak of it as a superior faculty, for in all natural affairs each of these three orders has a part to play, which is invalidated by application of an inappropriate order.

To take an early example, Descartes claimed to prove by pure reason that a vacuum could not exist in nature, thus supporting a cherished belief of Aristotelian (and Scholastic) philosophers, who based their faith on the authority of the great man and the tradition of centuries rather than on reason. For Pascal, a physical phenomenon is properly examined by physical means, that is the evidence of the senses, reading what the instruments actually record. Once the facts have been established, it is, of course, for reason to analyse and codify them, just as it is right for reason to formulate hypotheses for the senses to test experimentally. In neither case can the heart play a decisive role. Clearly in supernatural matters the senses are incompetent and it is only the arrogant delusion of men which attributes the last word to reason.

Pascal is thus in the paradoxical position of appealing to reason in order to communicate truths which, on his own showing, are outside its province. He is not, as has been sometimes claimed, trying to strike one spark of charity out of the great mass of rational arguments advanced. A better analogy would be that of the well; only when the drill has penetrated to a sufficient depth does the crust of reason and habit become thin enough for the flow of divine grace at last to break through. Pascal is no alchemist, transmuting elements, but a prospector, blasting away massive obstacles to reveal hidden treasure. The paradox is that only reason can persuade reason of its own inadequacy.

Pascal systematically eliminates the props with which man sustains himself in his illusions. Cherished values are shown to be purely imaginary, arbitrary concessions to the convenience or prejudice of the moment. Human relations and institutions are inconsistent, supposedly natural instincts can be completely changed, and habit plays so dominant a part in our lives that it can truly be called a second nature (126). Reason itself can work only from the raw material supplied by instinct or senses, for which no guarantee exists. Everything is inconstant, relative, uncertain. Much of this development is inspired by Montaigne, to whom Pascal is heavily indebted not only for examples but even for turns of phrase.

Defining the human condition as 'inconstancy, boredom, anxiety' (24), Pascal devotes the whole section on Diversion to showing how man tries to keep boredom, and with it anxiety, at bay. So long as he does not have to think, he may yet live out his days anaesthetized by activity, meaningless in itself, but strenuous enough to absorb his energies. Philosophers, searching for the sovereign good, have been no more successful than the ordinary man, whose only goal is happiness. From this Pascal argues that, wretched as he truly is, man would not so frantically pursue elusive happiness unless somewhere within him there remained a glimmer of past felicity. The impasse lies within man: only imperfection can be found in an imperfect being, and, until man looks outside himself for his goal, his problem can never be resolved. Quite simply, man must listen to God. Incredible as it may appear to so demoralized and puny a creature, God is not only able but willing to join himself to man.

Much of this is frankly emotive, but the brunt of the attack is borne by reason, whose shortcomings are remorselessly exposed. It is at this stage that Pascal invites his interlocutor at least to search for the truth, even if he does not find it, because this is more reasonable than persisting in indifference. What is more, only in Christ can the paradox wretchedness–greatness be resolved: 'It is not only impossible but useless to know God without Christ' (191). Thus deism, the religion of the philosophers, is for Pascal almost as far from Christianity as actual atheism (449). It is thought, and thought alone, that constitutes man's greatness, and it is thus the right and duty of reason to examine the facts of man's condition. The paradox and dualism of our nature is a riddle which true religion can and must solve. The doctrine of the Fall, inseparable from those of Incarnation and Redemption, is for Pascal the only possible answer. Without the Fall man would still be happy, without Redemption he could only remain wretched, and in the Incarnation God reveals himself in the only form comprehensible to a creature of finite understanding, balanced precariously between the infinitely small and the infinitely great. By partaking of humanity Christ sanctified a state which is neither that of beast nor that of angel, but both. Men will never be, as the serpent promised, like gods; God has become man and felicity will come from following Christ, both God and man.

The latter part of the *Pensées* is concerned to buttress the theological doctrines of the Fall and Redemption with proofs of various kinds from the Bible and other sources. Pascal took as literally as most of his contemporaries the Mosaic account of human history, and for him the Fall was a historical event, attested by writers in an unbroken line of contact with mankind's first parents. He was much impressed – and would be even more so today – by the tenacious survival of the Jewish people, regarding it as a clear sign of divine providence, not otherwise explicable, that the people to whom the Messianic hope was revealed and entrusted should both reject the Messiah when he came and be preserved to authenticate a tradition essential to Christianity. His use of rabbinical interpretation (at second-hand from a medieval book already centuries old when he read it) and of figures (or typology, as it is technically called) is the most obvious weakness of his argument. His quite uncritical reading of the prophetic books, especially Daniel, led him into open absurdity, but in the last analysis these errors, gross as they are, should increase our respect for him. If Christianity is more than a moral code or a pious legend, it must be related to historical fact and tradition, and, if Christians are to follow Christ in respecting the Old Testament, it is more meritorious to examine the credentials of the Jewish books, even getting them wrong, than to ignore the problem. For his day, and for an amateur, Pascal did very well. In passing, it is pertinent to observe the conspicuous failure of the Churches today in their task of explaining the Old Testament to believers, not to speak of unbelievers.

One or two further points in Pascal's argument should not be overlooked. First is the role allotted to the order of body. This has two quite different aspects. One, the more obvious, is represented by references to carnality, concupiscence and materialism as the enemies of charity, and shows what happens when the heart looks downwards to the beasts rather than upwards to God; in this sense man is betraying his nature by applying to spiritual truths material values, just as the arrogance of philosophers distorts it by applying only intellectual values. Pascal's main use of this aspect of the material order is to explain how most Jews (and some Christians) failed to interpret figures and prophecies in their correct, spiritual sense. The second role allotted to this order can be seen from the very beginning, and is most explicit in the section concluding the Wager. Here Pascal uses the word 'machine', meaning automatic, unthinking habit, or conditioned reflex. In this sense the bodily order has a vital part to play by supplying a second nature, by translating purely intellectual decision into action, and by humbling pride. Thus the unbeliever who

'takes holy water and has masses said' (418) will become more reconciled to apparently meaningless practices as he finds that they help to
overcome the passions, especially pride, which have been his greatest
obstacle to belief. These mechanical actions have no value in themselves, and to think that they have is to over-emphasize the letter of
the law, like the Pharisees, but they do bring into play the only form
of behaviour in which other people can join as a community of
worshippers. For it must be recognized that Pascal is trying to persuade his interlocutor not merely to believe, but in so doing to become
a full member of the Catholic Church, the body of Christ outside
which he saw no salvation.

This point has a direct social implication which is quite frequently
mentioned in the *Pensées*, notably in Section One, XXVI, on Christian
morality, but which comes out with particular force in the sentences
immediately following that just quoted from the Wager. Pascal
argues here that the unbeliever who withdraws his rational objections
to Christianity, and agrees to go through the motions, even though
he still has not faith, will on the purely human level be making himself a better citizen. By accepting a Christian way of life, he has
gone outside himself, abandoning at last the prison of self-love for
the freedom of charity to others.

Pascal's method is deliberately not linear, and consists of converging
arguments, all directed to the same end but with different starting-
points. In his own words: 'Jesus Christ is the object of all things, the
centre towards which all things tend' (449). This phrase must be
borne constantly in mind as one reads not only the *Pensées* but also the
Provincial Letters and Pascal's other religious writings. To return to
the *point de départ*, the wretchedness of man without God is the result
of making himself his own centre, the happiness of man with God is
the result of making Christ his centre, of trying to conform his life
to that of a perfect *man*. The creator of the universe must remain a
hidden God for finite creatures, but in God made man the model is
plain for all to follow who are not blinded by self-love and self-
interest. In these terms one can see how the *nuit de feu* underlies and
explains what followed. The *Pensées*, like the *Provincial Letters*, are as
much a denunciation of the false god of self as an apology for
Christianity. Such private texts as the *Mystery of Jesus* (919) show that
Pascal's meditations on the Passion brought him closer not only to

God but also to his fellow-men, with whom he shared both the guilt and the redemption. When insecurity and anxiety neuroses, arrogant intellectualism and unthinking materialism, selfishness and aggression have faded from the background of daily living Pascal may have fewer readers. In the meantime the *Pensées* will attract and even inspire countless men and women seeking to escape from a condition of 'inconstancy, boredom, anxiety' of which they are only too well aware.

4

A translator of Pascal must pick on one edition and stick to it; he will only make confusion worse confounded by introducing editorial variants of his own. At present there are more than half a dozen different arrangements of the *Pensées* on sale, and the number is not likely to diminish. So many different numberings exist that checking one version against another has become an intolerable chore, and none commands universal assent. Under these circumstances it seemed imperative to choose an order which would always correspond with one fixed arrangement, even if this entailed some undeniable disadvantages. The strict order of the *Copy* covers these requirements for the more than ninety per cent of the *Pensées* included in it, and the others are too few to pose any serious problems. Before his death in 1963, M. Louis Lafuma had produced four editions following the order of the *Copy*, and containing in addition all other authentic fragments known from other sources: 1952, in *Éditions du Luxembourg*; 1962 the very cheap and handy *Livre de Vie*, in *Éditions du Seuil*; 1963, from the same publisher, in the collection *L'Intégrale*, an excellent one-volume edition of Pascal's collected works, and also, in 1962, the magnificent photographic reproduction of Pascal's original manuscript, rearranged in the order of the *Copy*, published in a limited edition by *Libraires Associés* in commemoration of the tercentenary of Pascal's death.[1] It may well be that the edition promised by M. Jean Mesnard will win general acceptance, but for the present an order common to the four editions just mentioned has obvious advantages.

1. These editions must be distinguished from another to which M. Lafuma has also given his name (Delmas, 1952) and in which all fragments are classified either under one of Pascal's headings or in various appendices.

It must be repeated in this connexion that no order can ever, in the nature of things, be final, because only with publication (and not always then) does the form of a work become fixed. Not the least of the merits and attractions of the *Pensées* is the amount of active participation demanded of the reader. There is a lot to be said for cutting up all the fragments (at least of a cheap edition) and trying out alternative arrangements. It would be idle to deny that the confusion of the unclassified papers makes things hard for the reader, but the editions which make things easy for him are open to even more serious objections.

There would have been something to be said for omitting fragments intended for the *Provincial Letters* and other works, but having once chosen M. Lafuma's edition I decided to translate everything included in it. Apart from ease of reference between translation and original, such completeness gives so much better an idea of Pascal as man and writer. I have not followed the Lafuma edition in distinguishing typographically those passages erased or corrected by Pascal; such refinement is hardly appropriate to an edition of this kind. Spacing is that of the manuscript, with punctuation modified where necessary. On every doubtful point I have constantly consulted the photographic reproduction.

As regards the actual translation I have tried to follow one cardinal principle apparently rejected by most previous translators of Pascal: I know of no other author who repeats the same word with such almost obsessive frequency as Pascal, and failure to render this essential feature of his style makes a translation not only inadequate but positively misleading. Wherever possible, and especially within the same fragment or section, I have used one English word for the same keyword recurring in French. I am encouraged in my conviction that Pascal would have condemned change for the sake of mere variety or elegance by his clear statement to this effect (515). Some keywords, like '*juste*', cannot be treated with absolute consistency, but only '*honnête*' completely defied translation.

Though most of Pascal's Classical quotations are borrowed from Montaigne, I have only given references to the original. Biblical quotations have been wherever possible rendered by the Authorized Version, but, where Pascal's French or the Vulgate Latin diverges too widely from the Authorized Version, a literal translation has been supplied. Especially in the longer passages Pascal took considerable liberties with the text, and I have been obliged to effect some discreet reconstruction. The conscious archaism of Pascal's constant Biblical echoes has been copied as far as possible. The very first line of this book illustrates the special problem of such echoes: the French means both that the Psalms are sung *everywhere* on earth and *by* the whole earth, alluding to the several Psalms which exhort the whole world to sing a new song unto the Lord. In all such cases I have made every effort to render the implied double meaning. All textual references are to the Authorized Version, and where Pascal's own references are either different (e.g. for the Psalms) or incorrect, they have been brought into line. All translations from languages other than French are in italics, those from the French Bible in quotation marks. The number in brackets at the end of each fragment is that of the Brunschvicg edition, still widely used for reference.

It is a particular pleasure to pay tribute to the work of M. Lafuma, to whom all students of Pascal owe so much, as well as to that of M. Jean Mesnard, to whom I am indebted for permission to translate the additional *Pensées* recently discovered and published by him. I should like also to thank Mrs Annie Barnes for some very helpful advice and Miss Martha Livingston for helping to type an unusually troublesome manuscript.

January 1965   A.J.K.

PAPERS CLASSIFIED BY PASCAL
(Pascal's Titles)

I. ORDER

1   The whole world ringing out with Psalms.[1]

    Who bears witness to Mahomet? Himself.

    Jesus wants his witness to be nothing.

    The quality of witnesses is such that they must exist always, everywhere and wretched. He is alone.   (596)

2   *Order by dialogues.* 'What must I do? I see nothing but obscurities on every side.'

    'Shall I believe I am nothing? Shall I believe I am God?'   (227)

3   'There is change and succession in all things.'

    'You are wrong, there is . . .'

    'Why, do you not say yourself that the sky and the birds prove God?' – 'No.' – 'Does your religion not say so?' – 'No. For though it is true in a sense for some souls whom God has enlightened in this way, yet it is untrue for the majority.'   (244)

4   *Letter to induce men to seek God.* Then make them look for him among the philosophers, sceptics and dogmatists, who will worry the man who seeks.   (184)

5   *Order.* A letter of exhortation to a friend, to induce him to seek. He will reply: 'But what good will seeking do me? Nothing comes of it.' Answer: 'Do not despair.' Then he in turn would say that he would be happy to find some light, but according to religion itself it would do him no good even if he did thus believe, and so he would just as soon not look. The answer to that is 'the Machine'.   (247)

6   First part: Wretchedness of man without God.

  Second part: Happiness of man with God.

    otherwise

  First part: Nature is corrupt, proved by nature itself.

  Second part: There is a Redeemer, proved by Scripture.   (60)

1. Cf. Ps. xcviii. 4.

7 *Letter showing the usefulness of proofs, by the Machine.* Faith is different from proof. One is human and the other a gift of God. *The just shall live by faith.*[1] This is the faith that God himself puts into our hearts, often using proof as the instrument. *Faith cometh by hearing.*[2] But this faith is in our hearts, and makes us say not 'I know' but 'I believe'. (248)

8 *Order.* See what is clear and incontrovertible about the whole state of the Jews. (602)

9 In the letter on injustice perhaps include:

The absurdity of the eldest son having everything, 'My friend, you were born on this side of the mountain, so it is right that your elder brother should have everything.'

'Why are you killing me?' (291)

10 The basis of all this lies in the wretchedness of human existence. Realizing this they have taken to diversions. (167)

11 *Order.* After the letter urging men to seek God, write the letter about removing obstacles, that is the argument about the Machine, how to prepare it and how to use reason for the search. (246)

12 *Order.* Men despise religion. They hate it and are afraid it may be true. The cure for this is first to show that religion is not contrary to reason, but worthy of reverence and respect.

Next make it attractive, make good men wish it were true, and then show that it is.

Worthy of reverence because it really understands human nature.

Attractive because it promises true good. (187)

II. VANITY

13 Two faces are alike; neither is funny by itself, but side by side their likeness makes us laugh. (133)

1. Rom. I. 17. 2. Rom. x. 17.

14 True Christians are, however, obedient to these follies; not that they respect follies, but rather the divine order which has subjected men to follies as a punishment. *For the creature was made subject to vanity. He shall be delivered.*[1] So St Thomas explains the passage in St James[2] about the rich being preferred, by saying that if men do not do so in the sight of God they are transgressing the order of their religion. (138)

15 Perseus, King of Macedonia, Paulus Emilius.
Perseus was criticized for not killing himself. (410)

16 *Vanity.* That something so obvious as the vanity of the world should be so little recognized that people find it odd and surprising to be told that it is foolish to seek greatness; that is most remarkable. (161)

17 *Inconstancy and oddity.* To live by one's work alone and to reign over the most powerful state in the world are two very different things.
They are combined in the person of the Grand Turk. (113)

18 An inch or two of cowl can put 25,000 monks up in arms.[3] (955)

19 He has four lackeys. (318)

20 He lives across the water. (292)

21 If we are too young our judgement is impaired, just as it is if we are too old.
Thinking too little about things or thinking too much both make us obstinate and fanatical.
If we look at our work immediately after completing it, we are still too involved; if too long afterwards, we cannot pick up the thread again.
It is like looking at pictures which are too near or too far away. There is just one indivisible point which is the right place.
Others are too near, too far, too high, or too low. In painting the rules of perspective decide it, but how will it be decided when it comes to truth and morality? (381)

---

1. Rom. VIII. 20. 2. James II. 3.
3. Reference to a medieval dispute regarding the shape of the Franciscan habit.

22 Flies are so mighty that they win battles, paralyse our minds, eat up our bodies. (367)

23 *Vanity of science.* Knowledge of physical science will not console me for ignorance of morality in time of affliction, but knowledge of morality will always console me for ignorance of physical science. (67)

24 *Man's condition.* Inconstancy, boredom, anxiety. (127)

25 The fact that kings are habitually seen in the company of guards, drums, officers and all the things which prompt automatic responses of respect and fear has the result that, when they are sometimes alone and unaccompanied, their features are enough to strike respect and fear into their subjects, because we make no mental distinction between their person and the retinue with which they are normally seen to be associated. And the world, which does not know that this is the effect of habit, believes it to derive from some natural force, hence such sayings as: 'The character of divinity is stamped on his features.' (308)

26 The power of kings is founded on the reason and the folly of the people, but especially on their folly. The greatest and most important thing in the world is founded on weakness. This is a remarkably sure foundation, for nothing is surer than that the people will be weak. Anything founded on sound reason is very ill-founded, like respect for wisdom. (330)

27 It is not man's nature always to go in one direction; it has its ups and downs.

Fever makes us both shiver and sweat. The chill is as good an indication of how high the fever will go as the heat itself.

It is the same with human inventions from age to age, and with the good and evil in the world in general.

Change is usually pleasing to princes.[1] (354)

28 *Weakness.* Men are wholly occupied in pursuing their good, but they could not justify their claim to possession, because

---

1. Horace, *Odes*, III. 29.

they have nothing but human fancy and no strength to make its possession secure.

It is the same with knowledge, for illness removes it.

We are equally incapable of truth and good. (436)

29 *A warlike people who think life is not worth living if one cannot bear arms.*[1] They prefer death to peace, others prefer death to war.

Any opinion can be preferred to life, which it seems so natural to love dearly. (156)

30 We do not choose as captain of a ship the most highly born of those aboard. (320)

31 We do not care about our reputation in towns where we are only passing through. But when we have to stay some time we do care. How much time does it take? A time proportionate to our vain and paltry existence. (149)

32 *Vanity.* Respect means: put yourself out. (317b)

33 What amazes me most is to see that everyone is not amazed at his own weakness. We behave seriously, and everyone follows his calling, not because it is really a good thing to do so, in accordance with fashion, but as if everyone knew for certain where reason and justice lie. We are constantly disappointed and an absurd humility makes us blame ourselves and not the skill we always boast of having. But it is a good thing for the reputation of scepticism that there are so many people about who are not sceptics, to show that man is quite capable of the most extravagant opinions, since he is capable of believing that he is not naturally and inevitably weak, but is, on the contrary, naturally wise.

Nothing strengthens the case for scepticism more than the fact that there are people who are not sceptics. If they all were, they would be wrong. (374)

34 This sect derives more strength from its enemies than from its friends, for human weakness is much more obvious in those who do not realize it than in those who do. (376)

1. Livy, XXXIV. 17.

35 *Heel of a shoe.* 'How well-made that is! What a skilful work-man! What a brave soldier!' That is where our inclinations come from, and our choice of careers. 'What a lot that man drinks! How little that man drinks!' That is what makes people temperate or drunkards, soldiers, cowards, etc.   (117)

36 Anyone who does not see the vanity of the world is very vain himself. So who does not see it, apart from young people whose lives are all noise, diversions, and thoughts for the future?

But take away their diversion and you will see them bored to extinction. Then they feel their nullity without recognizing it, for nothing could be more wretched than to be intolerably depressed as soon as one is reduced to introspection with no means of diversion.   (164)

37 *Trades.* Fame is so sweet that we love anything with which we connect it, even death.   (158)

38 Too much and too little wine.

Do not give him any, he cannot find the truth. Give him too much; the same thing.   (71)

39 Men spend their time chasing a ball or a hare; it is the very sport of kings.   (141)

40 How vain painting is, exciting admiration by its resemblance to things of which we do not admire the originals!   (134)

41 *Two infinites, mean.* When we read too fast or too slowly we understand nothing.   (69)

42 How many kingdoms know nothing of us!   (207)

43 A trifle consoles us because a trifle upsets us.   (136)

44 *Imagination.* It is the dominant faculty in man, master of error and falsehood, all the more deceptive for not being invariably so; for it would be an infallible criterion of truth if it were infallibly that of lies. Since, however, it is usually false, it gives no indication of its quality, setting the same mark on true and false alike.

I am not speaking of fools, but of the wisest men, amongst whom imagination is best entitled to persuade. Reason may object in vain, it cannot fix the price of things.

This arrogant force, which checks and dominates its enemy, reason, for the pleasure of showing off the power it has in every sphere, has established a second nature in man. Imagination has its happy and unhappy men, its sick and well, its rich and poor; it makes us believe, doubt, deny reason; it deadens the senses, it arouses them; it has its fools and sages, and nothing annoys us more than to see it satisfy its guests more fully and completely than reason ever could. Those who are clever in imagination are far more pleased with themselves than prudent men could reasonably be. They look down on people with a lofty air; they are bold and confident in argument, where others are timid and unsure, and their cheerful demeanour often wins the verdict of their listeners, for those whose wisdom is imaginary enjoy the favour of judges similarly qualified. Imagination cannot make fools wise, but it makes them happy, as against reason, which only makes its friends wretched: one covers them with glory, the other with shame.

Who dispenses reputation? Who makes us respect and revere persons, works, laws, the great? Who but this faculty of imagination? All the riches of the earth are inadequate without its approval. Would you not say that this magistrate, whose venerable age commands universal respect, is ruled by pure, sublime reason, and judges things as they really are, without paying heed to the trivial circumstances which offend only the imagination of weaker men? See him go to hear a sermon in a spirit of pious zeal, the soundness of his judgement strengthened by the ardour of his charity, ready to listen with exemplary respect. If, when the preacher appears, it turns out that nature has given him a hoarse voice and an odd sort of face, that his barber has shaved him badly and he happens not to be too clean either, then, whatever great truths he may announce, I wager that our senator will not be able to keep a straight face.

Put the world's greatest philosopher on a plank that is wider than need be: if there is a precipice below, although his reason may convince him that he is safe, his imagination will prevail.

Many could not even stand the thought of it without going pale and breaking into sweat.

I do not intend to list all the effects of imagination. Everyone knows that the sight of cats, or rats, the crunching of a coal, etc., is enough to unhinge reason. The tone of voice influences the wisest of us and alters the force of a speech or a poem.

Love or hate alters the face of justice. An advocate who has been well paid in advance will find the cause he is pleading all the more just. The boldness of his bearing will make it seem all the better to the judges, taken in by appearances. How absurd is reason, the sport of every wind! I should list almost all the actions of men, who hardly stir except when jolted by imagination. For reason has had to yield, and at its wisest adopts those principles which human imagination has rashly introduced at every turn. Anyone who chose to follow reason alone would have proved himself a fool. We must, since reason so pleases, work all day for benefits recognized as imaginary, and, when sleep has refreshed us from the toils of our reason, we must at once jump up to pursue the phantoms and endure the impressions created by this ruler of the world. Here is one of the principles of error, but not the only one.

Man has been quite right to make these two powers into allies, although in this peace imagination enjoys an extensive advantage; for in conflict its advantage is more complete. Reason never wholly overcomes imagination, while the contrary is quite common.

Our magistrates have shown themselves well aware of this mystery. Their red robes, the ermine in which they swaddle themselves like furry cats, the law-courts where they sit in judgment, the fleurs de lys, all this august panoply was very necessary. If physicians did not have long gowns and mules, if learned doctors did not wear square caps and robes four times too large, they would never have deceived the world, which finds such an authentic display irresistible. If they possessed true justice, and if physicians possessed the true art of healing, they would not need square caps; the majesty of such sciences would command respect in itself. But, as they only possess imaginary science, they have to resort to these vain devices in order to strike the imagination, which is their real concern, and this, in fact, is how they win respect.

Soldiers are the only ones who do not disguise themselves in this way, because their role is really more essential; they establish themselves by force, the others by masquerade.

That is why our kings have not attempted to disguise themselves. They have not dressed up in extraordinary clothes to show what they are, but they have themselves escorted by guards, scarred veterans [?]. These armed troops whose hands and strength are theirs alone, the drums and trumpets that march before them, and these legions which surround them make the most resolute tremble. They do not wear the trappings, they simply have the power. It would take reason at its most refined to see the Grand Turk, surrounded in his superb seraglio by 40,000 janissaries, as a man like any other.

We have only to see a lawyer in cap and gown to form a favourable opinion of his competence.

Imagination decides everything: it creates beauty, justice and happiness, which is the world's supreme good. I should dearly like to see the Italian book, of which I know only the title, worth many books in itself, *Dell'opinione regina del mondo*. Without knowing the book, I support its views, apart from any evil it may contain.

Such, more or less, are the effects of this deceptive faculty, apparently given to us for the specific purpose of leading us inevitably into error. We have plenty of other principles of error.

Longstanding impressions are not the only ones that can mislead us; the charms of novelty have the same power. Hence all the debate among men, who accuse each other either of following the false impressions of childhood or of rashly pursuing new ones. If anyone has found the golden mean, let him appear and prove it. Any principle, however natural it may be, even implanted in childhood, may be treated as a false impression either of education or of the senses.

'Because,' they say, 'you have believed since you were a child that a box was empty when you could not see anything in it, you believed that a vacuum could exist. This is just an illusion of your senses, strengthened by habit, and it must be corrected by science.' Others say: 'When you were taught at school that there is no such thing as a vacuum, your common sense was corrupted; it was quite clear about it before being given the wrong impression, and now it must be corrected by reverting to your original state.' Who then is the deceiver, the senses or education?

We have another principle of error in illnesses, which impair our judgement and sense. If serious illnesses do considerable harm, I have no doubt that the less serious ones have a proportionate effect.

Our own interest is another wonderful instrument for blinding us agreeably. The fairest man in the world is not allowed to be judge in his own cause. I know of men who, to avoid the danger of partiality in their own favour, have leaned over to the opposite extreme of injustice. The surest way to lose a perfectly just case was to get close relatives to commend it to them. Justice and truths are two points so fine that our instruments are too blunt to touch them exactly. If they do make contact, they blunt the point and press all round on the false rather than the true.

Man, then, is so happily constituted that he has no exact principle of truth, and several excellent ones of falsehood. Let us now see how many.

But the most absurd cause of his errors is the war between the senses and the reason. (82)

45 Man is nothing but a subject full of natural error that cannot be eradicated except through grace. Nothing shows him the truth, everything deceives him. The two principles of truth, reason and senses, are not only both not genuine, but are engaged in mutual deception. The senses deceive reason through false appearances, and, just as they trick the soul, they are tricked by it in their turn: it takes its revenge. The senses are disturbed by passions, which produce false impressions. They both compete in lies and deception.

But, apart from such accidents, error arising from the failure of these heterogeneous faculties to reach understanding . . .

(This is where the chapter on powers of deception must start.) (83)

46 *Vanity*. The cause and effect of love. Cleopatra. (163)

47 We never keep to the present. We recall the past; we anticipate the future as if we found it too slow in coming and were trying to hurry it up, or we recall the past as if to stay its too rapid flight. We are so unwise that we wander about in times that do not belong to us, and do not think of the only one that does; so vain that we dream of times that are not and blindly flee the only one that is. The fact is that the present usually hurts. We thrust it out of sight because it distresses us, and if we find it enjoyable, we are sorry to see it slip away. We try to give it the support of the future, and think how we are going to arrange things over which we have no control for a time we can never be sure of reaching.

Let each of us examine his thoughts; he will find them wholly concerned with the past or the future. We almost never think of the present, and if we do think of it, it is only to see what light it throws on our plans for the future. The present is never our end. The past and the present are our means, the future alone our end. Thus we never actually live, but hope to live, and since we are always planning how to be happy, it is inevitable that we should never be so. (172)

48 The mind of this supreme judge of the world is not so independent as to be impervious to whatever din may be going on near by. It does not take a cannon's roar to arrest his thoughts; the noise of a weathercock or a pulley will do. Do not be surprised if his reasoning is not too sound at the moment, there is a fly buzzing round his ears; that is enough to render him incapable of giving good advice. If you want him to be able to find the truth, drive away the creature that is paralysing his reason and disturbing the mighty intelligence that rules over cities and kingdoms.

What an absurd god he is! Most ridiculous hero! (366)

49 Caesar was too old, it seems to me, to go off and amuse himself conquering the world. Such a pastime was all right for Augustus

and Alexander; they were young men, not easily held in check, but Caesar ought to have been more mature. (132)

50 *Raptus est* [?]. The Swiss take offence if anyone calls them noble, and prove their plebeian descent when they want to be considered eligible for high office. (305)

51 'Why are you killing me for your own benefit? I am unarmed.' 'Why, do you not live on the other side of the water? My friend, if you lived on this side, I should be a murderer, but since you live on the other side, I am a brave man and it is right.' (293)

52 *Good sense*. They are forced to say: 'You are not acting in good faith, we are not asleep, etc.' How I love to see this proud reason humbled and suppliant! For that is not how a man talks when you challenge his rights and he defends them by force of arms. He wastes no time saying that you are not acting in good faith, but punishes your bad faith with force. (388)

III. WRETCHEDNESS

53 Man is vile enough to bow down to beasts and even worship them. (429)

54 *Inconstancy*. Things have various qualities and the soul various tendencies, for nothing presented to the soul is simple, and the soul never applies itself simply to any subject. That is why the same thing makes us laugh and cry. (112)

55 *Inconstancy*. We think playing upon man is like playing upon an ordinary organ. It is indeed an organ, but strange, shifting and changeable. Those who only know how to play an ordinary organ would never be in tune on this one. You have to know where the keys are. (111)

56 We are so unhappy that we can only enjoy something which we should be annoyed to see go wrong, and that can and does constantly happen to thousands of things. Anyone who found the secret of rejoicing when things go well without being annoyed when they go badly would have found the point. It is perpetual motion. (181)

57 It is not good to be too free.
It is not good to have all one needs. (379)

58 Tyranny consists in the desire to dominate everything regardless
of order.

In the various departments for men of strength, beauty,
sense and piety, each man is master in his own house but nowhere else. Sometimes they meet and the strong and the handsome contend for mastery, but this is idiotic because their
mastery is of different kinds. They do not understand each other
and their mistake lies in wanting to rule everywhere. Nothing
can do that, not even strength: it is of no effect in the learned
world and only governs external actions. – So these arguments
are false. . . .

Tyranny. Tyranny is wanting to have by one means what can
only be had by another. We pay different dues to different kinds
of merit; we must love charm, fear strength, believe in knowledge.

These dues must be paid. It is wrong to refuse them and
wrong to demand any others. So these arguments are false and
tyrannical: 'I am handsome, so you must fear me. I am strong,
so you must love me, I am . . .' In the same way it is false and
tyrannical to say: 'He is not strong, so I will not respect him. He
is not clever, so I will not fear him.' (332)

59 When it comes to deciding whether we should make war, kill
so many men, condemn so many Spaniards to death, it is a
single man who decides, and an interested party at that; it
ought to be an impartial third party. (296)

60 In fact laws are so vain that he would break free of them, so it
is useful to deceive him.

What basis will he take for the economy of the world he
wants to rule? Will it be the whim of each individual? What
confusion! Will it be justice? He does not know what it is. If he
did know he would certainly never have laid down this most
commonly received of all human maxims: that each man
should follow the customs of his own country. True equity
would have enthralled all the peoples of the world with its

splendour, and lawgivers would not have taken as their model the whims and fancies of Persians and Germans in place of this consistent justice. We should see it planted in every country of the world, in every age, whereas what we do see is that there is nothing just or unjust but changes colour as it changes climate. Three degrees of latitude upset the whole of jurisprudence and one meridian determines what is true. Basic laws change when they have been in force only a few years, law has its periods, the entry of Saturn into the house of the Lion marks the origin of a given crime. It is a funny sort of justice whose limits are marked by a river; true on this side of the Pyrenees, false on the other.

They confess that justice does not lie in these customs, but resides in natural laws common to every country. They would certainly maintain this obstinately if the reckless chance which distributed human laws had struck on just one which was universal, but the joke is that man's whims have shown such great variety that there is not one.

Larceny, incest, infanticide, parricide, everything has at some time been accounted a virtuous action. Could there be anything more absurd than that a man has the right to kill me because he lives on the other side of the water, and his prince has picked a quarrel with mine, though I have none with him?

There no doubt exist natural laws, but once this fine reason of ours was corrupted, it corrupted everything. *Nothing more is ours (what we call ours is by convention).*[1] *It is by virtue of senatorial decrees and votes of the people that crimes are committed.*[2] *Just as we once used to suffer for our vices, we now suffer for our laws.*[3]

The result of this confusion is that one man says that the essence of justice is the authority of the legislator, another the convenience of the sovereign, another present custom, and that is the most reliable. Merely according to reason, nothing is just in itself, everything shifts with time. Custom is the whole of equity for the sole reason that it is accepted. That is the mystic basis of its authority. Anyone who tries to bring it back to its first principle destroys it. Nothing is so defective as those laws which correct defects. Anyone obeying them because they are just is obeying an imaginary justice, not the essence of the law,

1. Cicero, *De Fin.*, v. 21.   2. Seneca, *Ep.*, xcv.   3. Tacitus, *Ann.*, iii. 25

which is completely self-contained: it is law and nothing more. Anyone wishing to examine the reason for this will find it so trivial and feeble that, unless he is used to contemplating the marvels of human fancy, he will be amazed that in a century it has acquired so much pomp and reverence. The art of subversion, of revolution, is to dislodge established customs by probing down to their origins in order to show how they lack authority and justice. There must, they say, be a return to the basic and primitive laws of the state which unjust custom has abolished. There is no surer way to lose everything; nothing will be just if weighed in these scales. Yet the people readily listen to such arguments, they throw off the yoke as soon as they recognize it, and the great take the opportunity of ruining them and those whose curiosity makes them examine received customs. That is why the wisest of legislators used to say that men must often be deceived for their own good, and another sound politician: *When he asks about the truth that is to bring him freedom, it is a good thing that he should be deceived.*[1] The truth about the usurpation must not be made apparent; it came about originally without reason and has become reasonable. We must see that it is regarded as authentic and eternal, and its origins must be hidden if we do not want it soon to end.   (294)

61   *Justice.* Justice is as much a matter of fashion as charm is.   (309)

62   *Three hosts.* What man could enjoy the friendship of the King of England, the King of Poland and the Queen of Sweden,[2] and believe that he would one day nowhere find refuge and sanctuary?   (177)

63   *Glory.* Admiration spoils everything from our earliest youth. 'Well spoken! Well done! How good he is!'

The children of Port Royal who are not spurred on by envy and glory become indifferent.   (151)

64   *Mine, thine.* 'This is my dog,' said these poor children. 'That is my place in the sun.' There is the origin and image of universal usurpation.   (295)

1. St Augustine, *City of God*, IV. 27.
2. Charles I (executed 1649), John Casimir (deposed, but reinstated, 1656), Christina (abdicated 1654).

65 *Diversity*. Theology is a science, but at the same time how many sciences? A man is a substance, but if you dissect him, what is he? Head, heart, stomach, veins, each vein, each bit of vein, blood, each humour of blood?

A town or a landscape from afar off is a town and a landscape, but as one approaches it becomes houses, trees, tiles, leaves, grass, ants, ants' legs, and so on *ad infinitum*. All that is comprehended in the word 'landscape'. (115)

66 *Injustice*. It is dangerous to tell the people that laws are not just, because they obey them only because they believe them to be just. That is why they must be told at the same time that laws are to be obeyed because they are laws, just as superiors must be obeyed because they are superior. That is how to forestall any sedition, if people can be made to understand that, and that is the proper definition of justice. (326)

67 *Injustice*. Jurisdiction is not defined in terms of the one administering but the one administered; it is dangerous to tell that to the people. But the people have too much faith in you; it will not harm them and may help you. It should therefore be published abroad. *Feed my sheep,*[1] not *yours*. You owe me pasturage. (879)

68 When I consider the brief span of my life absorbed into the eternity which comes before and after – *as the remembrance of a guest that tarrieth but a day*[2] – the small space I occupy and which I see swallowed up in the infinite immensity of spaces of which I know nothing and which know nothing of me, I take fright and am amazed to see myself here rather than there: there is no reason for me to be here rather than there, now rather than then. Who put me here? By whose command and act were this time and place allotted to me? (205)

69 *Wretchedness*. Job and Solomon. (174b)

70 If our condition were truly happy we should not need to divert ourselves from thinking about it. (165b)

1. John XXI. 16.
2. Wisdom V. 15.

71   *Contradictions.* Pride counterbalances all these miseries; man either hides or displays them, and glories in his awareness of them.   (405)

72   One must know oneself. Even if that does not help in finding truth, at least it helps in running one's life, and nothing is more proper.   (66)

73   What causes inconstancy is the realization that present pleasures are false, together with the failure to realize that absent pleasures are vain.   (110)

74   *Injustice.* They have found no other way of satisfying their concupiscence without doing wrong to others. Job and Solomon.   (454)

75   Ecclesiastes shows that man without God is totally ignorant and inescapably unhappy, for anyone is unhappy who wills but cannot do. Now he wants to be happy and assured of some truth, and yet he is equally incapable of knowing and of not desiring to know. He cannot even doubt.   (389)

76   But perhaps this matter goes beyond the scope of reason. Let us then examine what it has devised in matters over which it has control. If there is one thing to which, in its own interest, it must most earnestly have applied itself, it is the search for the sovereign good. Let us see then where these powerful and penetrating souls have placed it, and whether they are in agreement.

   One says the sovereign good consists in virtue, another in sensual pleasure, another in following nature, another in truth – *Happy the man who could know the reasons for things*[1] – another in total ignorance, another in indolence, others in resisting appearances, another in never feeling surprise – *To be surprised at nothing is almost the only way to find happiness and keep it*[2] – and the good sceptics in their ataraxia, doubt and perpetual suspension of judgement. Others even wiser say that it cannot be found, not even by wishing. That is a fine answer!

   (Transpose after the laws the following article:)

1. Virgil, *Georgics*, II. 490.   2. Horace, *Ep.*, I. vi. 1.

So we must see whether this fine philosophy has come to any certain conclusions after such long and arduous toil. Perhaps at least the soul will come to know itself. Let us hear the regent masters of the world on this subject. What have they thought about its substance? 395. Have they been any luckier in locating it? 395. What have they discovered about its origin, duration, destination? 399. Could it be then that the soul is too noble a subject for its feeble understanding? Let us lower its gaze then on to matter. Let us see if it knows what its own body, to which it gives life, is made of, and the others it observes and moves at will. What have they known about it, these great dogmatists to whom no knowledge is denied? 393.[1]

Of these opinions [which is true].[2]

That would surely be enough if reason were reasonable. It is quite reasonable enough to admit that it has so far found no firm truth, but it has not yet given up hope of finding one. On the contrary, it pursues the quest as fervently as ever and is confident of possessing all the strength necessary for success.

We must then finish off the argument, and, after looking at its powers through their effects, examine them in themselves. Let us see if it lies within the powers and grasp of reason to seize the truth.   (73)

IV. BOREDOM

77   *Pride.* Curiosity is only vanity. We usually only want to know something so that we can talk about it; in other words, we would never travel by sea if it meant never talking about it, and for the sheer pleasure of seeing things we could never hope to describe to others.   (152)

78   *Description of man.* Dependence, desire for independence, needs.
                                                                   (126)

79   How tiresome it is to give up pursuits to which we have become attached. A man enjoying a happy home-life has only to see a

1. These numbers are references to pages in Pascal's edition of Montaigne.
2. Cicero, *Tusc.*, I. II.

woman who attracts him, or spend five or six pleasant days gambling, and he will be very sorry to go back to what he was doing before. It happens every day. (128)

V. CAUSES AND EFFECTS

80 Respect means; put yourself out. That may look pointless, but it is quite right, because it amounts to saying: I should certainly put myself out if you needed it, because I do so when you do not; besides, respect serves to distinguish the great. If respect meant sitting in an armchair we should be showing everyone respect and then there would be no way of marking distinction, but we make the distinction quite clear by putting ourselves out. (317)

81 The only universal rules are the law of the land in everyday matters and the will of the majority in others. How is that? Because of the power implied.

That is why kings, who have another source of power, do not follow the majority of their ministers.

Equality of possessions is no doubt right, but, as men could not make might obey right, they have made right obey might. As they could not fortify justice they have justified force, so that right and might live together and peace reigns, the sovereign good. (299)

82 Wisdom leads us back to childhood. *Except ye become as little children.*[1] (291)

83 The world is a good judge of things, because it is in the state of natural ignorance where man really belongs. Knowledge has two extremes which meet; one is the pure natural ignorance of every man at birth, the other is the extreme reached by great minds who run through the whole range of human knowledge, only to find that they know nothing and come back to the same ignorance from which they set out, but it is a wise ignorance which knows itself. Those who stand half-way have put their

---

1. Matt. XVIII. 3.

natural ignorance behind them without yet attaining the other; they have some smattering of adequate knowledge and pretend to understand everything. They upset the world and get everything wrong.

Ordinary people and clever people make up the run of the world; the former despise it and are despised in their turn. All their judgements are wrong and the world judges them rightly. (327)

84 *Descartes.* In general terms one must say: 'That is the result of figure and motion,' because it is true, but to name them and assemble the machine is quite ridiculous. It is pointless, uncertain, and arduous. Even if it were true we do not think that the whole of philosophy would be worth an hour's effort. (79)

85 *Extremes in the law are extremes of injustice.*[1] Majority opinion is the best way because it can be seen and is strong enough to command obedience, but it is the opinion of those who are least clever.

If it had been possible, men would have put might into the hands of right, but we cannot handle might as we like, since it is a palpable quality, whereas right is a spiritual quality which we manipulate at will, and so right has been put into the hands of might.

Thus the name of right goes to the dictates of might.

Hence the right of the sword, because the sword confers a genuine right.

Otherwise we should see violence on one side and justice on the other. (End of the 12th *Provincial Letter.*)

Hence the injustice of the Fronde, which sets up its alleged right against might. It is not the same thing with the Church, because there genuine justice exists without any violence. (878)

86 *Of true justice.*[2] We no longer have any. If we had, we should not accept it as a rule of justice that one should follow the customs of one's country.

That is why we have found might when we could not find right. (297)

1. Terence, *Heaut.*, IV. v. 47.
2. Cicero, *De Officiis*, III. 17.

87 The chancellor is a grave man, dressed in fine robes because his position is false; not so the king. He enjoys power, and has no use for imagination. Judges, doctors, etc., enjoy nothing but imagination. (307)

88 It is the effect of power, not of custom, for those capable of originality are rare. Those who are strongest in numbers only want to follow, and refuse recognition to those who seek it for their originality. If they persist in wanting recognition and despising those who are not original, the others will call them ridiculous names and may even beat them. So do not be conceited about your subtlety, or keep your satisfaction to yourself. (302)

89 *Cause and effect*. It is really remarkable; I am supposed not to honour a man dressed in brocade and attended by seven or eight lackeys. Why! He will have me thrashed if I do not bow to him. His clothes represent power. It is the same with a horse in fine harness compared to another. It is funny that Montaigne does not see what a difference there is, and asks in surprise why people find any. Indeed, he says, how does it happen, etc. (315)

90 *Cause and effect*. Gradation. Ordinary people honour those who are highly born, the half-clever ones despise them, saying that birth is a matter of chance, not personal merit. Really clever men honour them, not for the same reason as ordinary people, but for deeper motives. Pious folk with more zeal than knowledge despise them regardless of the reason which makes clever men honour them, because they judge men in the new light of piety, but perfect Christians honour them because they are guided by a still higher light.

So opinions swing back and forth, from pro to con, according to one's lights. (337)

91 *Cause and effect*. One must have deeper motives and judge everything accordingly, but go on talking like an ordinary person. (336)

92 *Cause and effect*. It is then true to say that everyone is the victim of illusion, because the ordinary person's opinions are sound

without being intellectually so, for he believes truth to be where it is not. There is certainly some truth in these opinions, but not as much as people imagine. It is true that we should honour the gentry but not because gentle birth is a real advantage.   (335)

93   *Cause and effect.* Constant swing from pro to con.

Thus we have shown that man is vain to pay so much attention to things which do not really matter, and all these opinions have been refuted.

Then we showed that all these opinions are perfectly sound, so that, all these examples of vanity being perfectly justified, ordinary people are not as vain as they are said to be. Thus we refuted the opinion which refuted that of the people.

But we must now refute this last proposition and show that it is still true that the people are vain, although their opinions are sound, because they do not see the truth when it is there, and assume things to be true when they are not, with the result that their opinions are always thoroughly wrong and unsound.

(328)

94   *Sound opinions of the people.* The greatest of evils is civil war.

It is bound to come if people want to reward merit, because everyone will claim to be meritorious. The evil to be feared if the succession falls by right of birth to a fool is neither so great nor so certain.   (313)

95   *Sound opinions of the people.* It is not mere vanity to be elegant, because it shows that a lot of people are working for you. Your hair shows that you have a valet, a perfumer, etc., bands, thread, braid, etc., show. . . . It means more than superficial show or mere accoutrement to have many hands in one's service.

The more hands one employs the more powerful one is. Elegance is a means of showing one's power.   (316)

96   *Cause and effect.* Human weakness is the reason for so many canons of beauty; for instance, being a good lute-player. It is only our weakness which makes it a bad thing [not to be one?].

(329)

97   *Cause and effect.* Concupiscence and force are the source of all our actions. Concupiscence causes voluntary, force involuntary actions.   (334)

98 How is it that a lame man does not annoy us while a lame mind does? Because a lame man recognizes that we are walking straight, while a lame mind says that it is we who are limping. But for that we should feel sorry rather than angry.

Epictetus goes much further when he asks: Why do we not lose our temper if someone tells us that we have a headache, while we do lose it if someone says there is anything wrong with our arguments or our choice? (80)

99 The reason for that is that we are quite certain that we have not got a headache, and are not limping, but we are not so sure we are making the right choice. Consequently, since the only thing that makes us sure is the evidence available to us, we hesitate and are taken aback when the evidence available to someone else makes him see just the opposite. All the more so when a thousand other people scoff at our choice, because we are obliged to prefer our judgement to that of so many others, and that is a bold and difficult thing to do. There is never such a clash of views over a lame man.

Man is so made that if he is told often enough that he is a fool he believes it. By telling himself so often enough he convinces himself, because when he is alone he carries on an inner dialogue with himself which it is important to keep under proper control. *Evil communications corrupt good manners.*[1] We must keep silence as far as we can and only talk to ourselves about God, whom we know to be true, and thus convince ourselves that he is. (536)

100 *Cause and effect.* Epictetus. Those who say: 'You have a headache.' It is not the same thing; we are sure about our health but not about being right, and he certainly talked plain nonsense.

All the same he thought he had proved his point by saying that it is either in our power or not, but he did not see that it is not in our power to control our heart, and he was wrong to conclude that it is from the existence of Christians. (467)

101 Ordinary people have some very sound opinions. For instance: 1. In choosing diversion and preferring the hunt to the capture.

1. I Cor. xv. 33.

The half-learned scoff and triumphantly use this to prove how foolish people are, but, for a reason these men cannot grasp, the people are right.

2. In distinguishing men by external things like noble birth and wealth. The world triumphs again in showing how unreasonable that is, but it is perfectly reasonable. Cannibals laugh at a child-king.

3. In taking offence at a slap on the face or being so eager for glory; but this is most desirable because of the other essential benefits it entails. A man who shows no resentment at being slapped is overwhelmed with insults and forced into need.

4. In taking chances, going to sea, crossing a plank. (324)

102 Either Jews or Christians must be wicked. (759)

103 *Right, might.* It is right to follow the right, it is necessary to follow the mighty.

Right without might is helpless, might without right is tyrannical.

Right without might is challenged, because there are always evil men about. Might without right is denounced. We must therefore combine right and might, and to that end make right into might or might into right.

Right is open to dispute, might is easily recognized and beyond dispute. Therefore right could not be made mighty because might challenged right, calling it unjust and itself claiming to be just.

Being thus unable to make right into might, we have made might into right. (298)

104 What a great advantage to be of noble birth, since it gives a man of eighteen the standing, recognition and respect that another man might not earn before he was fifty. That means winning thirty years start with no effort. (322)

VI. GREATNESS

105 If an animal did rationally what it does by instinct, and if it spoke rationally what it speaks by instinct when hunting, or

warning its fellows that the prey has been lost or found, it would certainly go on to talk about matters which affect it more seriously, and it would say, for instance: 'Bite through this cord; it is hurting me and I cannot reach it.'　　(342)

106　*Greatness.* Causes and effects show the greatness of man in producing such excellent order from his own concupiscence.
　　(403)

107·　The parrot wipes its beak although it is clean.　　(343)

108　What part of us feels pleasure? Is it our hand, our arm, our flesh, or our blood? It must obviously be something immaterial.
　　(339b)

109　*Against Scepticism.* It is odd that we cannot define these things without making them obscure; we talk about them all the time. We assume that everyone conceives of them in the same way, but that is a quite gratuitous assumption, because we have no proof that it is so. I see indeed that we apply these words on the same occasions; every time two men see a body change its position they both use the same word to express what they have seen, each of them saying that the body has moved. Such conformity of application provides a strong presumption of conformity of thought, but it lacks the absolute force of total conviction, although the odds are that it is so, because we know that the same conclusions are often drawn from different assumptions.

That is enough to cloud the issue, to say the least, though it does not completely extinguish the natural light which provides us with certainty in such matters. The Platonists would have wagered on it, but that makes the light dimmer and upsets the dogmatists, to the glory of the sceptical clique which stands for ambiguous ambiguity, and a certain dubious obscurity from which our doubts cannot remove every bit of light any more than our natural light can dispel all the darkness.

[Verso] The least thing is of this kind. God is the beginning and the end. Eccl.

　　1. Reason.　　(392)

110 We know the truth not only through our reason but also through our heart. It is through the latter that we know first principles, and reason, which has nothing to do with it, tries in vain to refute them. The sceptics have no other object than that, and they work at it to no purpose. We know that we are not dreaming, but, however unable we may be to prove it rationally, our inability proves nothing but the weakness of our reason, and not the uncertainty of all our knowledge, as they maintain. For knowledge of first principles, like space, time, motion, number, is as solid as any derived through reason, and it is on such knowledge, coming from the heart and instinct, that reason has to depend and base all its argument. The heart feels that there are three spatial dimensions and that there is an infinite series of numbers, and reason goes on to demonstrate that there are no two square numbers of which one is double the other. Principles are felt, propositions proved, and both with certainty though by different means. It is just as pointless and absurd for reason to demand proof of first principles from the heart before agreeing to accept them as it would be absurd for the heart to demand an intuition of all the propositions demonstrated by reason before agreeing to accept them.

Our inability must therefore serve only to humble reason, which would like to be the judge of everything, but not to confute our certainty. As if reason were the only way we could learn! Would to God, on the contrary, that we never needed it and knew everything by instinct and feeling! But nature has refused us this blessing, and has instead given us only very little knowledge of this kind; all other knowledge can be acquired only by reasoning.

That is why those to whom God has given religious faith by moving their hearts are very fortunate, and feel quite legitimately convinced, but to those who do not have it we can only give such faith through reasoning, until God gives it by moving their heart, without which faith is only human and useless for salvation. (282)

111 I can certainly imagine a man without hands, feet, or head, for it is only experience that teaches us that the head is more neces-

sary than the feet. But I cannot imagine a man without thought; he would be a stone or an animal. (339)

112   Instinct and reason, signs of two natures. (344)

113   *Thinking reed.* It is not in space that I must seek my human dignity, but in the ordering of my thought. It will do me no good to own land. Through space the universe grasps me and swallows me up like a speck; through thought I grasp it. (348)

114   Man's greatness comes from knowing he is wretched: a tree does not know it is wretched.

Thus it is wretched to know that one is wretched, but there is greatness in knowing one is wretched. (397)

115   *Immateriality of the soul.* When philosophers have subdued their passions, what material substance has managed to achieve this? (349)

116   All these examples of wretchedness prove his greatness. It is the wretchedness of a great lord, the wretchedness of a dispossessed king. (398)

117   *Man's greatness.* Man's greatness is so obvious that it can even be deduced from his wretchedness, for what is nature in animals we call wretchedness in man, thus recognizing that, if his nature is today like that of the animals, he must have fallen from some better state which was once his own.

Who indeed would think himself unhappy not to be king except one who had been dispossessed? Did anyone think Paulus Emilius was unhappy not to be consul? On the contrary, everyone thought he was happy to have been so once, because the office was not meant to be permanent. But people thought Perseus so unhappy at finding himself no longer king, because that was meant to be a permanent office, that they were surprised that he could bear to go on living. Who would think himself unhappy if he had only one mouth and who would not if he had only one eye? It has probably never occurred to anyone to be distressed at not having three eyes, but those who have none are inconsolable. (409)

118 Man's greatness even in his concupiscence. He has managed to produce such a remarkable system from it and make it the image of true charity. (402)

VII. CONTRADICTIONS

119 *Contradictions.* (After showing how vile and how great man is.) Let man now judge his own worth, let him love himself, for there is within him a nature capable of good; but that is no reason for him to love the vileness within himself. Let him despise himself because this capacity remains unfilled; but that is no reason for him to despise this natural capacity. Let him both hate and love himself; he has within him the capacity for knowing truth and being happy, but he possesses no truth which is either abiding or satisfactory.

I should therefore like to arouse in man the desire to find truth, to be ready, free from passion, to follow it wherever he may find it, realizing how far his knowledge is clouded by passions. I should like him to hate his concupiscence which automatically makes his decisions for him, so that it should not blind him when he makes his choice, nor hinder him once he has chosen. (423)

120 We are so presumptuous that we should like to be known all over the world, even by people who will only come when we are no more. Such is our vanity that the good opinion of half a dozen of the people around us gives us pleasure and satisfaction. (148)

121 It is dangerous to explain too clearly to man how like he is to the animals without pointing out his greatness. It is also dangerous to make too much of his greatness without his vileness. It is still more dangerous to leave him in ignorance of both, but it is most valuable to represent both to him.

Man must not be allowed to believe that he is equal either to animals or to angels, nor to be unaware of either, but he must know both. (418)

122 APR [At Port Royal] *Greatness and wretchedness.* Since wretchedness and greatness can be concluded each from the other, some people have been more inclined to conclude that man is wretched for having used his greatness to prove it, while others have all the more cogently concluded he is great by basing their proof on wretchedness. Everything that could be said by one side as proof of greatness has only served as an argument for the others to conclude he is wretched, since the further one falls the more wretched one is, and vice versa. One has followed the other in an endless circle, for it is certain that as man's insight increases so he finds both wretchedness and greatness within himself. In a word man knows he is wretched. Thus he is wretched because he is so, but he is truly great because he knows it. (416)

123 *Contradictions.* Contempt for our existence, dying for nothing, hatred of our existence. (157)

124 *Contradictions.* Man is naturally credulous, incredulous, timid, bold. (125)

125 What are our natural principles but habitual principles? In children it is the principles received from the habits of their fathers, like hunting in the case of animals.

A change of habit will produce different natural principles, as can be seen from experience, and if there are some principles which habit cannot eradicate, there are others both habitual and unnatural which neither nature nor a new habit can eradicate. It all depends on one's disposition. (92)

126 Fathers are afraid that their children's natural love may be eradicated. What then is this nature which is liable to be eradicated?

Habit is a second nature that destroys the first. But what is nature? Why is habit not natural? I am very much afraid that nature itself is only a first habit, just as habit is a second nature. (93)

127 Man's nature may be considered in two ways; either according to his end, and then he is great and beyond compare, or according to the masses, as the nature of horses and dogs is

judged by the masses from seeing how they run or ward off strangers, and then man is abject and vile. These are the two approaches which provoke such divergent views and such argument among philosophers, because each denies the other's hypothesis.

One says: 'Man was not born for this end, because everything he does belies it.' The other says: 'He is falling far short of his end when he acts so basely.' (415)

128 Two things teach man about his whole nature: instinct and experience. (396)

129 *Trade. Thoughts.* All is one, all is diversity.

How many natures lie in human nature! How many occupations! How fortuitously in the ordinary way each of us takes up the one that he has heard others praise. A well-turned heel. (116)

130 If he exalts himself, I humble him.
If he humbles himself, I exalt him.
And I go on contradicting him
Until he understands
That he is a monster that passes all understanding. (420)

131 The strongest of the sceptics' arguments, to say nothing of minor points, is that we cannot be sure that these principles are true (faith and revelation apart) except through some natural intuition. Now this natural intuition affords no convincing proof that they are true. There is no certainty, apart from faith, as to whether man was created by a good God, an evil demon, or just by chance, and so it is a matter of doubt, depending on our origin, whether these innate principles are true, false or uncertain.

Moreover, no one can be sure, apart from faith, whether he is sleeping or waking, because when we are asleep we are just as firmly convinced that we are awake as we are now. As we often dream we are dreaming, piling up one dream on another, is it not possible that this half of our life is itself just a dream, on to which the others are grafted, and from which we shall awake when we die? That while it lasts we are as little in possession of the principles of truth and goodness as during normal sleep? All this passage of time, of life, all these different bodies which we feel, the different thoughts which stir us, may be no more than illusions like the passage of time and vain phantoms of our dreams. We think we are seeing space, shape, movement, we feel time pass, we measure it, in fact we behave just as we do when we are awake. As a result, since half our life is spent in sleep, on our own admission and despite appearances we have no idea of the truth because all our intuitions are simply illusions during that time. Who knows whether the other half of our lives, when we think we are awake, is not another sleep slightly different from the first, on to which our dreams are grafted as our sleep appears, and from which we awake when we think we are sleeping? And who can doubt that, if we dreamed in the company of others and our dreams happened to agree, which is common enough, and if we were alone when awake, we should think things had been turned upside-down?

These are the main points on each side, to say nothing of minor arguments, like those the sceptics direct against the influences of habit, education, local customs, and so on, which the slightest puff of scepticism overturns, though they convince the majority of ordinary people, who have only this vain basis for their dogmas. You have only to look at their books; if you are not sufficiently persuaded you soon will be, perhaps too much so.

I pause at the dogmatists' only strong point, which is that we cannot doubt natural principles if we speak sincerely and in all good faith.

To which the sceptics reply, in a word, that uncertainty as to our origin entails uncertainty as to our nature. The dogmatists have been trying to answer that ever since the world began.

(Anyone wanting ampler information about scepticism should look at their books; he will soon be persuaded, perhaps too much so.)

This means open war between men, in which everyone is obliged to take sides, either with the dogmatists or with the sceptics, because anyone who imagines he can stay neutral is a sceptic *par excellence*. This neutrality is the essence of their clique. Anyone who is not against them is their staunch supporter, and that is where their advantage appears. They are not even for themselves; they are neutral, indifferent, suspending judgment on everything, including themselves.

What then is man to do in this state of affairs? Is he to doubt everything, to doubt whether he is awake, whether he is being pinched or burned? Is he to doubt whether he is doubting, to doubt whether he exists?

No one can go that far, and I maintain that a perfectly genuine sceptic has never existed. Nature backs up helpless reason and stops it going so wildly astray.

Is he, on the other hand, to say that he is the certain possessor of truth, when at the slightest pressure he fails to prove his claim and is compelled to loose his grasp?

What sort of freak then is man! How novel, how monstrous, how chaotic, how paradoxical, how prodigious! Judge of all things, feeble earthworm, repository of truth, sink of doubt and error, glory and refuse of the universe!

Who will unravel such a tangle? This is certainly beyond dogmatism and scepticism, beyond all human philosophy. Man transcends man. Let us then concede to the sceptics what they have so often proclaimed, that truth lies beyond our scope and is an unattainable quarry, that it is no earthly denizen, but at home in heaven, lying in the lap of God, to be known only in so far as it pleases him to reveal it. Let us learn our true nature from the uncreated and incarnate truth.

If we seek truth through reason we cannot avoid one of these three sects. You cannot be a sceptic or a Platonist without stifling nature, you cannot be a dogmatist without turning your back on reason.

Nature confounds the sceptics and Platonists, and reason confounds the dogmatists. What then will become of you, man, seeking to discover your true condition through natural reason? You cannot avoid one of these three sects nor survive in any of them.

Know then, proud man, what a paradox you are to yourself. Be humble, impotent reason! Be silent, feeble nature! Learn that man infinitely transcends man, hear from your master your true condition, which is unknown to you.

Listen to God.

Is it not as clear as day that man's condition is dual? The point is that if man had never been corrupted, he would, in his innocence, confidently enjoy both truth and felicity, and, if man had never been anything but corrupt, he would have no idea either of truth or bliss. But unhappy as we are (and we should be less so if there were no element of greatness in our condition) we have an idea of happiness but we cannot attain it. We perceive an image of the truth and possess nothing but falsehood, being equally incapable of absolute ignorance and certain knowledge; so obvious is it that we once enjoyed a degree of perfection from which we have unhappily fallen.

Let us then conceive that man's condition is dual. Let us conceive that man infinitely transcends man, and that without the aid of faith he would remain inconceivable to himself, for who cannot see that unless we realize the duality of human nature we remain invincibly ignorant of the truth about ourselves?

It is, however, an astounding thing that the mystery furthest from our ken, that of the transmission of sin, should be something without which we can have no knowledge of ourselves.

Without doubt nothing is more shocking to our reason than to say that the sin of the first man has implicated in its guilt men so far from the original sin that they seem incapable of sharing it. This flow of guilt does not seem merely impossible to us, but indeed most unjust. What could be more contrary to the rules of our miserable justice than the eternal damnation of a child, incapable of will, for an act in which he seems to have so little part that it was actually committed 6,000 years before he existed? Certainly nothing jolts us more rudely than this doctrine, and yet, but for this mystery, the most incomprehensible of all, we remain incomprehensible to ourselves. The knot of our condition was twisted and turned in that abyss, so that it is harder to conceive of man without this mystery than for man to conceive of it himself.

This shows that God, in his desire to make the difficulties of our existence unintelligible to us, hid the knot so high, or more precisely, so low, that we were quite unable to reach it. Consequently it is not through the proud activity of our reason but through its simple submission that we can really know ourselves.

These fundamental facts, solidly established on the inviolable authority of religion, teach us that there are in faith two equally constant truths. One is that man in the state of his creation, or in the state of grace, is exalted above the whole of nature, made like unto God and sharing in his divinity. The other is that in the state of corruption and sin he has fallen from that first state and has become like the beasts. These two propositions are equally firm and certain.

Scripture openly declares this when it says in certain places: *My delights were with the sons of men*[1] – *I will pour out my spirit upon all flesh*[2] – *Ye are gods*,[3] while saying in others: *All flesh is grass*[4] – *Man is like the beasts that perish*[5] – *I said in my heart concerning the estate of the sons of men.*[6]

Whence it is clearly evident that man through grace is made like unto God and shares his divinity, and without grace he is treated like the beasts of the field. (434)

VIII. DIVERSION

132 *Diversion.* If man were happy, the less he were diverted the happier he would be, like the saints and God. Yes: but is a man not happy who can find delight in diversion?

No: because it comes from somewhere else, from outside; so he is dependent, and always liable to be disturbed by a thousand and one accidents, which inevitably cause distress. (170)

133 *Diversion.* Being unable to cure death, wretchedness and ignorance, men have decided, in order to be happy, not to think about such things. (169)

134 Despite these afflictions man wants to be happy, only wants to be happy, and cannot help wanting to be happy.

1. Prov. VIII. 31.   2. Joel II. 28.   3. Ps. LXXXII. 6.
4. Is. XL. 6.   5. Ps. XLIX. 12.   6. Eccl. III. 18.

But how shall he go about it? The best thing would be to make himself immortal, but as he cannot do that, he has decided to stop himself thinking about it. (168)

135 I feel that it is possible that I might never have existed, for my self consists in my thought; therefore I who think would never have been if my mother had been killed before I had come to life; therefore I am not a necessary being. I am not eternal or infinite either, but I can see that there is in nature a being who is necessary, eternal, and infinite. (469)

136 *Diversion.* Sometimes, when I set to thinking about the various activities of men, the dangers and troubles which they face at Court, or in war, giving rise to so many quarrels and passions, daring and often wicked enterprises and so on, I have often said that the sole cause of man's unhappiness is that he does not know how to stay quietly in his room. A man wealthy enough for life's needs would never leave home to go to sea or besiege some fortress if he knew how to stay at home and enjoy it. Men would never spend so much on a commission in the army if they could bear living in town all their lives, and they only seek after the company and diversion of gambling because they do not enjoy staying at home.

But after closer thought, looking for the particular reasons for all our unhappiness now that I knew its general cause, I found one very cogent reason in the natural unhappiness of our feeble mortal condition, so wretched that nothing can console us when we really think about it.

Imagine any situation you like, add up all the blessings with which you could be endowed, to be king is still the finest thing in the world; yet if you imagine one with all the advantages of his rank, but no means of diversion, left to ponder and reflect on what he is, this limp felicity will not keep him going; he is bound to start thinking of all the threats facing him, of possible revolts, finally of inescapable death and disease, with the result that if he is deprived of so-called diversion he is unhappy, indeed more unhappy than the humblest of his subjects who can enjoy sport and diversion.

The only good thing for men therefore is to be diverted from thinking of what they are, either by some occupation which takes their mind off it, or by some novel and agreeable passion which keeps them busy, like gambling, hunting, some absorbing show, in short by what is called diversion.

That is why gaming and feminine society, war and high office are so popular. It is not that they really bring happiness, nor that anyone imagines that true bliss comes from possessing the money to be won at gaming or the hare that is hunted: no one would take it as a gift. What people want is not the easy peaceful life that allows us to think of our unhappy condition, nor the dangers of war, nor the burdens of office, but the agitation that takes our mind off it and diverts us. That is why we prefer the hunt to the capture.

That is why men are so fond of hustle and bustle; that is why prison is such a fearful punishment; that is why the pleasures of solitude are so incomprehensible. That, in fact, is the main joy of being a king, because people are continually trying to divert him and procure him every kind of pleasure. A king is surrounded by people whose only thought is to divert him and stop him thinking about himself, because, king though he is, he becomes unhappy as soon as he thinks about himself.

That is all that men have been able to devise for attaining happiness; those who philosophize about it, holding that people are quite unreasonable to spend all day chasing a hare that they would not have wanted to buy, have little knowledge of our nature. The hare itself would not save us from thinking about death and the miseries distracting us, but hunting it does so. Thus when Pyrrhus was advised to take the rest towards which he was so strenuously striving, he found it very hard to do so.

Telling a man to rest is the same as telling him to live happily. It means advising him to enjoy a completely happy state which he can contemplate at leisure without cause for distress. It means not understanding nature.

Thus men who are naturally conscious of what they are shun nothing so much as rest; they would do anything to be disturbed.

It is wrong then to blame them; they are not wrong to want excitement – if they only wanted it for the sake of diversion.

The trouble is that they want it as though, once they had the things they seek, they could not fail to be truly happy. That is what justifies calling their search a vain one. All this shows that neither the critics nor the criticized understand man's real nature.

When men are reproached for pursuing so eagerly something that could never satisfy them, their proper answer, if they really thought about it, ought to be that they simply want a violent and vigorous occupation to take their minds off themselves, and that is why they choose some attractive object to entice them in ardent pursuit. Their opponents could find no answer to that,

(Vanity, pleasure of showing off. Dancing, you must think where to put your feet.)

but they do not answer like that because they do not know themselves. They do not know that all they want is the hunt and not the capture. The nobleman sincerely believes that hunting is a great sport, the sport of kings, but his huntsman does not feel like that. They imagine that if they secured a certain appointment they would enjoy resting afterwards, and they do not realize the insatiable nature of cupidity. They think they genuinely want rest when all they really want is activity.

They have a secret instinct driving them to seek external diversion and occupation, and this is the result of their constant sense of wretchedness. They have another secret instinct, left over from the greatness of our original nature, telling them that the only true happiness lies in rest and not in excitement. These two contrary instincts give rise to a confused plan buried out of sight in the depths of their soul, which leads them to seek rest by way of activity and always to imagine that the satisfaction they miss will come to them once they overcome certain obvious difficulties and can open the door to welcome rest.

All our life passes in this way: we seek rest by struggling against certain obstacles, and once they are overcome, rest proves intolerable because of the boredom it produces. We must get away from it and crave excitement.

We think either of present or of threatened miseries, and even if we felt quite safe on every side, boredom on its own account would not fail to emerge from the depths of our hearts, where it is naturally rooted, and poison our whole mind.

Man is so unhappy that he would be bored even if he had no cause for boredom, by the very nature of his temperament, and he is so vain that, though he has a thousand and one basic reasons for being bored, the slightest thing, like pushing a ball with a billiard cue, will be enough to divert him.

'But,' you will say, 'what is his object in all this?' Just so that he can boast tomorrow to his friends that he played better than someone else. Likewise others sweat away in their studies to prove to scholars that they have solved some hitherto insoluble problem in algebra. Many others again, just as foolishly in my view, risk the greatest dangers so that they can boast afterwards of having captured some stronghold. Then there are others who exhaust themselves observing all these things, not in order to become wiser, but just to show they know them, and these are the biggest fools of the lot, because they know what they are doing, while it is conceivable that the rest would stop being foolish if they knew too.

A given man lives a life free from boredom by gambling a small sum every day. Give him every morning the money he might win that day, but on condition that he does not gamble, and you will make him unhappy. It might be argued that what he wants is the entertainment of gaming and not the winnings. Make him play then for nothing; his interest will not be fired and he will become bored, so it is not just entertainment he wants. A half-hearted entertainment without excitement will bore him. He must have excitement, he must delude himself into imagining that he would be happy to win what he would not want as a gift if it meant giving up gambling. He must create some target for his passions and then arouse his desire, anger, fear, for this object he has created, just like children taking fright at a face they have daubed themselves.

That is why this man, who lost his only son a few months ago and was so troubled and oppressed this morning by lawsuits and quarrels, is not thinking about it any more. Do not be surprised; he is concentrating all his attention on which way the boar will go that his dogs have been so hotly pursuing for the past six hours. That is all he needs. However sad a man may be, if you can persuade him to take up some diversion he will be happy while it lasts, and however happy a man may be, if he lacks diversion and has no absorbing passion or entertainment to keep boredom away, he will soon be depressed and unhappy. Without diversion there is no joy; with diversion there is no sadness. That is what constitutes the happiness of persons of rank, for they have a number of people to divert them and the ability to keep themselves in this state.

Make no mistake about it. What else does it mean to be Superintendent, Chancellor, Chief Justice, but to enjoy a position in which a great number of people come every morning from all parts and do not leave them a single hour of the day to think about themselves? When they are in disgrace and sent off to their country houses, where they lack neither wealth nor servants to meet their needs, they infallibly become miserable and dejected because no one stops them thinking about themselves. (139)

137   *Diversion.* Is not the dignity of kingship sufficiently great in itself to make its possessor happy by simply seeing what he is? Does he need to be diverted from such thoughts like ordinary people? I can quite see that it makes a man happy to be diverted from contemplating his private miseries by making him care about nothing else but dancing well, but will it be the same with a king, and will he be happier absorbed in such vain amusements than in contemplating his own greatness? What more satisfying object could his mind be offered? Would it not therefore be spoiling his delight to occupy his mind with thoughts of how to fit his steps to the rhythm of a tune or how to place a bar skilfully, instead of leaving him in peace to enjoy the contemplation of the majestic glory surrounding him? Put it to the test; leave a king entirely alone, with nothing to satisfy his senses, no care to occupy his mind, with no one to keep him company and no diversion, with complete leisure to think about himself, and you will see that a king without diversion is a very wretched man. Therefore such a thing is carefully avoided, and the persons of kings are invariably attended by a great number of people concerned to see that diversion comes after affairs of state, watching over

their leisure hours to provide pleasures and sport so that there should never be an empty moment. In other words they are surrounded by people who are incredibly careful to see that the king should never be alone and able to think about himself, because they know that, king though he is, he will be miserable if he does think about it.

In all this I am not speaking of Christian kings as Christian but merely as kings. (142)

138 *Diversion.* It is easier to bear death when one is not thinking about it than the idea of death when there is no danger. (166)

139 *Diversion.* From childhood on men are made responsible for the care of their honour, their property, their friends, and even of the property and honour of their friends; they are burdened with duties, language-training and exercises, and given to understand that they can never be happy unless their health, their honour, their fortune and those of their friends are in good shape, and that it needs only one thing to go wrong to make them unhappy. So they are given responsibilities and duties which harass them from the first moment of each day. You will say that is an odd way to make them happy: what better means could one devise to make them unhappy? What could one do? You would only have to take away all their cares, and then they would see themselves and think about what they are, where they come from, and where they are going. That is why men cannot be too much occupied and distracted, and that is why, when they have been given so many things to do, if they have some time off they are advised to spend it on diversion and sport, and always to keep themselves fully occupied.

How hollow and foul is the heart of man! (143)

IX. PHILOSOPHERS

140 Even if Epictetus did see the way quite clearly, he only told men: 'You are on the wrong track.' He shows that there is another, but he does not lead us there. The right way is to

want what God wants. Christ alone leads to it. *Via veritas.*[1]
The vices of Zeno himself.   (466)

141   *Philosophers.* All very well to cry out to a man who does not
know himself that he should make his own way to God! And
all very well to say that to a man who does know himself. (509)

142   (Against the philosophers who have God without Christ.)
Philosophers. They believe that God alone is worthy of love
and admiration; they too wanted to be loved and admired by
men and do not realize their own corruption. If their hearts
are filled with the desire to love and worship him, and if this
is their greatest joy, by all means let them think well of themselves. But if they find this repugnant, if their only inclination
is to win men's esteem, if their only perfection lies in persuading
men, without compelling them, that there is happiness in
loving them, then I say such perfection is horrible. Why,
they have known God and their sole desire has been, not that
men should love him, but that they should stop short at them!
They have wanted to be the object of the happiness which
men desire.   (463)

143   *Philosophers.* We are full of things that impel us outwards.
Our instinct makes us feel that our happiness must be sought
outside ourselves. Our passions drive us outwards, even without
objects to excite them. External objects tempt us in themselves
and entice us even when we do not think about them. Thus
it is no good philosophers telling us: Withdraw into yourselves
and there you will find your good. We do not believe them,
and those who do believe them are the most empty and silly
of all.   (464)

144   What the Stoics propose is so difficult and vain.
The Stoics claim that all those who fall short of the highest
degree of wisdom are equally foolish and vicious, as if those
who were in two inches of water [were to be called as wet as
those right in?][2]   (360)

---

1. 'I am the way, the truth, the life.' John XIV. 6.
2. Pascal did not complete the phrase, but it clearly amounts to this.

145 The three forms of concupiscence have created three sects, and all that philosophers have done is to follow one of these three sorts of concupiscence.   (461)

146 *Stoics.* They conclude that what one can sometimes do one can always do, and that, since the desire for glory certainly causes those who have it to do something, they think others could do the same.

Fever causes some movements which health cannot imitate.

Epictetus concludes from the fact that some Christians are steadfast that it is possible for everyone to be so.   (350)

X. THE SOVEREIGN GOOD

147 *The sovereign good.* Debate about the sovereign good.

That you may be content with yourself and the good things innate in you.[1]

There is some contradiction, because they finally advise suicide. Oh, how happy is a life we throw off like the plague!
(361)

148 *Second part.* Man without faith can know neither true good nor justice.

All men seek happiness. There are no exceptions. However different the means they may employ, they all strive towards this goal. The reason why some go to war and some do not is the same desire in both, but interpreted in two different ways. The will never takes the least step except to that end. This is the motive of every act of every man, including those who go and hang themselves.

Yet for very many years no one without faith has ever reached the goal at which everyone is continually aiming. All men complain: princes, subjects, nobles, commoners, old, young, strong, weak, learned, ignorant, healthy, sick, in every country, at every time, of all ages, and all conditions.

A test which has gone on so long, without pause or change,

1. Seneca, *Ep.*, xx. 8.

really ought to convince us that we are incapable of attaining the good by our own efforts. But example teaches us very little. No two examples are so exactly alike that there is not some subtle difference, and that is what makes us expect that our expectations will not be disappointed this time as they were last time. So, while the present never satisfies us, experience deceives us, and leads us on from one misfortune to another until death comes as the ultimate and eternal climax.

What else does this craving, and this helplessness, proclaim but that there was once in man a true happiness, of which all that now remains is the empty print and trace? This he tries in vain to fill with everything around him, seeking in things that are not there the help he cannot find in those that are, though none can help, since this infinite abyss can be filled only with an infinite and immutable object; in other words by God himself.

God alone is man's true good, and since man abandoned him it is a strange fact that nothing in nature has been found to take his place: stars, sky, earth, elements, plants, cabbages, leeks, animals, insects, calves, serpents, fever, plague, war, famine, vice, adultery, incest. Since losing his true good, man is capable of seeing it in anything, even his own destruction, although it is so contrary at once to God, to reason and to nature.

Some seek their good in authority, some in intellectual inquiry and knowledge, some in pleasure.

Others again, who have indeed come closer to it, have found it impossible that this universal good, desired by all men, should lie in any of the particular objects which can only be possessed by one individual and which, once shared, cause their possessors more grief over the part they lack than satisfaction over the part they enjoy as their own. They have realized that the true good must be such that it may be possessed by all men at once without diminution or envy, and that no one should be able to lose it against his will. Their reason is that this desire is natural to man, since all men inevitably feel it, and man cannot be without it, and they therefore conclude....

(428)

XI. AT PORT ROYAL

149 APR [At Port Royal] *Beginning, after explaining incomprehensibility.*

Man's greatness and wretchedness are so evident that the true religion must necessarily teach us that there is in man some great principle of greatness and some great principle of wretchedness.

It must also account for such amazing contradictions.

To make man happy it must show him that a God exists whom we are bound to love; that our true bliss is to be in him, and our sole ill to be cut off from him. It must acknowledge that we are full of darkness which prevents us from knowing and loving him, and so, with our duty obliging us to love God and our concupiscence leading us astray, we are full of unrighteousness. It must account to us for the way in which we thus go against God and our own good. It must teach us the cure for our helplessness and the means of obtaining this cure. Let us examine all the religions of the world on that point and let us see whether any but the Christian religion meets it.

Do the philosophers, who offer us nothing else for our good but the good that is within us? Have they found the cure for our ills? Is it curing man's presumption to set him up as God's equal? Have those who put us on the level of the beasts, have the Moslems, who offer nothing else for our good than earthly pleasures, even in eternity, brought us the cure for our concupiscence?

What religion, then, will teach us how to cure pride and concupiscence? What religion, in short, will teach us our true good, our duties, the weaknesses which lead us astray, the cause of these weaknesses, the treatment that can cure them, and the means of obtaining such treatment? All the other religions have failed to do so. Let us see what the wisdom of God will do.

'Men,' says his wisdom, 'do not expect either truth or consolation from men. It is I who have made you and I alone can teach you what you are.

'But you are no longer in the state in which I made you. I created man holy, innocent, perfect, I filled him with light and understanding, I showed him my glory and my wondrous works. Man's eye then beheld the majesty of God. He was not then in the darkness that now blinds his sight, nor subject to death and the miseries that afflict him.

'But he could not bear such great glory without falling into presumption. He wanted to make himself his own centre and do without my help. He withdrew from my rule, setting himself up as my equal in his desire to find happiness in himself, and I abandoned him to himself. The creatures who were subject to him I incited to revolt and made his enemies, so that today man has become like the beasts, and is so far apart from me that a barely glimmering idea of his author alone remains of all his dead or flickering knowledge. The senses, independent of reason and often its masters, have carried him off in pursuit of pleasure. All creatures either distress or tempt him, and dominate him either by forcibly subduing him or charming him with sweetness, which is a far more terrible and harmful yoke.

'That is the state in which men are today. They retain some feeble instinct from the happiness of their first nature, and are plunged into the wretchedness of their blindness and concupiscence, which has become their second nature.'

From this principle which I am disclosing to you, you can recognize the reason for the many contradictions which have amazed all mankind, and split them into such different schools of thought. Now observe all the impulses of greatness and of glory which the experience of so many miseries cannot stifle, and see whether they are not necessarily caused by another nature.

APR. *For tomorrow. Prosopopoeia.* 'Men, it is in vain that you seek within yourselves the cure for your miseries. All your intelligence can only bring you to realize that it is not within yourselves that you will find either truth or good.

'The philosophers made such promises and they have failed to keep them.

77

'They do not know what your true good is, nor what your true state is.

'How could they provide cures for ills which they did not even know? Your chief maladies are the pride that withdraws you from God, and the concupiscence that binds you to the earth; all they have done is to keep at least one of these maladies going. If they gave you God for object it was only to exercise your pride; they made you think that you were like him and of a similar nature. And those who saw the vanity of such a pretention cast you into the other abyss, by giving you to understand that your nature was like that of the beasts, and they induced you to seek your good in concupiscence, which is the lot of the animals.

'This is not the way to cure you of the unrighteousness which these wise men failed to recognize in you. Only I can make you understand what you are.

'I do not demand of you blind faith.'

Adam, Jesus Christ.

If you are united to God, it is by grace, and not by nature.

If you are humbled, it is by penitence, not by nature.

Hence this dual capacity.

You are not in the state of your creation.

With the disclosure of these two states it is impossible for you not to recognize them.

Follow your own impulses. Observe yourself, and see if you do not find the living characteristics of these two natures.

Would so many contradictions be found in a simple subject?

Incomprehensible. Everything that is incomprehensible does not cease to exist. Infinite number, an infinite space equal to the finite.

Incredible that God should unite himself to us.

This consideration derives solely from realizing our own vileness, but, if you sincerely believe it, follow it out as far as I do and recognize that we are in fact so vile that, left to ourselves, we are incapable of knowing whether his mercy may not make us capable of reaching him. For I should like to know by what right this animal, which recognizes his own weakness, measures God's mercy and keeps it within limits suggested by his own fancies. He has so little knowledge of what God is that he does not know what he is himself. Disturbed as he is by the contemplation of his own state, he dares to say that God cannot make him capable of communion with him. But I would ask him whether God demands anything but that he should love and know him, and why he thinks that God cannot enable man to know and love him, since man is naturally capable of love and knowledge. There is no doubt that he knows at least that he exists and loves something. Therefore, if he can see something in the darkness around him, and if he can find something to love among earthly things, why, if God reveals to him some spark of his essence, should he not be able to know and love him in whatever way it may please God to communicate himself to us? There is thus undoubtedly an intolerable presumption in such arguments, although they seem to be based on patent humility, which is neither sincere nor reasonable unless it makes us admit that, since we do not know of ourselves what we are, we can learn it only from God.

'I do not mean you to believe me submissively and without reason; I do not claim to subdue you by tyranny. Nor do I claim to account to you for everything. To reconcile these contradictions I mean to show you clearly, by convincing proofs, marks of divinity within me which will convince you of what I am, and establish my authority by miracles and proofs that you cannot reject, so that you will then believe the things I teach, finding no reason to reject them but your own inability to tell whether they are true or not.

'God's will has been to redeem men and open the way of salvation to those who seek it, but men have shown themselves so unworthy that it is right for God to refuse to some, for their hardness of heart, what he grants to others by a mercy they have not earned.

'If he had wished to overcome the obstinacy of the most hardened, he could have done so by revealing himself to them so plainly that they could not doubt the truth of his essence, as he will appear on the last day with such thunder and lightning and such convulsions of nature that the dead will rise up and the blindest will see him. This is not the way he wished to appear when he came in mildness, because so many men had shown themselves unworthy of his clemency, that he wished to deprive them of the good they did not desire. It was therefore not right that he should appear in a manner manifestly divine and absolutely capable of convincing all men, but neither was it right that his coming should be so hidden that he could not be recognized by those who sincerely sought him. He wished to make himself perfectly recognizable to them. Thus wishing to appear openly to those who seek him with all their heart and hidden from those who shun him with all their heart, he has qualified our knowledge of him by giving signs which can be seen by those who seek him and not by those who do not.

'There is enough light for those who desire only to see, and enough darkness for those of a contrary disposition.'   (430)

XII. BEGINNING

150   The ungodly who propose to follow reason must be singularly strong in reason.

What do they say then?

'Do we not see,' they say, 'animals live and die like men, Turks like Christians? They have their ceremonies, their prophets, their doctors, their saints, their religions like us, etc.'

'Is that contrary to Scripture? Does it not say all that?'

If you hardly care about knowing the truth, that is enough to leave you in peace, but if you desire with all your heart to know it, you have not looked closely enough at the details. This would do for a philosophical question, but here where everything is at stake. . . . And yet, after superficial reflection of this kind we amuse ourselves. . . .

Let us inquire of this religion; even if it does not explain the obscurity away, perhaps it will teach us about it.   (226)

151   It is absurd of us to rely on the company of our fellows, as wretched and helpless as we are; they will not help us; we shall die alone.

We must act then as if we were alone. If that were so, would we build superb houses, etc? We should unhesitatingly look for the truth. And, if we refuse, it shows that we have a higher regard for men's esteem than for pursuing the truth. (211)

152 Between us and heaven or hell there is only life half-way, the most fragile thing in the world. (213)

153 What after all do you promise me but ten years of self-love (for ten years is the stake), trying hard to please without succeeding, not to speak of certain anguish? (238)

154 *Choices.* Our life in the world must vary according to these different assumptions:
   1. (if it is certain that we shall always be here)[1] if we could always be here.
   2. (if it is uncertain whether we shall always be here or not).
   3. (if it is certain that we shall not always be here, but if we are sure of being here for a long time).
   4. (if it is certain that we shall not always be here and uncertain whether we shall be here for a long time: false).
   5. if it is certain that we shall not be here for long, and uncertain whether we shall be here even one hour.
   This last assumption is ours. (237)

155 Heart
   Instinct
   Principles. (281)

156 Pity the atheists who seek, for are they not unhappy enough? Inveigh against those who boast about it. (190)

157 Atheism indicates strength of mind, but only up to a certain point. (225)

158 As far as the choices go, you must take the trouble to seek the truth, for if you die without worshipping the true principle you are lost. 'But', you say, 'if he had wanted me to worship him, he would have left me some signs of his will.' So he did, but you pay no heed. Look for them then; it is well worth it. (236)

1. Pascal crossed out all the passages in brackets, but left the numbering from 1 to 5.

159 If we ought to give up one week of our life, we ought to give up a hundred years.　(204)

160 There are only three sorts of people: those who have found God and serve him; those who are busy seeking him and have not found him; those who live without either seeking or finding him. The first are reasonable and happy, the last are foolish and unhappy, those in the middle are unhappy and reasonable.

(257)

161 Atheists should say things that are perfectly clear. Now it is not perfectly clear that the soul is material.　(221)

162 Begin by pitying unbelievers; their condition makes them unhappy enough.

They ought not to be abused unless it does them good, but in fact it does them harm.　(189)

163 A man in a dungeon, not knowing whether sentence has been passed on him, with only an hour left to find out, and that hour enough, once he knows it has been passed, to have it revoked. It would be unnatural for him to spend that hour not finding out whether sentence has been passed but playing piquet.

So it is beyond all nature that man, etc. . . . It is weighing down the hand of God.

So it is not only the zeal of those who seek him that proves God's existence, but also the blindness of those who do not seek him.　(200)

164 *Beginning. Dungeon.* I agree that Copernicus' opinion need not be more closely examined. But this:

It affects our whole life to know whether the soul is mortal or immortal.　(218)

165 The last act is bloody, however fine the rest of the play. They throw earth over your head and it is finished for ever.　(210)

166 We run heedlessly into the abyss after putting something in front of us to stop us seeing it.　(183)

XIII. SUBMISSION AND USE OF REASON

167 Submission and use of reason; that is what makes true Christianity. (269)

168 How I hate such foolishness as not believing in the Eucharist, etc. If the Gospel is true, if Jesus Christ is God, where is the difficulty? (224)

169 I should not be a Christian but for the miracles, says St Augustine. (812)

170 *Submission.* One must know when it is right to doubt, to affirm, to submit. Anyone who does otherwise does not understand the force of reason. Some men run counter to these three principles, either affirming that everything can be proved, because they know nothing about proof, or doubting everything, because they do not know when to submit, or always submitting, because they do not know when judgement is called for.

Sceptic, mathematician, Christian; doubt, affirmation, submission. (268)

171 *They received the word with all readiness of mind, and searched the Scriptures daily, whether those things were so.*[1] (696)

172 The way of God, who disposes all things with gentleness, is to instil religion into our minds with reasoned arguments and into our hearts with grace, but attempting to instil it into hearts and minds with force and threats is to instil not religion but terror. *Terror rather than religion.* (185)

173 If we submit everything to reason our religion will be left with nothing mysterious or supernatural.

If we offend the principles of reason our religion will be absurd and ridiculous. (273)

174 St Augustine. Reason would never submit unless it judged that there are occasions when it ought to submit.[2]

1. Acts XVII. 11. 2. *Letters,* CXXII. 5.

It is right, then, that reason should submit when it judges that it ought to submit. (270)

175 One of the ways in which the damned will be confounded is that they will see themselves condemned by their own reason, by which they claimed to condemn the Christian religion. (563)

176 Those who do not love truth excuse themselves on the grounds that it is disputed and that very many people deny it. Thus their error is solely due to the fact that they love neither truth nor charity, and so they have no excuse. (261)

177 Contradiction is a poor indication of truth.
Many things that are certain are contradicted.
Many that are false pass without contradiction.
Contradiction is no more an indication of falsehood than lack of it is an indication of truth. (384)

178 See the two sorts of men under the title: *Perpetuity*. (747b)

179 There are few true Christians. I mean even as regards faith. There are plenty who believe, but out of superstition. There are plenty who do not believe, but because they are libertines; there are few in between.
I do not include those who lead a really devout life, nor all those who believe by intuition of the heart. (256)

180 Jesus Christ performed miracles, and then the apostles, and the early saints in great numbers, because, since the prophecies were not yet fulfilled, and were being fulfilled by them, there was no witness save that of miracles. It was foretold that the Messiah would convert the nations. How could this prophecy be fulfilled without the conversion of the nations, and how could the nations be converted to the Messiah when they could not see the final effect of the prophecies which prove him? Therefore, until he had died, risen again, and converted the nations, all things were not fulfilled and so miracles were needed throughout this time. Now there is no more need of miracles against the Jews, for the fulfilment of the prophecies is a continuing miracle. (838)

181 Piety is different from superstition.

>To carry piety to the point of superstition is to destroy it.

>Heretics reproach us for superstitious submission, and that is doing what they reproach us for.

>Impiety of not believing in the Eucharist because it cannot be seen.

>Superstition of believing certain propositions.

>Faith, etc. (255)

182 There is nothing so consistent with reason as this denial of reason. (272)

183 Two excesses: to exclude reason, to admit nothing but reason. (253)

184 It would have been no sin not to have believed in Jesus Christ without miracles.

>*Look upon me ... if I lie.*[1] (811)

185 Faith certainly tells us what the senses do not, but not the contrary of what they see; it is above, not against them. (265)

186 You abuse the trust people have in the Church and make them believe anything. (947)

187 There is nothing unusual in having to reproach people for being too docile. It is a vice as natural as incredulity and just as pernicious.

>Superstition. (254)

188 Reason's last step is the recognition that there are an infinite number of things which are beyond it. It is merely feeble if it does not go as far as to realize that.

>If natural things are beyond it, what are we to say about supernatural things? (267)

XIV. EXCELLENCE OF THIS MEANS OF PROVING GOD

189 *God through Jesus Christ.* We know God only through Jesus Christ. Without this mediator all communication with God is

1. Job VI. 28.

broken off. Through Jesus we know God. All those who have claimed to know God and prove his existence without Jesus Christ have only had futile proofs to offer. But to prove Christ we have the prophecies which are solid and palpable proofs. By being fulfilled and proved true by the event, these prophecies show that these truths are certain and thus prove that Jesus is divine. In him and through him, therefore, we know God. Apart from that, without Scripture, without original sin, without the necessary mediator, who was promised and came, it is impossible to prove absolutely that God exists, or to teach sound doctrine and sound morality. But through and in Christ we can prove God's existence, and teach both doctrine and morality. Therefore Jesus is the true God of men.

But at the same time we know our own wretchedness, because this God is nothing less than our redeemer from wretchedness. Thus we can know God properly only by knowing our own iniquities.

Those who have known God without knowing their own wretchedness have not glorified him but themselves.

For after that ... the world by wisdom knew not God, it pleased God by the foolishness of preaching to save them that believe.[1] (547)

190 *Preface.* The metaphysical proofs for the existence of God are so remote from human reasoning and so involved that they make little impact, and, even if they did help some people, it would only be for the moment during which they watched the demonstration, because an hour later they would be afraid they had made a mistake.

What they gained by curiosity they lost through pride.[2]

That is the result of knowing God without Christ, in other words communicating without a mediator with a God known without a mediator.

Whereas those who have known God through a mediator know their own wretchedness.   (543)

191 It is not only impossible but useless to know God without Christ. They are drawn closer to him, not further away. They

1. I Cor. I. 21.
2. St Augustine, *Sermons*, CXLI.

are not humbled but ... *The better one is the worse one becomes if one ascribes this excellence to oneself.*[1] (549)

192 Knowing God without knowing our own wretchedness makes for pride.

Knowing our own wretchedness without knowing God makes for despair.

Knowing Jesus Christ strikes the balance because he shows us both God and our own wretchedness. (527)

XV. TRANSITION FROM KNOWLEDGE OF MAN TO KNOWLEDGE OF GOD

193 *Prejudice leading to error.* It is deplorable to see everybody debating about the means, never the end. Everyone thinks about how he will get on in his career, but when it comes to choosing a career or a country it is fate that decides for us.

It is pitiful to see so many Turks, heretics, unbelievers follow in their fathers' footsteps, solely because they have all been brought up to believe that this is the best course. This is what makes each of us pick his particular career as locksmith, soldier, etc.

That is why savages do not care about Provence.[2] (98)

194 Why have limits been set upon my knowledge, my height, my life, making it a hundred rather than a thousand years? For what reason did nature make it so, and choose this rather than that mean from the whole of infinity, when there is no more reason to choose one rather than another, as none is more attractive than another? (208)

195 *Little of everything.* As we cannot be universal by knowing everything there is to be known about everything, we must know a little about everything, because it is much better to know something about everything than everything about something. Such universality is the finest. It would be still better if we could have both together, but, if a choice must be made,

1. St Bernard, *Sermons on the Canticles,* LXXXIV.
2. Cf. Montaigne, *Essays,* I/23.

this is the one to choose. The world knows this and does so, for the world is often a good judge. (37)

196 Some fancy makes me dislike people who croak or who puff while eating. Fancy carries a lot of weight. What good will that do us? That we indulge it because it is natural? No, rather that we resist it. (86)

197 There is no better proof of human vanity than to consider the causes and effects of love, because the whole universe can be changed by it. Cleopatra's nose. (163b)

198 H5. When I see the blind and wretched state of man, when I survey the whole universe in its dumbness and man left to himself with no light, as though lost in this corner of the universe, without knowing who put him there, what he has come to do, what will become of him when he dies, incapable of knowing anything, I am moved to terror, like a man transported in his sleep to some terrifying desert island, who wakes up quite lost and with no means of escape. Then I marvel that so wretched a state does not drive people to despair. I see other people around me, made like myself. I ask them if they are any better informed than I, and they say they are not. Then these lost and wretched creatures look around and find some attractive objects to which they become addicted and attached. For my part I have never been able to form such attachments, and considering how very likely it is that there exists something besides what I can see, I have tried to find out whether God has left any traces of himself.

I see a number of religions in conflict, and therefore all false, except one. Each of them wishes to be believed on its own authority and threatens unbelievers. I do not believe them on that account. Anyone can say that. Anyone can call himself a prophet, but I see Christianity, and find its prophecies, which are not something that anyone can do. (693)

199 H9. *Disproportion of man.* This is where unaided knowledge brings us. If it is not true, there is no truth in man, and if it is true, he has good cause to feel humiliated; in either case he is obliged to humble himself.

And, since he cannot exist without believing this knowledge, before going on to a wider inquiry concerning nature, I want him to consider nature just once, seriously and at leisure, and to look at himself as well, and judge whether there is any proportion between himself and nature by comparing the two.

Let man then contemplate the whole of nature in her full and lofty majesty, let him turn his gaze away from the lowly objects around him; let him behold the dazzling light set like an eternal lamp to light up the universe, let him see the earth as a mere speck compared to the vast orbit described by this star, and let him marvel at finding this vast orbit itself to be no more than the tiniest point compared to that described by the stars revolving in the firmament. But if our eyes stop there, let our imagination proceed further; it will grow weary of conceiving things before nature tires of producing them. The whole visible world is only an imperceptible dot in nature's ample bosom. No idea comes near it; it is no good inflating our conceptions beyond imaginable space, we only bring forth atoms compared to the reality of things. Nature is an infinite sphere whose centre is everywhere and circumference nowhere. In short it is the greatest perceptible mark of God's omnipotence that our imagination should lose itself in that thought.

Let man, returning to himself, consider what he is in comparison with what exists; let him regard himself as lost, and from this little dungeon, in which he finds himself lodged, I mean the universe, let him learn to take the earth, its realms, its cities, its houses and himself at their proper value.

What is a man in the infinite?

But, to offer him another prodigy equally astounding, let him look into the tiniest things he knows. Let a mite show him in its minute body incomparably more minute parts, legs with joints, veins in its legs, blood in the veins, humours in the blood, drops in the humours, vapours in the drops: let him divide these things still further until he has exhausted his powers of imagination, and let the last thing he comes down to now be the subject of our discourse. He will perhaps think that this is the ultimate of minuteness in nature.

I want to show him a new abyss. I want to depict to him not

only the visible universe, but all the conceivable immensity of nature enclosed in this miniature atom. Let him see there an infinity of universes, each with its firmament, its planets, its earth, in the same proportions as in the visible world, and on that earth animals, and finally mites, in which he will find again the same results as in the first; and finding the same thing yet again in the others without end or respite, he will be lost in such wonders, as astounding in their minuteness as the others in their amplitude. For who will not marvel that our body, a moment ago imperceptible in a universe, itself imperceptible in the bosom of the whole, should now be a colossus, a world, or rather a whole, compared to the nothingness beyond our reach? Anyone who considers himself in this way will be terrified at himself, and, seeing his mass, as given him by nature, supporting him between these two abysses of infinity and nothingness, will tremble at these marvels. I believe that with his curiosity changing into wonder he will be more disposed to contemplate them in silence than investigate them with presumption.

For, after all, what is man in nature? A nothing compared to the infinite, a whole compared to the nothing, a middle point between all and nothing, infinitely remote from an understanding of the extremes; the end of things and their principles are unattainably hidden from him in impenetrable secrecy.

Equally incapable of seeing the nothingness from which he emerges and the infinity in which he is engulfed.

What else can he do, then, but perceive some semblance of the middle of things, eternally hopeless of knowing either their principles or their end? All things have come out of nothingness and are carried onwards to infinity. Who can follow these astonishing processes? The author of these wonders understands them: no one else can.

Because they failed to contemplate these infinities, men have rashly undertaken to probe into nature as if there were some proportion between themselves and her.

Strangely enough they wanted to know the principles of things and go on from there to know everything, inspired by a presumption as infinite as their object. For there can be no

PENSÉES

doubt that such a plan could not be conceived without infinite presumption or a capacity as infinite as that of nature.

When we know better, we understand that, since nature has engraved her own image and that of her author on all things, they almost all share her double infinity. Thus we see that all the sciences are infinite in the range of their researches, for who can doubt that mathematics, for instance, has an infinity of infinities of propositions to expound? They are infinite also in the multiplicity and subtlety of their principles, for anyone can see that those which are supposed to be ultimate do not stand by themselves, but depend on others, which depend on others again, and thus never allow of any finality.

But we treat as ultimate those which seem so to our reason, as in material things we call a point indivisible when our senses can perceive nothing beyond it, although by its nature it is infinitely divisible.

Of these two infinites of science, that of greatness is much more obvious, and that is why it has occurred to few people to claim that they know everything. 'I am going to speak about everything,' Democritus used to say.

But the infinitely small is much harder to see. The philosophers have much more readily claimed to have reached it, and that is where they have all tripped up. This is the origin of such familiar titles as *Of the principles of things*, *Of the principles of philosophy*,[1] and the like, which are really as pretentious, though they do not look it, as this blatant one: *Of all that can be known*.[2]

We naturally believe we are more capable of reaching the centre of things than of embracing their circumference, and the visible extent of the world is visibly greater than we. But since we in our turn are greater than small things, we think we are more capable of mastering them, and yet it takes no less capacity to reach nothingness than the whole. In either case it takes an infinite capacity, and it seems to me that anyone who had understood the ultimate principles of things might also succeed in knowing infinity. One depends on the other, and one leads to the other. These extremes touch and join by going in opposite directions, and they meet in God and God alone.

1. By Descartes (1644). 2. By Pico della Mirandola (1486).

Let us then realize our limitations. We are something and we are not everything. Such being as we have conceals from us the knowledge of first principles, which arise from nothingness, and the smallness of our being hides infinity from our sight.

Our intelligence occupies the same rank in the order of intellect as our body in the whole range of nature.

Limited in every respect, we find this intermediate state between two extremes reflected in all our faculties. Our senses can perceive nothing extreme; too much noise deafens us, too much light dazzles; when we are too far or too close we cannot see properly; an argument is obscured by being too long or too short; too much truth bewilders us. I know people who cannot understand that 4 from o leaves o. First principles are too obvious for us; too much pleasure causes discomfort; too much harmony in music is displeasing; too much kindness annoys us: we want to be able to pay back the debt with something over. *Kindness is welcome to the extent that it seems the debt can be paid back. When it goes too far gratitude turns into hatred.*[1]

We feel neither extreme heat nor extreme cold. Qualities carried to excess are bad for us and cannot be perceived; we no longer feel them, we suffer them. Excessive youth and excessive age impair thought; so do too much and too little learning.

In a word, extremes are as if they did not exist for us nor we for them; they escape us or we escape them.

Such is our true state. That is what makes us incapable of certain knowledge or absolute ignorance. We are floating in a medium of vast extent, always drifting uncertainly, blown to and fro; whenever we think we have a fixed point to which we can cling and make fast, it shifts and leaves us behind; if we follow it, it eludes our grasp, slips away, and flees eternally before us. Nothing stands still for us. This is our natural state and yet the state most contrary to our inclinations. We burn with desire to find a firm footing, an ultimate, lasting base on which to build a tower rising up to infinity, but our whole foundation cracks and the earth opens up into the depth of the abyss.

Let us then seek neither assurance nor stability; our reason is

1. Tacitus, *Annals*, IV. 18.

always deceived by the inconsistency of appearances; nothing can fix the finite between the two infinites which enclose and evade it.

Once that is clearly understood, I think that each of us can stay quietly in the state in which nature has placed him. Since the middle station allotted to us is always far from the extremes, what does it matter if someone else has a slightly better understanding of things? If he has, and if he takes them a little further, is he not still infinitely remote from the goal? Is not our span of life equally infinitesimal in eternity, even if it is extended by ten years?

In the perspective of these infinites, all finites are equal and I see no reason to settle our imagination on one rather than another. Merely comparing ourselves with the finite is painful.

If man studied himself, he would see how incapable he is of going further. How could a part possibly know the whole? But perhaps he will aspire to know at least the parts to which he bears some proportion. But the parts of the world are all so related and linked together that I think it is impossible to know one without the other and without the whole.

There is, for example, a relationship between man and all he knows. He needs space to contain him, time to exist in, motion to be alive, elements to constitute him, warmth and food for nourishment, air to breathe. He sees light, he feels bodies, everything in short is related to him. To understand man therefore one must know why he needs air to live, and to understand air one must know how it comes to be thus related to the life of man, etc.

Flame cannot exist without air, so, to know one, one must know the other.

Thus, since all things are both caused or causing, assisted and assisting, mediate and immediate, providing mutual support in a chain linking together naturally and imperceptibly the most distant and different things, I consider it as impossible to know the parts without knowing the whole as to know the whole without knowing the individual parts.

The eternity of things in themselves or in God must still amaze our brief span of life.

The fixed and constant immobility of nature, compared to the continual changes going on in us, must produce the same effect.

And what makes our inability to know things absolute is that they are simple in themselves, while we are composed of two opposing natures of different kinds, soul and body. For it is impossible for the part of us which reasons to be anything but spiritual, and even if it were claimed that we are simply corporeal, that would still more preclude us from knowing things, since there is nothing so inconceivable as the idea that matter knows itself. We cannot possibly know how it could know itself.

Thus, if we are simply material, we can know nothing at all, and, if we are composed of mind and matter, we cannot have perfect knowledge of things which are simply spiritual or corporeal.

That is why nearly all philosophers confuse their ideas of things, and speak spiritually of corporeal things and corporeally of spiritual ones, for they boldly assert that bodies tend to fall, that they aspire towards their centre, that they flee from destruction, that they fear a void, that they have inclinations, sympathies, antipathies, all things pertaining only to things spiritual. And when they speak of minds, they consider them as being in a place, and attribute to them movement from one place to another, which are things pertaining only to bodies.

Instead of receiving ideas of these things in their purity, we colour them with our qualities and stamp our own composite being on all the simple things we contemplate.

Who would not think, to see us compounding everything of mind and matter, that such a mixture is perfectly intelligible to us? Yet this is the thing we understand least; man is to himself the greatest prodigy in nature, for he cannot conceive what body is, and still less what mind is, and least of all how a body can be joined to a mind. This is his supreme difficulty, and yet it is his very being. *The way in which minds are attached to bodies is beyond man's understanding, and yet this is what man is.*[1]

1. St Augustine, *City of God*, XXI. 10.

Finally to complete the proof of our weakness, I shall end
with these two considerations. . . . (72)

200 H3. Man is only a reed, the weakest in nature, but he is a thinking reed. There is no need for the whole universe to take up
arms to crush him: a vapour, a drop of water is enough to kill
him. But even if the universe were to crush him, man would
still be nobler than his slayer, because he knows that he is dying
and the advantage the universe has over him. The universe
knows none of this.

Thus all our dignity consists in thought. It is on thought that
we must depend for our recovery, not on space and time,
which we could never fill. Let us then strive to think well; that
is the basic principle of morality. (347)

201 The eternal silence of these infinite spaces fills me with dread.
(206)

202 Be comforted; it is not from yourself that you must expect it,
but on the contrary you must expect it by expecting nothing
from yourself.

(517)

XVb. NATURE IS CORRUPT

[though Pascal allowed for this heading he allotted no fragments to it.]

XVI. FALSENESS OF OTHER RELIGIONS

203 *Falseness of other religions.* Mahomet without authority.
So he had to have very powerful arguments since they had no
strength but their own.
What does he say then? That we must believe him. (595)

204 *Falseness of other religions.* They have no witnesses; these people
have.

God challenges other religions to produce such signs. Is.
XLIII. 9–XLIV. 8. (592)

205 If all things have a single principle, a single end – all things by
him, all things for him – true religion must then teach us to
worship and to love him alone. But, as we find ourselves unable to worship what we do not know or to love anything but
ourselves, the religion which teaches us these duties must also
teach us about our inability and tell us the remedy as well. It
teaches us that through one man all was lost and the bond
broken between God and man, and that through one man the
bond was restored.

We are born so opposed to this love of God, which is so
necessary for us, that we must be born guilty or God would be
unjust. (489)

206 *They saw the effect but not the cause.*[1] (235)

207 *Against Mahomet.* The Koran is no more Mahomet's than St
Matthew's Gospel. For it is quoted by many authors from one
century to another. Even its enemies, Celsus and Porphyry,
never denied it.

The Koran says that St Matthew was a good man, so he was a
false prophet either in calling good men evil or in disagreeing
with what they said about Christ. (597)

208 Without this divine knowledge how could men help feeling
either exalted at the persistent inward sense of their past greatness or dejected at the sight of their present weakness? For
unable to see the whole truth, they could not attain perfect
virtue. With some regarding nature as incorrupt, others as
irremediable, they have been unable to avoid either pride or
sloth, the twin sources of all vice, since the only alternative is
to give in through cowardice or escape through pride. For if
they realized man's excellence they did not know his corruption,
with the result that they certainly avoided sloth but sank into
pride, and if they recognized the infirmity of nature, they did
not know its dignity, with the result that they were certainly
able to avoid vanity, only to fall headlong into despair.

1. St Augustine, *Contra Pelagium*, IV. 60.

Hence the various sects of Stoics and Epicureans, Dogmatists and Academicians, etc.

The Christian religion alone has been able to cure these twin vices, not by using one to expel the other according to worldly wisdom, but by expelling both through the simplicity of the Gospel. For it teaches the righteous, whom it exalts, even to participation in divinity itself, that in this sublime state they still bear the source of all corruption, which exposes them throughout their lives to error, misery, death and sin; and it cries out to the most ungodly that they are capable of the grace of their redeemer. Thus, making those whom it justifies tremble and consoling those whom it condemns, it so nicely tempers fear with hope through this dual capacity, common to all men, for grace and sin, that it causes infinitely more dejection than mere reason, but without despair, and infinitely more exaltation than natural pride, but without puffing us up. This clearly shows that, being alone exempt from error and vice, it is the only religion entitled to teach and correct mankind.

Who then can refuse belief and worship to such heavenly enlightenment? For is it not clearer than day that we feel within ourselves the indelible marks of excellence, and is it not equally true that we constantly experience the effects of our deplorable condition?

What else then does this chaos and monstrous confusion proclaim but the truth about these two states in a voice too powerful to be gainsaid?   (435)

209 *Difference between Jesus Christ and Mahomet.* Mahomet not fore-told, Jesus foretold.

Mahomet slew, Jesus caused his followers to be slain.

Mahomet forbade reading, the Apostles commanded it.

In a word, the difference is so great that, if Mahomet followed the path of success, humanly speaking, Jesus followed that of death, humanly speaking, and, instead of concluding that where Mahomet succeeded Jesus could have done so too, we must say that, since Mahomet succeeded, Jesus had to die.   (599)

210 All men naturally hate each other. We have used concupiscence as best we can to make it serve the common good, but this is

mere sham and a false image of charity, for essentially it is just hate. (451)

211 We have established and developed out of concupiscence admirable rules of polity, ethics and justice, but at root, the evil root of man, this evil stuff of which we are made is only concealed; it is not pulled up. (453)

212 Jesus is a God whom we can approach without pride and before whom we can humble ourselves without despair. (528)

213 *More deserving of blows than kisses, I am not afraid because I love.*[1]
(551)

214 The sign of the true religion must be that it obliges men to love God. That is quite right, yet while none enjoined it, ours has done so.

It must also have understood about concupiscence and weakness; ours has done so.

It must have provided the remedies; one is prayer. No other religion has asked God to make us love and follow him.
(491)

215 (After hearing the whole nature of man.) For a religion to be true it must have known our nature; it must have known its greatness and smallness, and the reason for both. What other religion but Christianity has known this? (433)

216 True religion teaches us our duties, our weaknesses, pride and concupiscence, and the remedies, humility and mortification.
(493)

217 Some figures are clear and conclusive, but there are others which seem somewhat strained and only convince those who are already converted; they are like those of the Apocalyptics.

But the difference is that they have none that are wholly reliable; so much so that nothing is so wrong as when they point out that theirs are as well-founded as some of ours. For they have none that are conclusive, as some of ours are.

Thus it is not an even contest. These things must not be confused and treated as equal because they seem to be alike in one

1. St Bernard, *Sermons on the Canticles*, LXXXIV.

respect, while differing so much in others. What is clear, when it is divine, earns respect for what is obscure.

(It is like people who use a certain obscure language amongst themselves; those who cannot understand it only make nonsense of it.) (560)

218 It is not by what is obscure in Mahomet, and might be claimed to have a mystical sense, that I want him to be judged, but by what is clear, by his paradise and all the rest. That is what is ridiculous about him, and that is why it is not right to take his obscurities for mysteries, seeing that what is clear in him is ridiculous. It is not the same with Scripture. I admit that there are obscurities as odd as those of Mahomet, but some things are admirably clear, with prophecies manifestly fulfilled. So it is not an even contest. We must not confuse and treat as equal things which are only alike in their obscurities, and not in the clarity which earns respect for the obscurities. (598)

219 Other religions, like those of the heathen, are more popular, for they consist in externals, but they are not for clever men. A purely intellectual religion would be more appropriate to the clever, but would be no good for the people. The Christian religion alone is appropriate for all, being a blend of external and internal. It exalts the people inwardly, and humbles the proud outwardly, and is not perfect without both, for the people must understand the spirit of the letter while the clever must submit their spirit to the letter. (251)

220 No other religion has proposed that we should hate ourselves. No other religion therefore can please those who hate themselves and seek a being who is really worthy of love. And if they had never [before] heard of the religion of a humiliated God, they would at once embrace it. (468)

XVII. MAKE RELIGION ATTRACTIVE

221 Jesus Christ for all, Moses for one people.

The Jews blessed in Abraham: 'I will bless them that bless thee, and in thee shall all families of the earth be blessed.'[1]

1. Gen. XII. 3.

It is a light thing that thou shouldest be my servant (Isaiah).[1] *A light to lighten the Gentiles.*[2]

He hath not dealt so with any nation,[3] said David, speaking of the law, but speaking of Jesus Christ we must say: *He hath dealt so with every nation. It is a light thing,* etc. (Isaiah).

Thus it is for Jesus to be universal. The Church herself only offers her sacrifice for the faithful. Jesus offered that of the Cross for all. (774)

222 Carnal Jews and heathen have their miseries, and so have Christians. There is no redeemer for the heathen, for they do not even hope for one. There is no redeemer for the Jews; they hope for him in vain. Only for the Christians is there a redeemer. (See *Perpetuity*) (747)

XVIII. FOUNDATIONS

223 What is in the chapter on *Figures*, concerning the reason for using figures, must be put into the chapter on *Foundations*. Why was the first coming of Christ prophesied? Why prophesied in an obscure way? (570)

224 The incredulous are the most credulous. They believe in Vespasian's miracles only to disbelieve in those of Moses. (816)

225 Just as Jesus remained unknown among men, so the truth remains among popular opinions with no outward difference. Thus the Eucharist and ordinary bread. (789)

226 The whole of faith consists in Jesus Christ and Adam and the whole of morality in concupiscence and grace. (523)

227 What have they to say against the Resurrection, and against the Virgin Birth? Why is it more difficult to produce a man or an animal than to reproduce one? And if they had never seen a certain species of animal, could they guess whether or not they breed without intercourse? (223)

1. XLIX. 6. 2. Luke II. 32. 3. Ps. CXLVII. 20.

228 What do the prophets say about Jesus Christ? That he will plainly be God? No, but that he is a truly hidden God, that he will not be recognized, that people will not believe that it is he, that he will be a stumbling-block on which many will fall, etc.

Let us not then be criticized for lack of clarity, since we openly profess it. 'But,' they say, 'there are obscurities, and but for that Jesus would not have caused anyone to stumble.' And this is one of the formal intentions of the prophets. *Shut their eyes.*[1]

(751)

229 This religion taught its children what men had managed to know only at their most enlightened. (444)

230 Everything that is incomprehensible does not cease to exist.

(430b)

231 If we claim that man is too slight to deserve communion with God, we must indeed be great to be able to judge. (511)

232 We can understand nothing of God's works unless we accept the principle that he wished to blind some and enlighten others.

(566)

233 Jesus does not deny he is from Nazareth, nor that he is Joseph's son, so as to leave the wicked in their blindness. (796)

234 God wishes to move the will rather than the mind. Perfect clarity would help the mind and harm the will.

Humble their pride. (581)

235 Jesus came to blind those who have clear sight and to give sight to the blind; to heal the sick and let the healthy die; to call sinners to repentance and justify them, and to leave the righteous to their sins; to fill the hungry with good things and to send the rich empty away. (771)

236 *Blind, enlighten.* St Augustine, Montaigne, *Apology for Sebond.*
There is enough light to enlighten the elect and enough obscurity to humiliate them. There is enough obscurity to blind the reprobate and enough light to condemn them and deprive them of excuse.

1. Is. vi. 10.

The genealogy of Jesus in the Old Testament is mixed up with so many others that are irrelevant that it is indistinguishable. If Moses had recorded only the ancestors of Jesus it would have been too obvious; if he had not indicated Jesus's genealogy it would not have been obvious enough. But, after all, anyone who looks closely can see Jesus's genealogy easily distinguished through Thamar, Ruth, etc.

Those who ordained these sacrifices knew how useless they were and those who declared they were useless did not cease to perform them.

If God had permitted only one religion, it would have been too easily recognizable. But, if we look closely, it is easy to distinguish the true religion amidst all this confusion.

Principle: Moses was a clever man. Therefore, if he was governed by his intelligence, he must have put down nothing directly contrary to intelligence.

Thus all the most obvious weaknesses are really strengths. Example: the two genealogies of St Matthew and St Luke. What could be clearer than that there was no collaboration?

(578)

237 If Jesus had only come to sanctify, the whole of Scripture and everything else would tend that way, and it would be quite easy to convince unbelievers. If Jesus had only come to blind, all his behaviour would be unclear and we should have no means of convincing unbelievers, but as he came *for a sanctuary and a stone of stumbling*, as Isaiah says,[1] we cannot convince unbelievers and they cannot convince us. But we do convince them by that very fact, since we say that his whole behaviour proves nothing convincing either way.   (795)

238 *Figures.* Wishing to deprive his people of perishable goods, God made the Jewish people to show that it was not through any inability [to bestow them].   (645)

239 Man is not worthy of God but he is not incapable of being made worthy.

It is unworthy of God to unite himself to wretched man, but

1. Is. VIII. 14.

it is not unworthy of God to raise him out of his wretchedness.

(510)

240 *Proof.* Prophecy with fulfilment.
What preceded and what followed Jesus. (705)

241 *Source of contradictions.* A God humiliated even to death on the Cross. Two natures in Jesus Christ. Two comings. Two states of man's nature. A Messiah triumphing over death by his death. (765)

242 *That God wished to hide himself.* If there were only one religion, God would be clearly manifest. If there were no martyrs except in our religion, likewise.

God being thus hidden, any religion that does not say that God is hidden is not true, and any religion which does not explain why does not instruct. Ours does all this. *Verily thou art a God that hidest thyself.*[1] (585)

243 *Foundation of our faith.* Heathen religion has no foundations today. It is said that it once had them in oracles that spoke. But what are the books that assert this? Are they so reliable by virtue of their authors? Have they been so carefully preserved that we can be certain they have not become corrupt?

The Moslem religion has the Koran and Mahomet for foundation. But was this prophet, supposedly the world's last hope, foretold? And what signs does he show that are not shown by anyone else who wants to call himself a prophet? What miracles does he himself claim to have performed? What mystery did he teach according to his own tradition? What notions of morality? of bliss?

The Jewish religion must be regarded in two different ways in the tradition of the sacred books and in the tradition of the people. Its ideas of morality and bliss are ridiculous in popular tradition, but admirable in that of their sacred books. Its foundation is admirable. It is the oldest book in the world, and the most authentic, and, whereas Mahomet tried to preserve his book by forbidding anyone to read it, Moses tried to preserve his by ordering everyone to read it. And it is the same with

1. Is. XLV. 15.

every religion, for Christianity is two very different things in its sacred books and in those of the casuists.

Our religion is so divine that another divine religion merely provides its foundation. (601)

244 Objections by atheists.
'But we have no light.' (228)

XIX. FIGURATIVE LAW

245 That the law was figurative. (647)

246 *Figures.* The Jewish and Egyptian peoples visibly foretold by the two individuals whom Moses met: the Egyptian beating the Jew, Moses avenging him and killing the Egyptian, and the Jew being ungrateful. (657)

247 *Figurative things.* 'Look that thou make them after their pattern which was shewed thee in the mount,'[1] of which St Paul says that the Jews made an image of heavenly things.[2] (674)

248 *Figures.* The prophets prophesied in figures, like a girdle, beard, burned hair, etc. (653)

249 *Figurative things.* Key of the cipher.
True worshippers.[3] *Behold the Lamb of God which taketh away the sin of the world.*[4] (681)

250 *Figurative.* Terms like sword, shield, *o most mighty.*[5] (667)

251 Anyone who wishes to give the meaning of Scripture without taking it from Scripture is the enemy of Scripture. St Augustine, *De Doctrina Christiana* [III–27]. (900)

252 Two errors: 1. to take everything literally, 2. to take everything spiritually. (648)

253 *Figures.* Jesus opened their minds to understand the Scriptures.

1. Ex. XXV. 40.   2. Heb. VIII. 4–5.   3. John IV. 23.
4. John I. 29.   5. Ps. XLV. 3.

The following are two great revelations: 1. Everything happened to them in figures – *An Israelite indeed, free indeed,* 'true bread from heaven.'[1]

2. A God humiliated even unto the Cross. Christ had to suffer to enter into his glory, 'that through death he might destroy death.'[2] Two comings. (679)

254 Speak against excessive use of figures. (649)

255 In order to make the Messiah recognizable to the good and unrecognizable to the wicked God caused him to be foretold in this way. If the manner of the Messiah had been clearly foretold, there would have been no obscurity even for the wicked.

If the time had been foretold obscurely, there would have been obscurity even for the good, for the goodness of their heart would not have made them understand, for example, that the closed *mem*[3] signified 600 years. But the time was foretold clearly, while the manner was figurative.

As a result, the wicked, taking the promised good to be a material one, have gone astray, although the time was clearly foretold, while the good have not gone astray.

For an understanding of the promised good depends on the heart, which calls good that which it loves, but an understanding of the promised time does not depend on the heart. Thus foretelling the time clearly and the good obscurely deceived none but the wicked. (758)

256 The carnal Jews understood neither the greatness nor the lowliness of the Messiah foretold in their prophecies. They failed to recognize him in his greatness as foretold, as when it is written that the Messiah will be David's lord, though his son,[4] that he is before Abraham and Abraham has seen him.[5] They did not believe he was so great as to be eternal and they similarly failed to recognize him in his humiliation and death. 'Christ,' they said, 'abideth for ever' but this man says he will die.[6] Thus they believed neither that he was mortal nor that he was eternal; they sought in him only a carnal greatness. (662)

1. John I. 47, VIII. 36, VI. 32.   2. Heb. II. 14.
3. A Hebrew letter whose form varies according to its position.
4. Matt. XXII. 45.   5. John VIII. 56, 58.   6. John XII. 34.

257 *Contradictions.* A good portrait can only be made by reconciling all our contradictory features, and it is not enough to follow through a series of mutually compatible qualities without reconciling their opposites; to understand an author's meaning all contradictory passages must be reconciled.

Thus to understand Scripture a meaning must be found which reconciles all contradictory passages; it is not enough to have one that fits a number of compatible passages, but one which reconciles even contradictory ones.

Every author has a meaning which reconciles all contradictory passages, or else he has no meaning at all, and that cannot be said of Scripture and the prophets; they were certainly too sensible. We must therefore look for a meaning which reconciles all contradictions.

Thus the true meaning is not that of the Jews, but in Christ all contradictions are reconciled.

The Jews could not reconcile the end of the kings and princes prophesied by Hosea with the prophecy of Jacob.[1]

If we take the law, the sacrifices and the kingdom for realities, these passages cannot all be reconciled; it necessarily follows that they are only figurative. It would not even be possible to reconcile passages by the same author, in the same book, sometimes in the same chapter, which makes it only too clear what the author intended; as when Ezekiel, xx, says that man shall live by the commandments of God and that he shall not live by them. (684)

258 It was not permitted to sacrifice outside Jerusalem, which was the place the Lord had chosen, nor even to eat the tithes anywhere else. (Deut. xii. 5, Deut. xiv. 23, xv. 20, xvi. 2, 7, 11, 15).

Hosea[2] prophesied that they would be without a king, without a prince, without sacrifices, etc., without idols, all of which has come to pass today, since no lawful sacrifice can be made outside Jerusalem. (728

259 *Figures.* If the law and the sacrifices are the truth, they must be

1. Hos. iii. 4 and Gen. xlix. 10.
2. Hos. iii. 4.

106

pleasing to God and not displeasing. If they are figurative, they must both please and displease him.

Now throughout Scripture they both please and displease. It is written that the law will be changed, that the sacrifice will be changed, that they will be without a king, without princes and without sacrifices, that a new covenant will be made, that the law will be renewed, that the precepts they have received are no good, that their sacrifices are abominable, that God did not ask for them.

It is written on the other hand that the law will last for ever, that this covenant will be eternal, that the sacrifice will be eternal, that the sceptre will never leave their midst, since it is not to go until the coming of the everlasting king.

Are all these passages meant literally? No. Are they all meant figuratively? No, but either literally or figuratively. But by excluding the possibility of a literal meaning, the first passages show that there is merely a figurative one.

All these passages together cannot be literal statements; they can all be figurative statements. They are thus not literal but figurative statements.

The Lamb slain from the foundation of the world,[1] *perpetual sacrifice.*[2]
(685)

260 A picture includes absence and presence, pleasant and unpleasant. Reality excludes absence and unpleasantness.

Figures. To know whether the law and the sacrifices are literal or figurative, we must see whether the prophets in speaking of these things thought and looked no further, so that they saw only the old covenant, or whether they saw something else of which it was the image, for in a picture we see the thing represented. To know this we need only examine what they say about it.

When they say it will be everlasting, do they mean the same covenant which they say will be changed? And the same with the sacrifices, etc.

A cipher has two meanings. When we come upon an important letter, whose meaning is clear but where we are told

1. Rev. XIII. 8.   2. Ezek. XLVI. 14 and elsewhere.

that the meaning is veiled and obscure, that it is hidden so that seeing we shall not see and hearing we shall not hear, what else are we to think but that this is a cipher with a double meaning?

And all the more when we find obvious contradictions in the literal meaning.

The prophets clearly said that Israel would always be beloved of God and that the law would be everlasting, and they also said that none would understand their meaning, but that it was veiled.

How highly then should we esteem those who break the cipher for us and teach us to understand the hidden meaning, especially when the principles they derive from it are completely natural and clear? That is what Jesus and the Apostles did. They broke the seal, he rent the veil and revealed the spirit. They have taught us to this effect that man's enemies are his passions, that the redeemer will be spiritual and his kingdom of the spirit, that there will be two comings, one in wretchedness to humble the proud, the other in glory to exalt the humble, that Jesus is God and man. (678)

261 The time of the first coming was deliberately foretold, the time of the second was not, because the first was meant to be hidden, the second full of glory and so plain that even his enemies have to recognize him. But he had first to come in obscurity and be recognizable only to those who probed the Scriptures. (757)

262 What could his enemies, the Jews, do?

If they accepted him, they proved him by their acceptance, for it would mean that those entrusted with the Messianic hope were accepting him, and if they rejected him they proved him by their rejection. (762)

263 *Contradictions.* Sceptre until the time of the Messiah, but no kings or princes.

> Everlasting law, changed law.
> Everlasting covenant, new covenant.
> Good law, bad precepts. (Ezek. xx). (686)

264 The Jews were used to great and glorious miracles, and so, having had the great wonders of the Red Sea and the land of Canaan as an epitome of the great things to be done by their Messiah, they expected something more glorious, of which the miracles performed by Moses were only a sample.   (746)

265 Figure includes absence and presence, pleasant and unpleasant.
Cipher with a double meaning, of which one is clear and says that the meaning is hidden.   (677)

266 We might perhaps think that, when the prophets foretold that the sceptre would not pass from Judah until the coming of the everlasting king, they were speaking to flatter the people, and that their prophecy was proved false by Herod. But to prove that they did not mean this, and on the contrary knew perfectly well that the temporal kingdom must cease, they said that they would be without kings or princes, and for a long time. (Hosea)   (719)

267 *Figures.* Once this secret is revealed it is impossible not to see it. Read the Old Testament in this light and see whether the sacrifices were true, if the line of Abraham was the true reason for God's friendship, if the promised land was the true place of rest. No? then they were all figurative.
In the same way look at all the prescribed ceremonies and all the commandments not directed towards charity, and it will be seen that they are figurative.
All these sacrifices and ceremonies were therefore either figurative or nonsense. Now some things are too clear and lofty to be considered nonsense.
See whether the prophets looked no further than the Old Testament or whether they saw something else in it.   (680)

268 *Figures.* The letter kills – Everything happened figuratively – Christ had to suffer – A humiliated God – This is the cipher St Paul gives us.[1]
Circumcision of the heart, true fasting, true sacrifice, true temple;[2] the prophets showed that all this must be spiritual.
Not the flesh that perishes, but that which does not perish.[3]

1. II Cor. III. 6.   2. Rom. II. 29.   3. John VI. 53-7.

'Ye shall be free indeed.'[1] So the other freedom is just a figurative freedom.

'I am the true bread from heaven.'[2] (683)

269 There are some who see clearly that man has no other enemy but concupiscence, which turns him away from God, and not [human] enemies, no other good but God, and not a rich land. Let those who believe that man's good lies in the flesh and his evil in whatever turns him away from sensual pleasures take their fill and die of it. But those who seek God with all their hearts, whose only pain is to be deprived of the sight of him, whose only desire is to possess him, whose only enemies are those who turn them away from him, who grieve at finding themselves surrounded and dominated by such enemies, let them take heart, for I bring them glad tidings. There is one who will set them free, I will show him to them, I will prove to them that there is a God for them, I will not show him to others. I will show them that a Messiah was promised to deliver them from their enemies, and that one has come to deliver them from their iniquities, but not from their enemies.

When David foretold that the Messiah would deliver his people from their enemies, we may believe that, according to the flesh, he meant the Egyptians. And in that case I could not prove the fulfilment of the prophecy, but we may also very well believe that he meant iniquities, because in fact the Egyptians are not enemies, while iniquities are.

The word 'enemy' is therefore ambiguous, but if he says elsewhere, as he does, that he will deliver his people from their sins,[3] as do Isaiah[4] and others, the ambiguity is removed, and the double meaning of enemies reduced to the single meaning of iniquities. For, if he had sins in mind, he might quite well describe them as enemies, but if he was thinking of enemies he could not refer to them as iniquities.

Now, Moses, David and Isaiah used the same terms. Who can say then that they did not mean the same thing, and that the meaning of David, who patently meant iniquities when

1. John VII. 36. 2. John VI. 51.
3. Ps. CXXX. 8. 4. Is. XLIII. 25.

PENSÉES

he spoke of enemies, was not the same as that of Moses speaking of enemies?

Daniel IX prays that the people may be delivered from the captivity of their enemies. But he was thinking about sins, and to prove it he says that Gabriel came to tell him that his prayer had been granted and that there were only seventy more weeks to wait. After that the people would be delivered from iniquity, sin would come to an end, and the Redeemer, the holy of holies, would bring in everlasting righteousness; not the righteousness of the law, but everlasting righteousness.

(692)

270 A. *Figures.* The Jews had grown old in these earthly thoughts: that God loved their father Abraham, his flesh and what came forth from it; that because of this he had caused them to multiply and had distinguished them from all other peoples without suffering them to intermingle; that when they were languishing in Egypt he brought them out, with many great signs of his favour towards them; that he fed them with manna in the desert; that he led them into a very rich land; that he gave them kings and a well-built temple in which to offer beasts and be purified by the shedding of their blood; that finally he was to send them the Messiah to make them masters over the whole world and that he had foretold the time of his coming.

When the world had grown old in these carnal errors, Jesus Christ came at the time appointed, but not in the expected blaze of glory, and thus they did not think it was he. After Christ's death St Paul came to teach them that all these things had happened figuratively,[1] that the kingdom of God was not in the flesh but the spirit, that the enemies of men were not the Babylonians but their passions, that God did not delight in temples made with hands but in a pure and humble heart,[2] that the circumcision of the body was useless, but that there must be circumcision of the heart;[3] that Moses had not given them the bread from heaven, etc.

1. I Cor. X. 11.
2. Heb. IX. 24. 3. Rom. III. 29.

III

But God being unwilling to reveal these things to these people who were unworthy of them, and yet wishing to effect them so that they should be believed, foretold the time clearly and at times expressed them clearly, but very often in a figurative way, so that those who loved the symbols should go no further and those who loved what was symbolized should see it.

Everything which does not lead to charity is figurative.

The sole object of Scripture is charity.

Everything that does not lead to this sole good is figurative. For, since there is only one goal, everything that does not lead to it explicitly is figurative.

Thus God diversified this single precept of charity to satisfy our curiosity, which seeks diversity, through a diversity which always leads us to the one thing that is necessary for us. For, while one thing only is necessary, we like diversity, and God meets both needs by this diversity which leads to the one thing necessary. The Jews were so fond of symbols and so fully expected them, that they failed to recognize the real thing when it came at the time and in the way foretold.

The Rabbis take the breasts of the bride figuratively,[1] like everything else which does not express their sole aim, that of temporal goods.

Christians even take the Eucharist as figurative of the glory to which they aspire. (670)

271   All Jesus did was to teach men that they loved themselves, that they were slaves, blind, sick, unhappy and sinful, that he had to deliver, enlighten, sanctify and heal them, that this would be achieved by men hating themselves and following him through his misery and death on the Cross. (545)

272   *Figures.* When the word of God, which is true, is false in the letter it is true in the spirit. *Sit thou at my right hand*[2] is false literally, so it is true spiritually.

In such expressions God is spoken of in human terms. And that simply means that what men intend when they seat some-

1. Song of Solomon IV. 5.   2. Ps. CX. I.

one at their right hand, God will also intend. Thus it indicates God's intention, not the way he will carry it out.

Thus when it is written: 'The Lord smelled a sweet savour'[1] and will reward you with a rich land, it means that he has the same intention as a man who smells your sweet savour and rewards you with a rich land. God will have the same intention towards you because you have the same intention towards him as a man has towards the person to whom he offers his sweet savours.

Thus *the anger of the Lord is kindled,*[2] 'jealous God', etc. For as the things of God are inexpressible, they cannot be said in any other way and the Church still uses them today: *for he hath strengthened the bars,*[3] etc.

It is not permissible to attribute to Scripture meanings which it has not revealed itself to have, like saying that the closed *mem*[4] of Isaiah means 600: that is not revealed truth. It is not written that the final *tsadhe*[4] and defective *he*[4] indicate mysteries, and so it is not permissible to say so, still less to say that this is the manner of the philosophers' stone. But we do say that the literal meaning is not true because the prophets themselves said so. (687)

273 Those who find it hard to believe seek an excuse in the fact that the Jews do not believe. 'If it is so clear,' they say, 'why do they not believe?' They would almost like them to believe so that they should not be deterred by the example of the Jews' refusal. But it is the very fact of their refusal that is the basis of our belief. We should be much less inclined to believe if they were on our side; we should then have a much better excuse.

It is a wonderful thing to have made the Jews so fond of prophecies and so hostile to their fulfilment. (745)

274 *Proofs of both Testaments at the same time.* In order to prove both at one stroke we need only see whether the prophecies of the one are fulfilled in the other.

1. Gen. VIII. 21.   2. Is. v. 25.   3. Ps. CXLVII. 13.

4. These references to Hebrew letters, and most others like them, come from the *Pugio Fidei* of the thirteenth-century Dominican Raymond Martini, of which an edition came out in 1651.

To examine the prophecies we must understand them.

For, if we believe they have only one meaning, it is certain that the Messiah has not come, but if they have two meanings, it is certain that he has come in Jesus Christ.

Thus the whole question is to know whether they have two meanings.

Here are the proofs that Scripture has two meanings, which Jesus Christ and the Apostles have given.

1. Proof by Scripture itself.

2. Proofs by the Rabbis. Moses Maimonides says that Scripture certainly has two aspects and that the prophets foretold only Jesus Christ.

3. Proof by the Kabbala.

4. Proofs by the mystic interpretation which the Rabbis themselves give to Scripture.

5. Proofs by the Rabbis' principles that there are two meanings – that there are two comings of the Messiah, glorious or lowly according to their deserts – that the prophets only foretold the Messiah – the law is not eternal but due to change with the coming of the Messiah – that then no one will remember the Red Sea any more – that the Jews and the Gentiles will be intermingled.

6. Proofs by the key provided by Christ and the Apostles.

(642)

275   A. *Figures*. Is. LI. The Red Sea image of the redemption.

That ye may know that the Son of man hath power on earth to forgive sins . . . I say unto thee, Arise.[1]

Wishing to show that he could create a people holy with an invisible holiness and fill them with eternal glory, God created visible things. As nature is an image of grace, he created in natural gifts what he was to do in gifts of grace, so that men should judge him able to create invisible things from seeing him create visible ones.

Thus he saved the people from the Flood, he caused them to be born of Abraham, he redeemed them from the midst of their enemies and gave them rest.

1. Mark II. 10.

God's object was not to save them from the Flood and cause a whole people to be born of Abraham just to lead us into a rich land.

And even grace is only figurative of glory, for it is not the ultimate end. It was prefigured by the law and itself prefigures glory, but it is both the figure and the origin or cause.

The ordinary life of men is like that of saints. They all seek satisfaction, and differ only according to the object in which they locate it. Those they call their enemies are those that prevent them, etc. Thus God showed the power he has for conferring invisible gifts by showing the power he has over visible ones. (643)

276 If two people are talking nonsense, and one sees a double meaning understood by adepts, while the other sees only a single meaning, any uninitiated person who heard them talking like this would judge them alike. But if the first goes on to say angelic things and the other always banal commonplaces, he would judge that one was talking mystically, but not the other, since one has shown clearly enough that he is incapable of such nonsense and capable of a mystic meaning, while the other has shown himself incapable of a mystic meaning and capable of nonsense.

The Old Testament is a cipher. (691)

XX. RABBINISM

277 *Chronology of Rabbinism.* (Page references are from the book *Pugio*.)

p. 27 Rabbi Hakadosh, author of the *Mishna* or oral law, or second law – year 200.

$$\text{Commentaries on the } \textit{Mishna} \quad \left\{ \begin{array}{l} \text{one Siphra} \\ \text{Baraitot} \\ \textit{Talmud} \text{ of Jerusalem} \\ \textit{Tosephta} \end{array} \right\} \text{year 340}$$

Bereshith Rabbah, by R. Hoshaiah Rabbah, commentary on the *Mishna*.

Bereshith Rabbah, Bar Nachoni, are subtle and agreeable discourses on history and theology.

The same author wrote books called *Rabboth.*

A hundred years after the *Talmud* of Jerusalem the *Talmud* of Babylon was written by R. Ashi, by universal consent of all Jews, who are necessarily obliged to observe all that is contained therein.

R. Ashi's addition is called *Gemara,* that is 'the commentary' on the *Mishna,* and the *Talmud* comprises the *Mishna* and *Genara* together. (635)

278 Ample tradition of original sin according to the Jews.

On the text of Gen. VIII: 'the imagination of man's heart is evil from his youth.'.

R. Moses Hadarshan: 'This evil leaven is put into man from the moment of his creation.'

Massachet Sukkah: 'This evil leaven has seven names; in the Scriptures it is called evil, foreskin, unclean, enemy, scandal, heart of stone, icy blast, which all represent the wickedness hidden and imprinted in the heart of man.' *Midrash Tehillim* says the same thing, and also that God will deliver man's good nature from his bad.

This wickedness is renewed against man every day, as it is written in Ps. XXXVII. 32: 'The wicked watcheth the righteous and seeketh to slay him, but the Lord will not leave him.'

This wickedness tempts man's heart in this life and will denounce him in the next.

All this is found in the *Talmud.*

Midrash Tehillim on Ps. IV: 'Stand in awe and sin not.' Stand in awe and frighten your concupiscence and it will not lead you into sin. And on Ps. XXXVI: 'The wicked hath said in his heart that there is no fear of God before his eyes,' in other words the natural wickedness of man has said that to the wicked man.

Midrash el Kohelet: 'The poor wise child is better than the foolish old king who cannot foresee the future.' The child is the virtue and the king the wickedness of man. It is called king because all the members obey it and old because it has been in man's heart from his childhood until old age, and foolish because it leads man into the way of damnation that he does not foresee.

The same thing is in *Midrash Tehillim*.

Bereshith Rabbah on Ps. XXXV: 'All my bones shall say, Lord, who is like unto thee, which deliverest the poor from him that is too strong for him?' and is there any greater tyrant than the evil leaven?

And on Prov. XXV. 21: 'If thine enemy be hungry, give him bread to eat,' that is, if the evil leaven is hungry, give him the bread of wisdom spoken of in Prov. IX, and if he thirsts give him the water mentioned in Is. LV.

Midrash Tehillim says the same thing, and adds that Scripture at this point, when speaking of our enemy, means the evil leaven and that by [giving] him this bread and this water we shall heap coals of fire on his head.

Midrash el Kohelet on Eccl. IX: 'A great king besieged a little city'; the great king is the evil leaven, the great bulwarks with which he surrounds it are temptations. 'And there was found a poor wise man and he delivered the city,' that is virtue.

And on Ps. XLI: 'Blessed is he that considereth the poor.'

And on Ps. LXXVIII. 39: 'A wind that passeth away and cometh not again,' which has led some into error against the immortality of the soul,[1] but the meaning is that this wind is the bad leaven which goes with man until his death and will not come back at the resurrection.

And on Ps. CIII[16] likewise, and on Ps. XVI[10].

Principles of the Rabbis: two Messiahs. (446)

XXI PERPETUITY

279 A single saying of David or Moses, such as 'God will circumcise their hearts,' is a test of their way of thinking.

All their other arguments may be ambiguous and leave it uncertain whether they are philosophers or Christians, but one saying of this kind settles all the others, just as one saying of

1. Because the Hebrew word (like Latin *spiritus*) means both 'soul', or 'breath' and 'wind'.

Epictetus settles everything else in a contrary sense. Ambiguity goes just so far and no further. (690)

280 States would perish if their laws were not often stretched to meet necessity, but religion has never tolerated or practised such a thing. So either compromise or miracles are needed.

There is nothing strange in securing survival through flexibility, but this is not strictly speaking preservation, and in any case they all perish completely in the end. None of them has lasted a thousand years. But the fact that this religion has always been preserved inflexibly shows that it is divine. (614)

281 *Perpetuity.* This religion consists in believing that man has fallen from a state of glory and communion with God into a state of gloom, penitence and estrangement from God, but that after this life we shall be restored by a promised Messiah, and it has always existed on earth.

All things have passed away, but this, through which all things are, has endured.

In the first age of the world men were led into all kinds of misdeeds, and yet there were holy men like Enoch, Lamech and others who patiently awaited the Christ promised since the world began. Noah saw men's wickedness at its height, and he had the merit to save the world in his person, through hoping in the Messiah, whom he prefigured. Abraham was surrounded by idolaters when God showed him the mystery of the Messiah whom he hailed from afar. In the time of Isaac and Jacob abomination spread over the whole earth but these holy men lived in their faith, and Jacob on his deathbed, as he was blessing his children, cried out in a rapture which made him interrupt his speech: 'I await the saviour whom thou hast promised, O Lord.'[1]

The Egyptians were riddled with idolatry and magic, and even the people of God were carried away by their example. Yet Moses and others saw him they did not see, and worshipped as they looked to the eternal gifts he was preparing for them.

Next the Greeks and Latins set up false gods. The poets invented a hundred different theologies, the philosophers split

1. Gen. XLIX. 18.

up into a thousand different sects. And yet in the heart of Judaea there were always chosen men foretelling the coming of the Messiah who was known only to them. He came at last in the fullness of time, and since then we have seen so many schisms and heresies arise, so many states overthrown, so many changes of every kind, while the Church which worships him who has always been has continued without a break. What is wonderful, incomparable and wholly divine is that this religion which has always survived has always been under attack. Times without number it has been on the verge of total destruction, and every time it has been in such a state God has rescued it by extraordinary manifestations of his power. For what is amazing is that it has continued without bending and bowing to the will of tyrants, for there is nothing strange in a state still surviving when its laws are sometimes made to give way to necessity, but that. . . . (See the circle in Montaigne.)   (613)

282   *Perpetuity.* The Messiah has always been believed in. The tradition of Adam was still fresh in Noah and Moses. Then the prophets foretold him, always by foretelling other things, which, coming to pass from time to time for men to see, established the truth of their mission and consequently of the promises they had made concerning the Messiah. Jesus Christ performed miracles, as did the Apostles, which converted all the heathen. Thus with the fulfilment of all the prophecies the Messiah has been proved for ever.   (616)

283   The six ages, the six fathers of the six ages, the six wonders at the beginning of the six ages, the six orients at the beginning of the six ages.   (655)

284   The only religion which is against nature, against common sense and against our pleasures is the only one which has always existed.   (605)

285   If the ancient Church was in error, the Church [today] is a fallen one. If she should fall into error today it is not the same thing, because there is always the overriding principle of tradition, of the faith of the ancient Church, so that submission and conformity to the ancient Church prevails and corrects

everything. But the ancient Church did not presuppose or regard a future Church as we presuppose and regard the ancient Church.

(867)

286   Two kinds of men in every religion.

Among the heathen those who worship animals and others who worship the one God of natural religion.

Among the Jews those who were carnal and those who were spiritual, the Christians of the old law.

Among the Christians the gross ones, who are the Jews of the new law.

The carnal Jews awaited a carnal Messiah, and the gross Christians believe that the Messiah has dispensed them from loving God. True Jews and true Christians worship a Messiah who makes them love God.   (609)

287   Anyone who tries to judge the Jewish religion by its grosser members will misunderstand it. It can be seen in the sacred books and in the tradition of the prophets, who made it clear enough that they did not interpret the law literally. So too our religion is divine in the Gospel, the Apostles and tradition, but ridiculous in those who misuse it.

The Messiah, according to the carnal Jews, was to be a great temporal ruler. Jesus Christ, according to carnal Christians, came to dispense us from loving God, and to give us sacraments which are fully efficacious without our help: neither of these is the Christian nor Jewish religion.

True Jews and true Christians have always awaited a Messiah who would make them love God and by this love overcome their enemies.   (607)

288   Moses, Deut. xxx, promises that God will circumcise their heart to make them capable of loving him.   (689)

289   Carnal Jews are midway between Christians and heathen. The heathen do not know God and love only earthly things, the Jews know the true God and love only earthly things, Christians know the true God and do not love earthly things. Jews and heathen love the same goods; Jews and Christians know the same God.

The Jews were of two kinds: some only had heathen, others had Christian impulses. (608)

XXII. PROOFS OF MOSES

290 *Another circle*. The longevity of the patriarchs, instead of causing the history of past events to be lost, served on the contrary to preserve it. For the reason that we are sometimes not well-informed about the history of our ancestors is that we have barely lived with them at all, and they have often died before we reach the age of reason. Now, when men lived for such a long time, children lived for a long time with their fathers, and spent a long time talking to them. Now what else would they have talked about but the history of their ancestors? For all history came down to that, and they had no studies, sciences or arts, such as bulk large in the conversations of our daily life. Thus we see that people at that time took particular care to preserve their genealogy. (626)

291 This religion so great in miracles, in men holy, pure and irreproachable, in scholars, great witnesses and martyrs, established kings – David – Isaiah, a prince of the blood; so great in knowledge, after displaying all its miracles and all its wisdom, rejects it all and says that it offers neither wisdom nor signs, but only the Cross and folly.

For those who by this wisdom and these signs have deserved your trust, and who have proved their character, declare to you that none of this can change us and make us capable of knowing and loving God, except the virtue contained in the folly of the Cross, without wisdom or signs, and not the signs without this virtue.

Thus our religion is foolish judged by its effective cause, and wise judged by the wisdom which prepares for it. (587)

292 *Proofs of Moses*. Why does Moses make men's lives so long and their generations so few?

For it is not the length of the years but the number of the

generations which makes things obscure, for truth is only altered when men change.

And yet the two most memorable events that have ever been imagined, namely the Creation and the Flood, he brings so close that we seem to touch them both. (624)

293 If we ought to give up a week we ought to give up our whole life. (204b)

294 While the prophets were there to maintain the law, the people paid no attention, but, once there were no more prophets, zeal took their place. (703)

295 Josephus conceals the shame of his nation.
Moses does not conceal his own shame nor. . . .
Would God that all the Lord's people were prophets![1]
He was weary with the people. (629)

296 Shem, who saw Lamech, who saw Adam, also saw Jacob, who saw those who saw Moses; therefore the Flood and Creation are true. This evidence is conclusive among certain people who really understand the matter. (625)

297 Zeal of the Jewish people for their law, and especially since there have been no more prophets. (702)

XXIII. PROOFS OF JESUS CHRIST

298 *Order.* Against the objection that there is no order in Scripture.
The heart has its order, the mind has its own, which uses principles and demonstrations. The heart has a different one. We do not prove that we ought to be loved by setting out in order the causes of love; that would be absurd.

Jesus Christ and St Paul possess the order of charity, not of the mind, for they wished to humble, not to teach.

The same with St Augustine. This order consists mainly in digressions upon each point which relates to the end, so that this shall be kept always in sight. (283)

1. Num. XI. 29.

299 The Gospel only speaks of the Virgin's virginity up to the birth of Jesus. Everything in relation to Jesus. (742)

300 Jesus in such obscurity (according to what the world calls obscurity) that historians writing only of important political events hardly noticed him. (786)

301 *I will pour out my spirit.*[1] All nations were given up to unbelief and concupiscence; the whole earth burned with charity; princes laid aside their rank, maidens suffered martyrdom. Whence did this strength arise? The Messiah had come. These are the signs and effects of his coming. (772)

302 Combination of miracles. (809)

303 An artisan speaking of riches, a lawyer speaking of war, or kingship, etc., but the rich man can well speak of riches, the king can speak indifferently of some great gift he has just bestowed, and God can well speak of God. (799)

304 *Proofs of Jesus Christ.* Why was the book of Ruth preserved? Why the story of Thamar? (743)

305 *Proofs of Jesus Christ.* It was no real captivity when there was the certainty of being delivered in seventy years, but now they are captive and without hope.

God promised them that though he scattered them to the ends of the earth, yet, if they remained faithful to his law, he would gather them in again. They remain most faithful to it, but still oppressed. (638)

306 By trying to prove whether he was God the Jews proved he was man. (763)

307 The Church has had as much difficulty in proving that Jesus was man, against those who denied it, as in proving that he was God, and both were equally evident. (764)

308 The infinite distance between body and mind symbolizes the infinitely more infinite distance between mind and charity, for charity is supernatural.

1. Joel II. 28.

All the splendour of greatness lacks lustre for those engaged in pursuits of the mind.

The greatness of intellectual people is not visible to kings, rich men, captains, who are all great in a carnal sense.

The greatness of wisdom, which is nothing if it does not come from God, is not visible to carnal or intellectual people. They are three orders differing in kind.

Great geniuses have their power, their splendour, their greatness, their victory and their lustre, and do not need carnal greatness, which has no relevance for them. They are recognized not with the eyes but with the mind, and that is enough.

Saints have their power, their splendour, their victory, their lustre, and do not need either carnal or intellectual greatness, which has no relevance for them, for it neither adds nor takes away anything. They are recognized by God and the angels, and not by bodies or by curious minds. God is enough for them.

Archimedes in obscurity would still be revered. He fought no battles visible to the eyes, but enriched every mind with his discoveries. How splendidly he shone in the minds of men!

Jesus without wealth or any outward show of knowledge has his own order of holiness. He made no discoveries; he did not reign, but he was humble, patient, thrice holy to God, terrible to devils, and without sin. With what great pomp and marvellously magnificent array he came in the eyes of the heart, which perceive wisdom!

It would have been pointless for Archimedes to play the prince in his mathematical books, prince though he was.

It would have been pointless for Our Lord Jesus Christ to come as a king with splendour in his reign of holiness, but he truly came in splendour in his own order.

It is quite absurd to be shocked at the lowliness of Jesus, as if his lowliness was of the same order as the greatness he came to reveal.

If we consider his greatness in his life, his passion, his obscurity, his death, in the way he chose his disciples, in their desertion, in his secret resurrection and all the rest, we shall see that it is so great that we have no reason to be shocked at a lowliness which has nothing to do with it.

But there are some who are only capable of admiring carnal greatness, as if there were no such thing as greatness of the mind. And others who only admire greatness of the mind, as if there were not infinitely higher greatness in wisdom.

All bodies, the firmament, the stars, the earth and its kingdoms are not worth the least of minds, for it knows them all and itself too, while bodies know nothing.

All bodies together and all minds together and all their products are not worth the least impulse of charity. This is of an infinitely superior order.

Out of all bodies together we could not succeed in creating one little thought. It is impossible, and of a different order. Out of all bodies and minds we could not extract one impulse of true charity. It is impossible, and of a different, supernatural, order. (793)

309 *Proofs of Jesus Christ.* Jesus said great things so simply that he seems not to have thought about them, and yet so clearly that it is obvious what he thought about them. Such clarity together with such simplicity is wonderful. (797)

310 *Proofs of Jesus Christ.* The hypothesis that the Apostles were knaves is quite absurd. Follow it out to the end and imagine these twelve men meeting after Jesus's death and conspiring to say that he had risen from the dead. This means attacking all the powers that be. The human heart is singularly susceptible to fickleness, to change, to promises, to bribery. One of them had only to deny his story under these inducements, or still more because of possible imprisonment, tortures and death, and they would all have been lost. Follow that out. (801)

311 It is amazing and peculiarly remarkable to see the Jewish people survive for so many years and see them always wretched, but it is necessary as a proof of Christ that they should survive to prove him and be wretched, since they crucified him. And although it is contradictory to be wretched and to survive, they still survive, despite their wretchedness. (640)

312 *Read the prophets.*
See what has been accomplished.
Collate what is still to be accomplished. (697)

313 *Canonical books.* The heretics at the beginning of the Church
serve to prove the canonical books.   (569)

314 When Nebuchadnezzar led the people away, lest they should
think the sceptre had been removed from Judah, he [God] told
them first that they would not be there long; that they would
both be there and be restored.[1]

They were always consoled by the prophets; their kings
continued.

But their second destruction was without any promise of
restoration, without prophets, without kings, without consolation, without hope, because the sceptre had been removed
for ever.   (639)

315 Moses first teaches the Trinity, original sin, the Messiah.
David a great witness.

Good, merciful king, noble soul, wise and mighty. He
prophesies and his miracle takes place. That is infinite.

He had only to say he was the Messiah if he had been vain
enough, because the prophecies were clearer about him than
about Christ.

And the same thing with St John.   (752)

316 Who taught the evangelists the qualities of a perfectly heroic
soul, so that they could depict one so perfectly in Jesus? Why
do they make him weak in his agony? Do they not know how
to describe a steadfast death? Yes, because the same St Luke
describes the death of St Stephen more heroically than that of
Jesus.[2]

They make him capable of fear before death had become
inevitable and then absolutely steadfast.

But when they show him so distressed it is when he distresses
himself; when men distress him he is steadfast.   (800)

317 The zeal of the Jews for their law and their temple. Josephus and
Philo the Jew, *ad Caium.*

What other people were so zealous? They had to be so.

Jesus foretold as to the time and state of the world. 'The

1. Jer. XXIX. 10.
2. Acts VII. 58.

lawgiver from between his feet'[1] and the fourth monarchy.[2]

How fortunate we are to have this light in our darkness!

How good it is to see with the eyes of faith Darius and Cyrus, Alexander, the Romans, Pompey and Herod, working unwittingly for the glory of the Gospel! (701)

318 Apparent discrepancies between the Gospels. (755)

319 The synagogue preceded the Church, the Jews the Christians; the prophets foretold the Christians, St John Jesus Christ. (699)

320 Macrobius. The innocents slain by Herod. (178)

321 Any man can do what Mahomet did. For he performed no miracles and was not foretold. No man can do what Christ did. (600)

322 The Apostles were either deceived or deceivers. Either supposition is difficult, for it is not possible to imagine that a man has risen from the dead.

While Jesus was with them he could sustain them, but afterwards, if he did not appear to them, who did make them act? (802)

XXIV. PROPHECIES

323 Jews and heathen ruined by Jesus Christ: *All the kindreds of the nations shall worship before thee.*[3] *It is a light thing . . .*[4] *Ask of me.*[5]
Yea, all kings shall fall down before him.[6]
False witnesses.[7]
He giveth his cheek to him that smiteth him.[8] *They gave me also gall for my meat.*[9] (773)

324 That idolatry would then be overthrown, that the Messiah would cast down all idols, and would bring men to worship the true God.[10]

1. Gen. XLIX. 10.   2. Dan. II. 40.   3. Ps. XXII. 27.   4. Is. XLIX. 6.
5. Ps. II. 8.   6. Ps. LXXII. 11.   7. Ps. XXXV. 11.   8. Lam. III. 30.
9. Ps. LXIX. 21.   10. Ezek. XXX. 13.

That the temples of the idols would be cast down, and that amongst all the nations and in every place throughout the world a pure sacrifice would be offered up to him, and not that of animals.[1]

That he would be king of the Jews and Gentiles. And here is this king of Jews and Gentiles oppressed by both, who plot his death, ruling over both of them, and destroying both Mosaic worship in Jerusalem, its centre, where he creates his first church, and the worship of idols in Rome, its centre, where he creates his chief church. (730)

325 That he would teach men the way of perfection.

And never before or since has any man come who taught anything nearly as divine as this. (733)

326 And what crowns it all is that it was foretold, so that no one could say it was the effect of chance.

Anyone with only a week to live will not find it in his interest to believe that all this is just a matter of chance.

Now, if we were not bound by our passions, a week and a hundred years would come to the same thing. (694)

327 After many people had gone before him, Jesus finally came to say: 'Here am I and now is the time. What the prophets said was to happen in the fullness of time, I tell you my apostles will accomplish. The Jews will be rejected, Jerusalem will soon be destroyed, and the heathen will enter into the knowledge of God. My apostles will accomplish this after you have killed the heir to the vineyard.'[2]

And then the Apostles told the Jews: 'You will be accursed.' (Celsus laughed at this.) And they told the heathen: 'You will enter into the knowledge of God.' And then it came to pass. (770)

328 'That then they shall teach no more every man his neighbour saying: "Know the Lord" for God will make himself known to all.'[3] 'Your sons shall prophesy.'[4] 'I will put my spirit and my fear in your heart.'[5]

1. Mal. I. 11.   2. Cf. Mark XII. 8.   3. Jer. XXXI. 34.
4. Joel II. 28.   5. Jer. XXXII. 40.

This is all the same thing.

To prophesy is to speak of God, not by outward proofs, but from an inward immediate feeling. (732)

329   That Jesus would be small in his beginning and grow afterwards. The little stone of Daniel [II. 35].

If I had never heard anything at all about the Messiah, none the less, after seeing the fulfilment of such wonderful prophecies about the order of the world, I should see that this is divine. And if I knew that these same books foretold a Messiah, I should feel certain that he should surely come, and seeing that they put the time before the destruction of the second temple, I should say that he had come. (734)

330   *Prophecies.* Conversion of the Egyptians.
    Is. XIX. 19.
    An altar in Egypt to the true God. (725)

331   At the time of the Messiah the people were divided.

The spiritual ones embraced the Messiah, the grosser ones remained to bear witness to him. (748)

332   *Prophecies.* If a single man had written a book foretelling the time and manner of Jesus's coming and Jesus had come in conformity with these prophecies, this would carry infinite weight.

But there is much more here. There is a succession of men over a period of 4,000 years, coming consistently and invariably one after the other, to foretell the same coming; there is an entire people proclaiming it, existing for 4,000 years to testify in a body to the certainty they feel about it, from which they cannot be deflected by whatever threats and persecutions they may suffer. This is of a quite different order of importance. (710)

333   *Prophecies.* The time foretold by the state of the Jewish people, by the state of the heathen people, by the state of the temple, by the number of years. (708)

334   Hos. III.

Is. XLIV, XLVIII. 'I foretold it of old so that they might know it was I.' LIV, LX, LXI, and last.

Jaddus to Alexander. (716)

335 The most weighty proofs of Jesus are the prophecies. It is for them that God made most provision, for the event which fulfilled them is a miracle, continuing from the birth of the Church to the end. Thus God raised up prophets for 1,600 years and for 400 years afterwards dispersed all the prophecies with all the Jews, who carried them into every corner of the world. Such was the preparation for the birth of Christ, and, since his Gospel had to be believed by the whole world, there not only had to be prophecies to make men believe it, but these prophecies had to be spread throughout the world so that the whole world should embrace it.   (706)

336 It takes boldness to foretell the same thing in so many ways.

The four monarchies, idolatrous or heathen, the end of the reign of Judah, and the seventy weeks, all had to take place at the same time, and before the second temple was destroyed.
                                                                    (709)

337 Herod believed to be the Messiah. He had taken away the sceptre from Judah, but he was not of Judah. This created an important sect.

And Bar Kochba and another accepted by the Jews. And the rumour to be heard everywhere at that time.

Suetonius. Tacitus. Josephus.

What kind of man had the Messiah to be, since through him the sceptre was to remain for ever in Judah, but at his coming the sceptre was to be removed from Judah?

To ensure that seeing they should not see and hearing they should not hear, nothing could be better devised.

Anathema of the Greeks against those who compute the periods of time.   (753)

338 *Prediction.* That under the fourth monarchy, before the destruction of the second temple, before the Jews lost their supremacy in the seventieth week of Daniel, while the second temple lasted, the heathen would be instructed and brought to the knowledge of the God worshipped by the Jews, that those who loved him should be delivered from their enemies and filled with the fear and love of God.

And it came to pass that under the fourth monarchy, before the destruction of the second temple, etc., the mass of the heathen worshipped God and led the life of angels.

Their maidens consecrated their virginity and their life to God, and the men renounced all pleasures. What Plato had not been able to make a few chosen and highly educated men believe, a secret force made hundreds of thousands of ignorant men believe by the power of a few words.

Rich men abandoned their wealth, children abandoned the luxury of their parents' home for thē austerity of the desert. (See Philo the Jew.)

What does all this mean? It was what was foretold so long beforehand: for 2,000 years no heathen had worshipped the God of the Jews and at the time predicted the mass of the heathen worshipped this one and only God. Temples are destroyed, even kings make their submission to the Cross. What does this all mean? It is the spirit of God spreading over the earth.

No heathen believed from the time of Moses to that of Christ, according to the rabbis themselves, and then after Christ the mass of the heathen believed in the books of Moses, observing their essence and spirit and rejecting only what was useless. (724)

339   Since the prophets had given various signs which were all to appear at the coming of the Messiah, all these signs had to appear at the same time. Thus the fourth kingdom had to come in when Daniel's seventy weeks were up and the sceptre had then to be removed from Judah.

And all this came to pass without any difficulty. And then the Messiah had to come, and Christ came then, calling himself the Messiah, and this again without any difficulty. This clearly proves the truth of prophecy. (738)

340   *We have no king but Caesar.*[1] Therefore Jesus was the Messiah, because they no longer had any king but a foreigner, and they did not want any other. (720)

341   *Prophecies.* The seventy weeks of Daniel are ambiguous as

1. John XIX. 15.

regards their beginning, because of the terms of the prophecy, and as regards their end, because of the variations between the chronologists. But all the difference only amounts to 200 years. (723)

342 *Prophecies.* The kingdom was not interrupted by the captivity in Babylon, because their return was prompt and foretold. (637)

343 *Prophecies.* The great Pan is dead.[1] (695)

344 What can one feel but reverence for a man who clearly fore-tells things that come to pass, who declares his intention of both blinding and enlightening, and who mixes in obscurities with clear things that come to pass? (756)

345 *It is a light thing. . . .*[2] Vocation of the Gentiles. (Is. LII. 15.) (727b)

346 *Predictions.* It was foretold that at the time of the Messiah he would come to establish a new covenant which would make them forget how they came out of Egypt. (Jer. XXIII. 7, Is. XLIII. 16.). That he would implant his law not in outward things but in their hearts, that he would implant his fear, which had only been in outward things, in their inmost hearts.
Who cannot see the Christian law in all this? (729)

347 *Prophecies.* That the Jews would reject Jesus and that they would be rejected of God because the chosen vine would yield only sour grapes; that the chosen people would be unfaithful, ungrateful, and unbelieving.[3] *A disobedient and gainsaying people.*[4]
That God would strike them with blindness and that they would grope at noonday like blind men.[5]
That one should come before to prepare his way.[6] (735)

348 The eternal reign of David's race. II Chron. by all the pro-phecies and with an oath. And not fulfilled temporally. Jer. XXXIII. 20. (718)

1. Plutarch, *De Defectu*, XVII, a favourite story for Christian apologists (and others) from Eusebius onwards.
2. Is. XLIX. 6.   3. Is. V. 1–7.   4. Rom. X. 21.   5. Deut. XXVIII. 28.
6. Mal. III. 1.

XXV. PARTICULAR FIGURES

349 *Particular figures.* Double law, double tables of the law, double temple, double captivity. (652)

350 Japhet begins the genealogy.
Joseph crosses his arms and prefers the younger.[1] (623)

XXVI. CHRISTIAN MORALITY

351 Christianity is strange; It bids man to recognize that he is vile, and even abominable, and bids him want to be like God. Without such a counterweight his exaltation would make him horribly vain or his abasement horribly abject. (537)

352 Wretchedness induces despair.
Pride induces presumption.
The Incarnation shows man the greatness of his wretchedness through the greatness of the remedy required. (526)

353 Neither an abasement which makes us incapable of good nor a holiness free from evil. (529)

354 There is no doctrine better suited to man than that which teaches him his dual capacity for receiving and losing grace, on account of the dual danger to which he is always exposed of despair or pride. (524)

355 Of all that is on earth, he shares only the pains and not the pleasures. He loves those near to him, but his charity does not keep within these limits and extends to his enemies, and then to God's enemies. (767)

356 What difference is there between a soldier and a Carthusian as regards obedience? For they are equally obedient and dependent and engaged in equally arduous exercises. But the soldier always hopes to become his own master, and never does, for even captains and princes are always slaves and dependent, but

1. i.e. Ephraim. Gen. XLVIII. 13–14.

he always hopes, and always strives to achieve his object, whereas the Carthusian vows never to be anything but dependent. Thus they do not differ in their perpetual servitude, which is always their common lot, but in the hope that one always and the other never entertains. (539)

357 No one is so happy as a true Christian, or so reasonable, virtuous, and lovable. (541)

358 How little pride the Christian feels in believing himself united to God! How little he grovels when he likens himself to the earthworm! A fine way to meet life and death, good and evil! (538)

359 Example of noble deaths of Spartans and others hardly affects us, for what good does it do us?

But the example of the deaths of martyrs affects us for they are our members, we have a common bond with them, their resolution can inspire ours, not only by example, but because it has perhaps deserved ours.

There is none of this in heathen examples. We have no connexion with them, just as we do not become rich through seeing a rich stranger, but through seeing a father or husband rich. (481)

360 *Beginning of thinking members. Morality.* When God had made heaven and earth, which are not conscious of the happiness of their existence, he wanted to create beings who would realize it and compose a body of thinking members. For our own members are not conscious of the happiness of their union, their wonderful understanding, the care taken by nature to infuse them with spirits and make them grow and endure. How happy they would be if they could feel and see all this! But for that they would have to have the intelligence to know it and the good will to fall in with that of the universal soul. If, when they had been given intelligence, they used it to retain nourishment for themselves without letting it pass on to the other members, they would be not only wrong but wretched, and would hate rather than love themselves; for their delight as much as their duty consists in consenting to the guidance of the whole soul to

which they belong, which loves them better than they love themselves. (482)

361 'Are you less of a slave for being liked and flattered by your master? You are really well off, slave, your master flatters you! He will beat you in a while.' (209)

362 The will itself will never bring satisfaction, even if it had power over everything it wanted, but we are satisfied the moment we give it up. Without it we can never be discontented, with it we can never be content. (472)

363 They give free reign to concupiscence and check scruples, whereas they ought to do the opposite. (914)

364 It is superstitious to put one's hopes in formalities, but arrogant to refuse to submit to them. (249)

365 Experience shows us an enormous difference between piety and goodness. (496)

366 Two sorts of men in every religion. (See *Perpetuity*.) Superstition, concupiscence. (747c)

367 *Not formalists*. When St Peter and the Apostles discussed abolishing circumcision, where it was a question of going against the law of God, they did not look to the prophets but simply to the reception of the Holy Spirit in the person of the uncircumcised.

They judged it more certain that God approved those whom he fills with his spirit than that the law must be observed.

They knew that the only purpose of the law was the Holy Spirit, and that since he could certainly be received without circumcision, this was not necessary. (672)

368 *Members. Begin there.* In order to control the love we owe to ourselves, we must imagine a body full of thinking members (for we are members of the whole), and see how each member ought to love itself, etc. (474)

369 *Republic.* The Christian and even the Jewish republic had no master but God, as Philo the Jew observes, *On Monarchy*.

When they fought it was only for God, and their chief hope

was in God alone. They considered their towns as belonging to God alone and preserved them for God. I Chron. XIX. 13. (611)

370 To ensure that the members are happy they must have a will and make it conform to the body. (480)

371 Imagine a body of thinking members. (473)

372 To be a member is to have no life, no being and no movement except through the spirit of the body and for the body. The separated member, no longer seeing the body to which it belongs, has only a wasting and moribund being left. However, it believes itself to be a whole, and, seeing no body on which it depends, believes itself to be dependent only on itself and tries to make itself its own centre and body. But, not having in itself any principle of life, it only wanders about and becomes bewildered at the uncertainty of its existence, quite conscious that it is not the body and yet not seeing that it is member of a body. Eventually, when it comes to know itself, it has returned home, as it were, and only loves itself for the body's sake. It deplores its past aberrations.

It could not by its very nature love anything else except for selfish reasons and in order to enslave it, because each thing loves itself more than anything else.

But in loving the body it loves itself, because it has no being except in the body, through the body, and for the body. *But he that is joined unto the Lord is one spirit.*[1]

The body loves the hand and if it had a will the hand ought to love itself in the same way as the soul loves it; any love that goes beyond that is wrong.

He that is joined to the Lord is one spirit, we love ourselves because we are members of Christ. We love Christ because he is the body of which we are members. All are one. One is in the other like the three persons [of the Trinity]. (483)

373 We must love God alone and hate ourselves alone.

If the foot had never known it belonged to the body, and that there was a body on which it depended, if it had only known

1. I Cor. VI. 17.

and loved itself, and if it then came to know that it belonged to a body on which it depended, what regret, what shame it would feel for its past life, for having been useless to the body which poured life into it, and would have annihilated it if it had rejected and cut it off as the foot cut itself off from the body! How it would pray to be kept on! How submissively it would let itself be governed by the will in charge of the body, to the point of being amputated if necessary! Otherwise it would cease to be a member, for every member must be willing to perish for the sake of the body, for whose sake alone everything exists.   (476)

374   If the feet and hands had their own wills, they would never be properly in order except when submitting this individual will to the primal will governing the whole body. Otherwise they would be disorganized and unhappy, but in desiring only the good of the body they achieve their own good.   (475)

375   The philosophers made vices holy by attributing them to God himself. Christians have made virtues holy.   (503)

376   Two laws are enough to rule the whole Christian republic better than all political laws.   (484)

XXVII. CONCLUSION

377   What a long way it is between knowing God and loving him!
(280)

378   'If I had seen a miracle,' they say, 'I should be converted.' How can they be positive that they would do what they know nothing about? They imagine that such a conversion consists in a worship of God conducted, as they picture it, like some exchange or conversation. True conversion consists in self-annihilation before the universal being whom we have so often vexed and who is perfectly entitled to destroy us at any moment, in recognizing that we can do nothing without him and that we have deserved nothing but his disfavour. It consists in knowing that there is an irreconcilable opposition between

God and us, and that without a mediator there can be no exchange. (470)

379 'Miracles do not serve to convert but to condemn.' I.p. q. 113 a. 10 ad 2.[1] (825)

380 Do not be astonished to see simple people believing without argument. God makes them love him and hate themselves. He inclines their hearts to believe. We shall never believe, with an effective belief and faith, unless God inclines our hearts, and we shall believe as soon as he does so.

And that is what David knew very well: *Incline my heart unto thy testimonies*.[2] (284)

381 Those who believe without having read the Testaments do so because their inward disposition is truly holy and what they hear about our religion matches it. They feel that a God made them, they only want to love God, they only want to hate themselves. They feel that they are not strong enough to do this by themselves, that they are incapable of going to God, and that if God does not come to them they are incapable of communicating with him at all. They hear it said in our religion that we must only love God and only hate ourselves, but that, since we are all corrupt and incapable of reaching God, God made himself man in order to unite himself with us. It takes no more than this to convince men whose hearts are thus disposed and who have such an understanding of their duty and incapacity. (286)

382 *Knowledge of God.* Those whom we see to be Christians without knowledge of the prophecies and proofs are no less sound judges than those who possess such knowledge. They judge with their hearts as others judge with their minds. It is God himself who inclines them to believe and thus they are most effectively convinced.

It may be said that this way of judging is not certain, and that it is by following such a method that heretics and unbelievers go astray.

1. In the *Summa Theologica* of St Thomas.
2. Ps. CXIX. 36.

'The reply to that might be that heretics and unbelievers say the same thing.' To that I answer that God truly inclines those whom he loves to believe in the Christian religion, that the unbelievers have no proof of what they say and therefore, though our propositions employ the same terms, they differ in that one lacks any proof while the other is very solidly proved.

(*Of those who love*[1] – *God inclines the hearts of those whom he loves* – of him who loves him, him whom he loves.)

I freely admit that one of these Christians who believe without proof will perhaps not have the means of convincing an unbeliever, who might say as much for himself, but those who do know the proofs of religion can easily prove that this believer is truly inspired by God, although he cannot prove it himself.

For since God said in his prophets (who are unquestionably prophets) that in the reign of Jesus Christ he would spread his spirit over the nations, and that the sons, daughters and children of the Church would prophesy, there can be no doubt that the spirit of God is upon them and that it is not upon the others.

(287)

1. Ps. CXIX. 36.

SECTION TWO

PAPERS NOT CLASSIFIED BY PASCAL
(Translator's Titles)

[VARIOUS]

383 To be so insensitive as to despise the things of interest, and to become insensitive to the point that most interests us. (197)

384 Maccabees, once there had ceased to be prophets. Massorah, since the coming of Christ. (630)

385 But it was not enough that there should be such prophecies: they had to be distributed throughout the world and preserved through every age.

And so that his coming should not be taken for the effect of chance it had to be foretold.

It is much more to the Messiah's glory that they [Jews] should be the spectators, and even the instruments, of his glory, apart from the fact that God reserved them for this. (707)

386 *The enchantment of vanity.*[1] To render passion harmless let us behave as though we had only a week to live. (386)

387 *Order.* I should be much more afraid of being mistaken and then finding out that Christianity is true than of being mistaken in believing it to be true. (241)

388 Jesus Christ with whom both Testaments are concerned; the Old as its hope, the New as its model, both as their centre. (740)

389 Why did Christ not come in an obvious way, instead of proving himself by previous prophecies?

Why did he have himself foretold figuratively? (794)

390 *Perpetuity.* Let us consider that from the beginning of the world the Messiah has been awaited or worshipped continuously; that there were men who said that God had revealed to them that a redeemer would be born and would save his people; that Abraham then came to say that it had been revealed to him

1. Wisdom IV. 12.

that he [redeemer] would be born of his line through a son he would have; that Jacob declared that of his twelve children it would be of Judah that the redeemer would be born; that Moses and the prophets came next to declare the time and manner of his coming; that they said that the law which they had was only to last until the Messiah gave them his; that it would be permanent until then but that the other would last for ever; that in this way their law or that of the Messiah, of which it was the pledge, would always be upon the earth; that it has in fact always endured; finally, that Jesus Christ did come exactly in the circumstances foretold. This is all very remarkable. (617)

391 'If this was so clearly foretold to the Jews, how could they fail to believe, or why were they not wiped out for resisting something so obvious?'

I reply: first, that it was foretold that they would fail to believe something so obvious and also that they would not be wiped out. And nothing redounds more to the glory of the Messiah, for it was not enough that there should be prophets, they had to be kept above suspicion, now. . . . (749)

392 *Figures.* God wishing to create for himself a holy people, whom he would keep apart from all other nations, whom he would deliver from their enemies, whom he would bring to a place of rest, promised to do so and foretold by his prophets the time and manner of his coming. And yet to strengthen the hope of his chosen people in every age he showed them an image of all this, never leaving them without assurances of his power and will for their salvation, for in the creation of man Adam was witness to this and received the promise of a saviour who should be born of woman.

When men were still so close to Creation that they had not been able to forget their creation and fall; when those who had seen Adam were no longer in this world, God sent Noah, saving him and drowning the whole earth by a miracle which clearly showed his power to save the world, and his will to do so, and to cause to be born from the seed of woman the one he had promised.

This miracle was sufficient to strengthen the hope of the elect.

The memory of the Flood being still so fresh among men, while Noah was still alive, God made his promises to Abraham, and while Shem was still alive, God sent Moses. .... (644)

393 Man's true nature, his true good and true virtue, and true religion are things which cannot be known separately. (442)

394 Instead of complaining that God has hidden himself, you will give him thanks for revealing himself as much as he has, and you will thank him too for not revealing himself to wise men full of pride and unworthy of knowing so holy a God.

Two sorts of persons know him: those who are humble of heart and love their lowly state, whatever the degree of their intelligence, high or low, and those who are intelligent enough to see the truth, however much they may be opposed to it. (288)

395 When we wish to think of God, is there not something which distracts us and tempts us to think of something else? All this is evil and innate in us. (478)

396 It is wrong that anyone should become attached to me even though they do so gladly and of their own accord. I should be misleading those in whom I aroused such a desire, for I am no one's goal nor have I the means of satisfying anyone. Am I not ready to die? Then the object of their attachment will die. Thus, just as I should be culpable if I made someone believe a falsehood, even though I used gentle means of persuasion, and it gave them pleasure to believe it and me pleasure that they should: in the same way I am culpable if I make anyone love me. And, if I attract people to become attached to me, I must warn those who might be ready to consent to the lie that they must not believe it, whatever benefit I might derive from it: and likewise that they must not become attached to me, because they must devote their lives and efforts to pleasing God or seeking him. (Mlle Périer has the original of this note.) (471)

397 Since [man's] true nature has been lost, anything can become his nature: similarly, true good being lost, anything can become his true good. (426)

398 The philosophers did not prescribe feelings proportionate to the two states.

They inspired impulses of pure greatness, and this is not the state of man.

They inspired impulses of pure abasement, and this is not the state of man.

There must be impulses of abasement prompted not by nature but by penitence, not as a lasting state but as a stage towards greatness. There must be impulses of greatness, prompted not by merit but by grace, and after the stage of abasement has been passed. (525)

399 If man was not made for God, why is he only happy in God? If man was made for God, why is he so opposed to God? (438)

400 Man does not know the place he should occupy. He has obviously gone astray; he has fallen from his true place and cannot find it again. He searches everywhere, anxiously but in vain, in the midst of impenetrable darkness. (427)

401 We desire truth and find in ourselves nothing but uncertainty. We seek happiness and find only wretchedness and death.
We are incapable of not desiring truth and happiness and incapable of either certainty or happiness.
We have been left with this desire as much as a punishment as to make us feel how far we have fallen. (437)

402 *Proofs of religion.* Morality / Doctrine / Miracles / Prophecies / Figures. (290)

403 *Wretchedness.* Solomon and Job have known and spoken best about man's wretchedness, one the happiest, the other the unhappiest of men; one knowing by experience the vanity of pleasure, and the other the reality of afflictions. (174)

404 All those contradictions which seemed to take me furthest from the knowledge of any religion are what led me most directly to the true religion. (424)

405 I condemn equally those who choose to praise man, those who

choose to condemn him and those who choose to divert themselves, and I can only approve of those who seek with groans.

(421)

406 *Instinct, reason.* We have an incapacity for proving anything which no amount of dogmatism can overcome.

We have an idea of truth which no amount of scepticism can overcome. (395)

407 The Stoics say: 'Withdraw into yourself, that is where you will find peace.' And that is not true.

Others say: 'Go outside: look for happiness in some diversion.' And that is not true: we may fall sick.

Happiness is neither outside nor inside us: it is in God, both outside and inside us. (465)

408 A letter on the folly of human knowledge and philosophy.
This letter to be put before the section on '*Diversion*'.
'*Happy the man who could.* . . .'[1]
'Happy he who is surprised at nothing.'[2]
280 kinds of sovereign good in Montaigne.[3] (74)

409 Falseness of the philosophers who did not discuss the immortality of the soul.

Falseness of their dilemma in Montaigne. (220)

410 This internal war of reason against the passions has made those who wanted peace split into two sects. Some wanted to renounce passions and become gods, others wanted to renounce reason and become brute beasts. (Des Barreaux.)[4] But neither side has succeeded, and reason always remains to denounce the baseness and injustice of the passions and to disturb the peace of those who surrender to them. And the passions are always alive in those who want to renounce them. (413)

411 *Greatness of man.* Our idea of man's soul is so lofty that we cannot bear to be despised and not enjoy the esteem of a given soul. All the happiness of men lies in this esteem. (400)

1. '. . . know the reasons for things.' Virgil, *Georg.*, 11, 490.
2. Horace, *Ep.*, 1. vi, 1. 3. *Essays*, 11. 12.
4. 1602–73. A celebrated libertine.

412   Men are so inevitably mad that not to be mad would be to give a mad twist to madness. (414)

413   Anyone who wants to know the full extent of man's vanity has only to consider the causes and effects of love. The cause is a *je ne sais quoi*. (Corneille.)[1] And its effects are terrifying. This indefinable something, so trifling that we cannot recognize it, upsets the whole earth, princes, armies, the entire world.

Cleopatra's nose: if it had been shorter the whole face of the earth would have been different. (162)

414   *Wretchedness.* The only thing that consoles us for our miseries is diversion. And yet it is the greatest of our miseries. For it is that above all which prevents us thinking about ourselves and leads us imperceptibly to destruction. But for that we should be bored, and boredom would drive us to seek some more solid means of escape, but diversion passes our time and brings us imperceptibly to our death. (171)

415   *Activity.* When a soldier complains of his hard life (or a labourer, etc.) try giving him nothing to do. (130)

416   *Nature is corrupt.* Without Christ man can only be vicious and wretched. With Christ man is free from vice and wretchedness.

In him is all our virtue and all our happiness.

Apart from him there is only vice, wretchedness, error, darkness, death, despair. (546)

417   Not only do we only know God through Jesus Christ, but we only know ourselves through Jesus Christ; we only know life and death through Jesus Christ. Apart from Jesus Christ we cannot know the meaning of our life or our death, of God or of ourselves.

Thus without Scripture, whose only object is Christ, we know nothing, and can see nothing but obscurity and confusion in the nature of God and in nature itself. (548)

1. *Médée*, II. v.

SERIES II
[THE WAGER]

418 *Infinity – nothing.* Our soul is cast into the body where it finds number, time, dimensions; it reasons about these things and calls them natural, or necessary, and can believe nothing else.

Unity added to infinity does not increase it at all, any more than a foot added to an infinite measurement: the finite is annihilated in the presence of the infinite and becomes pure nothingness. So it is with our mind before God, with our justice before divine justice. There is not so great a disproportion between our justice and God's as between unity and infinity.

God's justice must be as vast as his mercy. Now his justice towards the damned is less vast and ought to be less startling to us than his mercy towards the elect.

We know that the infinite exists without knowing its nature, just as we know that it is untrue that numbers are finite. Thus it is true that there is an infinite number, but we do not know what it is. It is untrue that it is even, untrue that it is odd, for by adding a unit it does not change its nature. Yet it is a number, and every number is even or odd. (It is true that this applies to every finite number.)

Therefore we may well know that God exists without knowing what he is.

Is there no substantial truth, seeing that there are so many true things which are not truth itself?

Thus we know the existence and nature of the finite because we too are finite and extended in space.

We know the existence of the infinite without knowing its nature, because it too has extension but unlike us no limits.

But we do not know either the existence or the nature of God, because he has neither extension nor limits.

But by faith we know his existence, through glory we shall know his nature.

Now I have already proved that it is quite possible to know that something exists without knowing its nature.

Let us now speak according to our natural lights.

If there is a God, he is infinitely beyond our comprehension, since, being indivisible and without limits, he bears no relation to us. We are therefore incapable of knowing either what he is or whether he is. That being so, who would dare to attempt an answer to the question? Certainly not we, who bear no relation to him.

Who then will condemn Christians for being unable to give rational grounds for their belief, professing as they do a religion for which they cannot give rational grounds? They declare that it is a folly, *stultitiam*, in expounding it to the world, and then you complain that they do not prove it. If they did prove it they would not be keeping their word. It is by being without proof that they show they are not without sense. 'Yes, but although that excuses those who offer their religion as such, and absolves them from the criticism of producing it without rational grounds, it does not absolve those who accept it.' Let us then examine this point, and let us say: 'Either God is or he is not.' But to which view shall we be inclined? Reason cannot decide this question. Infinite chaos separates us. At the far end of this infinite distance a coin is being spun which will come down heads or tails. How will you wager? Reason cannot make you choose either, reason cannot prove either wrong.

Do not then condemn as wrong those who have made a choice, for you know nothing about it. 'No, but I will condemn them not for having made this particular choice, but any choice, for, although the one who calls heads and the other one are equally at fault, the fact is that they are both at fault: the right thing is not to wager at all.'

Yes, but you must wager. There is no choice, you are already committed. Which will you choose then? Let us see: since a choice must be made, let us see which offers you the least interest. You have two things to lose: the true and the good; and two things to stake: your reason and your will, your knowledge and your happiness; and your nature has two things to avoid: error and wretchedness. Since you must necessarily choose, your reason is no more affronted by choosing one rather than the other. That is one point cleared up. But your happiness? Let us weigh up the gain and the loss involved in calling heads that God exists. Let us assess the two cases: if you win you win everything, if you lose you lose nothing. Do not hesitate then; wager that he does exist. 'That is wonderful. Yes, I must wager, but perhaps I am wagering too much.' Let us see: since there is an equal chance of gain and loss, if you stood to win only two lives for one you could still wager, but supposing you stood to win three?

You would have to play (since you must necessarily play) and it would be unwise of you, once you are obliged to play, not to risk your life in order to win three lives at a game in which there is an equal chance of losing and winning. But there is an eternity of life and happiness. That being so, even though there were an infinite number of chances, of which only one were in your favour, you would still be right to wager one in order to win two; and you would be acting wrongly, being obliged to play, in refusing to stake one life against three in a game, where out of an infinite number of chances there is one in your favour, if there were an infinity of infinitely happy life to be won. But here there is an infinity of infinitely happy life to be won, one chance of winning against a finite number of chances of losing, and what you are staking is finite. That leaves no choice; wherever there is infinity, and where there are not infinite chances of losing against that of winning, there is no room for hesitation, you must give everything. And thus, since you are obliged to play, you must be renouncing reason if you hoard your life rather than risk it for an infinite gain, just as likely to occur as a loss amounting to nothing.

For it is no good saying that it is uncertain whether you will win, that it is certain that you are taking a risk, and that the infinite distance between the certainty of what you are risking and the uncertainty of what you may gain makes the finite good you are certainly risking equal to the infinite good that you are not certain to gain. This is not the case. Every gambler takes a certain risk for an uncertain gain, and yet he is taking a certain finite risk for an uncertain finite gain without sinning against reason. Here there is no infinite distance between the certain risk and the uncertain gain: that is not true. There is, indeed, an infinite distance between the certainty of winning and the certainty of losing, but the proportion between the uncertainty of winning and the certainty of what is being risked is in proportion to the chances of winning or losing. And hence if there are as many chances on one side as on the other you are playing for even odds. And in that case the certainty of what you are risking is equal to the uncertainty of what you may win; it is by no means infinitely distant from it. Thus our argument carries infinite weight, when the stakes are finite in a game where there are even chances of winning and losing and an infinite prize to be won.

This is conclusive and if men are capable of any truth this is it.

'I confess, I admit it, but is there really no way of seeing what the cards are?' – 'Yes. Scripture and the rest, etc.' – 'Yes, but my hands are tied and my lips are sealed; I am being forced to wager and I am not free; I am being held fast and I am so made that I cannot believe. What do you want me to do then?' – 'That is true, but at least get it into your head that, if you are unable to believe, it is because of your passions, since reason impels you to believe and yet you cannot do so. Concentrate then not on convincing yourself by multiplying proofs of God's existence but by diminishing your passions. You want to find faith and you do not know the road. You want to be cured of unbelief and you ask for the remedy: learn from those who were once bound like you and who now wager all they have. These are people who know the road you wish to follow, who have been cured of the affliction of which you wish to be cured: follow the way by which they began. They behaved just as if they did believe, taking holy water, having masses said, and so on. That will make you believe quite naturally, and will make you more docile.'[1] – 'But that is what I am afraid of.' – 'But why? What have you to lose? But to show you that this is the way, the fact is that this diminishes the passions which are your great obstacles. . . .'

1. *abêtira*. That is, the unbeliever will act unthinkingly and mechanically, and in this become more like the beasts, from whom man was differentiated, according to contemporary philosophy, by his faculty of reason.

End of this address.

'Now what harm will come to you from choosing this course? You will be faithful, honest, humble, grateful, full of good works, a sincere, true friend. . . . It is true you will not enjoy noxious pleasures, glory and good living, but will you not have others?

'I tell you that you will gain even in this life, and that at every step you take along this road you will see that your gain is so certain and your risk so negligible that in the end you will realize that you have wagered on something certain and infinite for which you have paid nothing.'

'How these words fill me with rapture and delight! – '

'If my words please you and seem cogent, you must know that they come from a man who went down upon his knees before and after to pray this infinite and indivisible being, to whom he submits his own, that he might bring your being also to submit to him for your own good and for his glory: and that strength might thus be reconciled with lowliness.'   (233)

419 Custom is our nature. Anyone who grows accustomed to faith believes it, and can no longer help fearing hell, and believes nothing else.

Anyone accustomed to believe that the king is to be feared. . . .

Who then can doubt that our soul, being accustomed to see number, space, movement, believes in this and nothing else?

(419)

420 'Do you believe that it is impossible for God to be infinite and indivisible?' – 'Yes.' – 'Very well, I will show you something infinite and indivisible: it is a point moving everywhere at an infinite speed.

'For it is one and the same everywhere and wholly present in every place. From this natural phenomenon which previously seemed impossible to you you should realize that there may be others which you do not yet know. Do not conclude from your apprenticeship that there is nothing left for you to learn, but that you still have an infinite amount to learn.'   (231)

421 It is untrue that we are worthy to be loved by others. It is unfair

that we should want such a thing. If we were born reasonable and impartial, with a knowledge of ourselves and others, we should not give our wills this bias. However, we are born with it, and so we are born unfair.

For everything tends towards itself: this is contrary to all order.

The tendency should be towards the general, and the bias towards self is the beginning of all disorder, in war, politics, economics, in man's individual body.

The will is therefore depraved. If the members of natural and civil communities tend to the good of the whole body, the communities themselves should tend towards another more general body of which they are members. We should therefore tend towards the general. Thus we are born unfair and depraved. (477)

No religion except our own has taught that man is born sinful, no philosophical sect has said so, so none has told the truth.

No sect and no religion has always existed on earth except Christianity. (606)

422 We are greatly indebted to those who point out our faults, for they mortify us, they teach us that we have incurred contempt, but they do not prevent us incurring it in the future, for we have plenty of other faults to deserve it. They prepare us for the exercise of correcting and eradicating a given fault. (535)

423 The heart has its reasons of which reason knows nothing: we know this in countless ways.

I say that it is natural for the heart to love the universal being or itself, according to its allegiance, and it hardens itself against either as it chooses. You have rejected one and kept the other. Is it reason that makes you love yourself? (277)

424 It is the heart which perceives God and not the reason. That is what faith is: God perceived by the heart, not by the reason. (278)

425 The only knowledge which is contrary alike to common sense and human nature is the only one always to have existed among men. (604)

426 Only Christianity makes men both happy and lovable: the
code of the gentleman[1] does not allow you to be both happy
and lovable.   (542)

SERIES III

[AGAINST INDIFFERENCE]

427 Let them at least learn what this religion is which they are
attacking before attacking it. If this religion boasted that it had
a clear sight of God and plain and manifest evidence of his
existence, it would be an effective objection to say that there
is nothing to be seen in the world which proves him so obviously. But since on the contrary it says that men are in darkness and remote from God, that he has hidden himself from
their understanding, that this is the very name which he gives
himself in Scripture: *Deus absconditus* [the hidden God];[2] and,
in a word, if it strives equally to establish these two facts: that
God has appointed visible signs in the Church so that he shall
be recognized by those who genuinely seek him, and that he
has none the less hidden them in such a way that he will only
be perceived by those who seek him with all their heart, then
what advantage can they derive when, unconcerned to seek the
truth as they profess to be, they protest that nothing shows it to
them? For the obscurity in which they find themselves, and
which they use as an objection against the Church, simply
establishes one of the things the Church maintains without
affecting the other, and far from proving her teaching false,
confirms it.

In order really to attack the truth they would have to protest
that they had made every effort to seek it everywhere, even in
what the Church offers by way of instruction, but without any
satisfaction. If they talked like that they would indeed be
attacking one of Christianity's claims. But I hope to show here
that no reasonable person could talk like that. I even venture

1. *honnêteté*.
2. Is. XLV. 15.

to say that no one has ever done so. We know well enough how people in this frame of mind behave. They think they have made great efforts to learn when they have spent a few hours reading some book of the Bible, and have questioned some ecclesiastic about the truths of the faith. After that they boast that they have sought without success in books and among men. But, in fact, I should say to them what I have often said: such negligence is intolerable. It is not a question here of the trifling interest of some stranger prompting such behaviour: it is a question of ourselves, and our all.

The immortality of the soul is something of such vital importance to us, affecting us so deeply, that one must have lost all feeling not to care about knowing the facts of the matter. All our actions and thoughts must follow such different paths, according to whether there is hope of eternal blessings or not, that the only possible way of acting with sense and judgement is to decide our course in the light of this point, which ought to be our ultimate objective.

Thus our chief interest and chief duty is to seek enlightenment on this subject, on which all our conduct depends. And that is why, amongst those who are not convinced, I make an absolute distinction between those who strive with all their might to learn and those who live without troubling themselves or thinking about it.

I can feel nothing but compassion for those who sincerely lament their doubt, who regard it as the ultimate misfortune, and who, sparing no effort to escape from it, make their search their principal and most serious business.

But as for those who spend their lives without a thought for this final end of life and who, solely because they do not find within themselves the light of conviction, neglect to look elsewhere, and to examine thoroughly whether this opinion is one of those which people accept out of credulous simplicity or one of those which, though obscure in themselves, none the less have a most solid and unshakeable foundation: as for them, I view them very differently.

This negligence in a matter where they themselves, their eternity, their all are at stake, fills me more with irritation than pity; it astounds and appals me; it seems quite monstrous to me. I do not say this prompted by the pious zeal of spiritual devotion. I mean on the contrary that we ought to have this feeling from principles of human interest and self-esteem. For that we need only see what the least enlightened see.

One needs no great sublimity of soul to realize that in this life there is no true and solid satisfaction, that all our pleasures are mere vanity, that our afflictions are infinite, and finally that death which threatens us at every moment must in a few years infallibly face us with the inescapable and appalling alternative of being annihilated or wretched throughout eternity.

Nothing could be more real, or more dreadful than that. Let us put on as bold a face as we like: that is the end awaiting the world's most illustrious life. Let us ponder these things, and then say whether it is not beyond doubt that the only good thing in this life is the hope of another life, that we become happy only as we come nearer to it, and that, just as no more unhappiness awaits those who have been quite certain of eternity, so there is no happiness for those who have no inkling of it.

It is therefore quite certainly a great evil to have such doubts, but it is at least an indispensable obligation to seek when one does thus doubt; so the doubter who does not seek is at the same time very unhappy and very wrong. If in addition he feels a calm satisfaction, which he openly professes, and even regards as a reason for joy and vanity, I can find no terms to describe so extravagant a creature.

What can give rise to such feelings? What reason for joy can be found in the expectation of nothing but helpless wretchedness? What reason for vanity in being plunged into impenetrable darkness? And how can such an argument as this occur to a reasonable man?

'I do not know who put me into the world, nor what the world is, nor what I am myself. I am terribly ignorant about everything. I do not know what my body is, or my senses, or my soul, or even that part of me which thinks what I am saying, which reflects about everything and about itself, and does not know itself any better than it knows anything else.

'I see the terrifying spaces of the universe hemming me in, and I find myself attached to one corner of this vast expanse without knowing why I have been put in this place rather than that, or why the brief span of life allotted to me should be assigned to one moment rather than another of all the eternity which went before me and all that which will come after me. I see only infinity on every side, hemming me in like an atom or like the shadow of a fleeting instant. All I know is that I must soon die, but what I know least about is this very death which I cannot evade.

'Just as I do not know whence I come, so I do not know whither I am going. All I know is that when I leave this world I shall fall for ever into nothingness or into the hands of a wrathful God, but I do not know which of these two states is to be my eternal lot. Such is my state, full of weakness and uncertainty. And my conclusion from all this is that I must pass my days without a thought of seeking what is to happen to me. Perhaps I might find some enlightenment in my doubts, but I do not want to take the trouble, nor take a step to look for it: and afterwards, as I sneer at those who are striving to this end – (whatever certainty they have should arouse despair rather than vanity) – I will go without fear or foresight to face so momentous an event, and allow myself to be carried off limply to my death, uncertain of my future state for all eternity.'

Who would wish to have as his friend a man who argued like that? Who would choose him from among others as a confidant in his affairs? Who would resort to him in adversity? To what use in life could he possibly be turned?

It is truly glorious for religion to have such unreasonable men as enemies: their opposition represents so small a danger that it serves on the contrary to establish the truths of religion. For the Christian faith consists almost wholly in establishing these two things: The corruption of nature and the redemption of Christ. Now, I maintain that, if they do not serve to prove the truth of the redemption by the sanctity of their conduct, they do at least admirably serve to prove the corruption of nature by such unnatural sentiments.

Nothing is so important to man as his state: nothing more

fearful than eternity. Thus the fact that there exist men who are indifferent to the loss of their being and the peril of an eternity of wretchedness is against nature. With everything else they are quite different; they fear the most trifling things, foresee and feel them; and the same man who spends so many days and nights in fury and despair at losing some office or at some imaginary affront to his honour is the very one who knows that he is going to lose everything through death but feels neither anxiety nor emotion. It is a monstrous thing to see one and the same heart at once so sensitive to minor things and so strangely insensitive to the greatest. It is an incomprehensible spell, a supernatural torpor that points to an omnipotent power as its cause.

Man's nature must have undergone a strange reversal for him to glory in being in a state in which it seems incredible that any single person should be. Yet experience has shown me so many like this that it would be surprising if we did not know that most of those concerned in this are pretending and are not really what they seem. They are people who have heard that it is good form to display such extravagance. This is what they call shaking off the yoke, and what they are trying to imitate. But it would not be difficult to show them how mistaken they are to court esteem in this way. That is not how to acquire it, not even, I would say, among worldly people, who judge things sensibly and who know that the only way to succeed is to appear honest, faithful, judicious and capable of rendering useful service to one's friends, because by nature men only like what may be of use to them. Now what advantage is it to us to hear someone say he has shaken off the yoke, that he does not believe that there is a God watching over his actions, that he considers himself sole master of his behaviour, and that he proposes to account for it to no one but himself? Does he think that by so doing he has henceforth won our full confidence, and made us expect from him consolation, counsel and assistance in all life's needs? Do they think that they have given us great pleasure by telling us that they hold our soul to be no more than wind or smoke, and saying it moreover in tones of pride and satisfaction? Is this then something to be said gaily? Is it not on the contrary something to be said sadly, as being the saddest thing in the world?

If they thought seriously, they would see that this is so misguided, so contrary to good sense, so opposed to decency, so remote in every way from the good form they seek, that they would be more likely to reform than corrupt those who might feel inclined to follow them. And, indeed, make them describe the feeling and reasons which inspire their doubts about religion: what they say will be so feeble and cheap as to persuade you of the contrary. As someone said to them very aptly one day: 'If you go on arguing like that,' he said, 'you really will convert me.' And he was right, for who would not shrink from finding himself sharing the feelings of such contemptible people?

Thus those who only pretend to feel like this would be indeed unhappy if they did violence to their nature in order to become the most impertinent of men. If they are vexed in their inmost heart at not seeing more clearly, they should not try to pretend otherwise: it would be no shame to admit it. There is no shame except in having none. There is no surer sign of extreme weakness of mind than the failure to recognize the unhappy state of a man without God; there is no surer sign of an evil heart than failure to desire that the eternal promises be true; nothing is more cowardly than to brazen it out with God. Let them then leave such impiety to those ill-bred enough to be really capable of it; let them at least be decent people if they cannot be Christians; let them, in short, acknowledge that there are only two classes of persons who can be called reasonable: those who serve God with all their heart because they know him and those who seek him with all their heart because they do not know him.

As for those who live without either knowing or seeking him, they consider it so little worth while to take trouble over themselves that they are not worth other people's trouble, and it takes all the charity of that religion they despise not to despise them to the point of abandoning them to their folly. But as this religion obliges us always to regard them, as long as they live, as being capable of receiving grace which may enlighten them, and to believe that in a short time they may be filled with more faith than we are, while we on the contrary may be stricken by the same blindness which is theirs now, we must do for them what we would wish to be done for us in their place, and appeal to them to have pity on themselves, and to take at least a few steps in an attempt to find some light. Let them spend on reading about it a few of the hours they waste on other things: however reluctantly they may approach the task they will perhaps hit upon something, and at least they will not be losing much. But as for those who approach it with absolute sincerity and a real desire to find the truth, I hope that they will be satisfied, and convinced by the proofs of so divine a religion which I have collected here, following more or less this order. . . . (194)

428 Before going into the proofs of the Christian religion, I find it necessary to point out how wrong are those men who live unconcerned to seek the truth about something of such importance to them, and affecting them so closely.

Of all their aberrations it is no doubt this which most convicts them of folly and blindness, and where they can most easily be confounded by the first application of common sense and by natural instincts. For it is indubitable that this life is but an instant of time, that the state of death is eternal, whatever its nature may be, and thus that all our actions and thoughts must follow such different paths according to the state of this eternity, that the only possible way of acting with sense and judgement is to decide our course in the light of this point, which ought to be our ultimate objective.

There is nothing more obvious than this, and it follows, according to rational principles, that men are behaving quite reasonably if they do not choose another path. Let us then judge on that score those who live without a thought for the final end of life, drifting wherever their inclinations and pleasures may take them, without reflection or anxiety, as if they could annihilate eternity by keeping their minds off it, concerned solely with attaining instant happiness.

However, eternity exists, and death, which must begin it

and which threatens at every moment, must infallibly face them with the inescapable and appalling alternative of being either eternally annihilated or wretched, without their knowing which of these two forms of eternity stands ready to meet them for ever.

The consequences are undeniably terrible. They risk an eternity of wretchedness; whereupon, as if the matter were not worth their trouble, they omit to consider whether this is one of those opinions which are accepted by the people with too ready credulity or one of those which, though obscure in themselves, have a very solid, though concealed, foundation. Thus they do not know whether the fact is true or false, nor whether the proofs are strong or weak. The proofs lie before their eyes, but they refuse to look, and in this state of ignorance they choose to do everything necessary to fall into this calamity, if it exists, to wait for death before testing the proofs, while yet remaining highly satisfied in that state, professing it openly, and indeed with pride. Can we seriously think how important this matter is without being horrified at such extravagant behaviour?

To settle down in such ignorance is a monstrous thing, and those who spend their lives thus must be made to feel how extravagant and stupid it is by having it pointed out to them so that they are confounded by the sight of their own folly. For this is how men argue when they choose to live without knowing what they are and without seeking enlightenment. 'I do not know,' they say. (195)

429 This is what I see and what troubles me. I look around in every direction and all I see is darkness. Nature has nothing to offer me that does not give rise to doubt and anxiety. If I saw no sign there of a Divinity I should decide on a negative solution: if I saw signs of a Creator everywhere I should peacefully settle down in the faith. But, seeing too much to deny and not enough to affirm, I am in a pitiful state, where I have wished a hundred times over that, if there is a God supporting nature, she should unequivocally proclaim him, and that, if the signs in nature are deceptive, they should be completely erased;

that nature should say all or nothing so that I could see what course I ought to follow. Instead of that, in the state in which I am, not knowing what I am nor what I ought to do, I know neither my condition nor my duty. My whole heart strains to know what the true good is in order to pursue it: no price would be too high to pay for eternity.

I envy those of the faithful whom I see living so unconcernedly, making so little use of a gift which, it seems to me, I should turn to such different account. (229)

430 No other has realized that man is the most excellent of creatures. Some, fully realizing how real his excellence is, have taken for cowardice and ingratitude men's natural feelings of abasement; while others, fully realizing how real this abasement is, have treated with haughty ridicule the feelings of greatness which are just as natural to man.

'Lift up your eyes to God,' say some of them, 'look at him whom you resemble and who created you to worship him. You can make yourself like him: wisdom will make you his equal, if you want to follow him.' – 'Hold your heads high, free men,' said Epictetus. And others say, 'Cast down your eyes towards the ground, puny worm that you are, and look at the beasts whose companion you are.'

What then is to become of man? Will he be the equal of God or the beasts? What a terrifying distance! What then shall he be? Who cannot see from all this that man is lost, that he has fallen from his place, that he anxiously seeks it, and cannot find it again? And who then is to direct him there? The greatest men have failed. (431)

431 We cannot conceive Adam's state of glory, or the nature of his sin, or the way it has been transmitted to us. These are things which took place in a state of nature quite different from our own and which pass our present understanding.

Knowing all this does not help us to escape. All that it is important for us to know is that we are wretched, corrupt, separated from God but redeemed by Christ; and that is what is wonderfully proved to us on earth.

Thus the two proofs of corruption and redemption are drawn

from the ungodly, who live indifferent to religion, and from the Jews, who are its irreconcilable enemies. (560)

SERIES IV
[ETERNAL JUDGMENT. CHRIST]

432   ¹ – self-interest, and because it is something of sufficient interest to move us that we should be certain that after all the ills of this life, an inevitable death, which threatens us at every moment, must infallibly in a few years face us with the inescapable and appalling alternative of being annihilated or wretched for all eternity.

The three conditions:

This must not be claimed as evidence of reason.

It is all a man could do if he were certain that this news were false, and even then he ought not to be delighted about it but dejected.

Nothing else matters, and nothing is so neglected.

Our imagination so magnifies the present, because we are continually thinking about it, and so reduces eternity, because we do not think about it, that we turn eternity into nothing and nothing into eternity, and all this is so strongly rooted within us that all our reason cannot save us from it and. . . .

I should ask them if it is not true that they confirm in themselves the foundation of the faith they are attacking, which is that man's nature lies in corruption. (194b, c)

433   . . . Then Jesus Christ comes to tell men that they have no enemies but themselves, that it is their passions that cut them off from God, that he has come to destroy these passions, and to give men his grace, so as to make them all into one holy Church, that he has come to bring into this Church heathen and Jews, to destroy the idols of the former and the superstitions of the latter. All men range themselves in opposition to this, not only through the natural opposition of concupiscence: but above all the kings of the earth unite to abolish this religion

1. Cf. 427. The rest of this fragment is filed in Series XXX, after 821.

at birth as it had been foretold (Proph: *Why do the heathen rage? . . . The kings of the earth . . . against his anointed.*)[1]

All the great ones on earth unite, scholars, sages, kings. They write, they condemn, they slay. And, despite opposition from all these quarters, these simple powerless people resist all these powers and bring to their knees even the kings, scholars, sages, and sweep idolatry from the face of the earth. And all this is accomplished by the power which had foretold it.   (783)

434   Imagine a number of men in chains, all under sentence of death, some of whom are each day butchered in the sight of the others; those remaining see their own condition in that of their fellows, and looking at each other with grief and despair await their turn. This is an image of the human condition.   (199)

435   When the Creation and Flood had taken place, and God was no more going to destroy the world than create it anew, or show himself in such great signs, he began to establish a people upon the earth, specially created, who were to last until the Messiah should create a people through his own spirit. (621)

SERIES V

[TWO ESSENTIAL TRUTHS OF CHRISTIANITY]

436   *Antiquity of the Jews.* What a difference there is between one book and another! I am not surprised that the Greeks composed the *Iliad*, nor the Egyptians and Chinese their histories. You have only to see how that came about. These historians of fable were not contemporary with the things they wrote about. Homer composed a tale, offered and accepted as such: for no one ever doubted that Troy and Agamemnon had never really existed any more than the golden apple. He never meant to write history about it, but only a diversion; he is the only writer of his times, the beauty of the work makes it survive; everyone learns it and talks about it; it is something that has

1. Ps. II. 1, 2.

to be known and everyone knows it off by heart. Four hundred years later the witnesses of these things are no longer alive; no one knows any longer from his own knowledge whether the work is fable or history; it has simply been learned from earlier generations; it may pass for truth.

Any history that is not contemporary is suspect: thus the Sibylline books and those of Trismegistus, and many others which have enjoyed credit in the world, are false and have been found to be false in the course of time. This is not the case with contemporary authors.

There is a great difference between a book composed by an individual, which he hands over to the people, and a book that a people composes itself. It is beyond doubt that the book is as old as the people. (628)

437 Only sentient beings can be wretched: a ruined house is not. Only man is wretched. *I am the man that hath seen affliction.*[1]

(399)

438 That if God's mercy is so great that he gives us salutary instruction even when he hides himself, what enlightenment ought we not to expect when he reveals himself? (848)

439 Acknowledge then the truth of religion in its very obscurity, in the little light we can throw on it, in our indifference regarding knowledge of it. (565)

440 The eternal being exists for ever if he once exists. (559b)

441 All the objections of both sides only tell against themselves, not against religion. Everything the ungodly say. . . . (201)

442 . . . Thus the whole universe teaches man either that he is corrupt or redeemed. Everything teaches him his greatness or his wretchedness. God's abandonment can be seen in the heathen: God's protection in the Jews. (560b)

443 Their error is all the more dangerous because each man follows his own truth: their mistake is not in following a falsehood but in failing to follow another truth. (863)

1. Lam. III. 1.

444 It is true then that everything teaches man his condition, but there must be no misunderstanding, for it is not true that everything reveals God, and it is not true that everything conceals God. But it is true at once that he hides from those who tempt him and that he reveals himself to those who seek him, because men are at once unworthy and capable of God: unworthy through their corruption, capable through their original nature.

(557)

445 What are we to conclude from all our darkness but our unworthiness?

(558)

446 If there were no obscurity man would not feel his corruption: if there were no light man could not hope for a cure. Thus it is not only right but useful for us that God should be partly concealed and partly revealed, since it is equally dangerous for man to know God without knowing his own wretchedness as to know his wretchedness without knowing God.

(586)

447 The conversion of the heathen was solely reserved for the grace of the Messiah. The Jews had been attacking them for so long without success: everything that Solomon and the prophets said was useless. Wise men, like Plato and Socrates, failed to persuade them.

(769)

448 If no sign of God had ever appeared, such an eternal deprivation would be ambiguous and might equally well be ascribed to the absence of any divinity as to the fact that man was unworthy to know about it; but the fact that he appears sometimes but not always removes all ambiguity. If he appears once, he exists for ever. Thus the only possible conclusion is that there is a God and that men are unworthy of him.

(559)

449 ... They blaspheme against what they do not know. The Christian religion consists of two points, which it is equally important for man to know and equally dangerous not to know; and it is equally merciful of God to have given signs of both.

And yet they take occasion to conclude that one of these points is not true from facts which should lead them to conclude the other. Wise men who said there was only one God were persecuted, the Jews were hated, Christians still more so. They saw by the light of nature that, if there is a true religion on earth, the conduct of all things must tend to centre upon it. The way all things are conducted ought to be directed towards establishing religion and making it great: men ought to have within themselves feelings conforming to its teaching: in a word it ought to be so much the goal and centre towards which all things tend that anyone knowing its principles would be able to explain the whole nature of man in particular and the whole conduct of the world in general.

And on this basis they take occasion to blaspheme against the Christian religion, because they know so little about it. They imagine that it simply consists in worshipping a God considered to be great and mighty and eternal, which is properly speaking deism, almost as remote from the Christian religion as atheism, its complete opposite. And thence they conclude that this religion is not true, because they cannot see that all things combine to establish the point that God does not manifest himself to men as obviously as he might.

But let them conclude what they like against deism, their conclusions will not apply to Christianity, which properly consists in the mystery of the Redeemer, who, uniting in himself the two natures, human and divine, saved men from the corruption of sin in order to reconcile them with God in his divine person.

It teaches men then these two truths alike: that there is a God, of whom men are capable, and that there is a corruption in nature which makes them unworthy. It is of equal importance to men to know each of these points: and it is equally dangerous for man to know God without knowing his own wretchedness as to know his own wretchedness without knowing the Redeemer who can cure him. Knowing only one of these points leads either to the arrogance of the philosophers, who have known God but not their own wretchedness, or to the despair of the atheists, who know their own wretchedness without knowing their Redeemer.

And thus, as it is equally necessary for man to know these

two points, so it is equally merciful of God to have let us know them. The Christian religion does so, and it consists indeed of this.

Let us go on to examine the order of the world, and see whether all things do not tend to establish the two main tenets of this religion: Jesus Christ is the object of all things, the centre towards which all things tend. Whoever knows him knows the reason for everything.

Those who go astray only do so for want of seeing one of these two things. It is then perfectly possible to know God but not our own wretchedness, or our own wretchedness but not God; but it is not possible to know Christ without knowing both God and our wretchedness alike.

And that is why I shall not undertake here to prove by reasons from nature either the existence of God, or the Trinity or the immortality of the soul, or anything of that kind: not just because I should not feel competent to find in nature arguments which would convince hardened atheists, but also because such knowledge, without Christ, is useless and sterile. Even if someone were convinced that the proportions between numbers are immaterial, eternal truths, depending on a first truth in which they subsist, called God, I should not consider that he had made much progress towards his salvation.

The Christian's God does not consist merely of a God who is the author of mathematical truths and the order of the elements. That is the portion of the heathen and Epicureans. He does not consist merely of a God who extends his providence over the life and property of men so as to grant a happy span of years to those who worship him. That is the portion of the Jews. But the God of Abraham, the God of Isaac, the God of Jacob, the God of the Christians is a God of love and consolation: he is a God who fills the soul and heart of those whom he possesses: he is a God who makes them inwardly aware of their wretchedness and his infinite mercy: who unites himself with them in the depths of their soul: who fills it with humility, joy, confidence and love: who makes them incapable of having any other end but him.

All those who seek God apart from Christ, and who go no

furthet than nature, either find no light to satisfy them or come to devise a means of knowing and serving God without a mediator, thus falling into either atheism or deism, two things almost equally abhorrent to Christianity.

But for Christ the world would not go on existing, for it would either have to be destroyed or be a kind of hell.

If the world existed in order to teach man about God, his divinity would shine out on every hand in a way that could not be gainsaid: but as it only exists through Christ, for Christ, and to teach men about their corruption and redemption, everything in it blazes with proofs of these two truths.

What can be seen on earth indicates neither the total absence, nor the manifest presence of divinity, but the presence of a hidden God. Everything bears this stamp.

Shall the only being who knows nature know it only in order to be wretched? Shall the only one to know it be the only one to be unhappy?

He must not see nothing at all, nor must he see enough to think that he possesses God, but he must see enough to know that he has lost him. For, to know that one has lost something one must see and not see: such precisely is the state of nature.

Whatever course he adopts I will not leave him in peace. . . .

(556)

450 The true religion would have to teach greatness and wretchedness, inspire self-esteem and self-contempt, love and hate. (494)

SERIES VI

[ADVANTAGES OF JEWISH PEOPLE]

451 *Advantages of the Jewish people.* In this inquiry the Jewish people first attract my attention through a number of striking and singular features apparent in them.

I see first of all that they are a people wholly composed of brothers, and, whereas all other peoples are made up of an infinite collection of families, these people, though unusually numerous, are entirely descended from one individual, and being thus all one flesh and members one of another comprise a powerful state of a single family: this is unique.

This family, or people, is the oldest known to man, which seems to me to earn it special respect. And above all in the inquiry we are conducting, since if God has throughout time held communication with men, it is to these that we must resort to know the tradition.

This people is not only of remarkable antiquity but has also lasted for a singularly long time, extending continuously from its origin to the present day. For whereas the peoples of Greece and Italy, of Sparta, Athens, Rome, and others who came so much later have perished so long ago, these still exist, despite the efforts of so many powerful kings who have tried a hundred times to wipe them out, as their historians testify, and as can easily be judged by the natural order of things over such a long spell of years. They have always been preserved, however, and their preservation was foretold. And extending from the earliest to the most recent times their history includes in its range that of all our histories.

The law by which this people is governed is at once the oldest law in the world, the most perfect, and the only one which has been continuously observed in any state. Josephus proves this admirably (*Against Apion*), as also Philo the Jew, in various places where they show that it is so ancient that the very name of law was not known in earliest antiquity until a thousand years later, so that Homer, who wrote the history of so many states, never used it. And it is easy to judge how perfect it is just by reading it, when it can be seen to have provided for everything with such wisdom, equity and judgement that the oldest Greek and Roman lawgivers, having some inkling of it, borrowed from it their chief laws. This appears from what they call the twelve tables and other proofs adduced by Josephus.

But this law is at the same time the most severe and rigorous of all as regards the practice of their religion, holding this people to its duty by imposing a host of peculiar and arduous observations on pain of death. Thus it is a really amazing thing that the law has been constantly preserved for so many centuries, by a people as rebellious and impatient as this one, while all other states have from time to time changed their laws, although they were very much more lenient.

The book containing this first of all laws is itself the oldest book in the world; those of Homer, Hesiod, and others coming only six or seven hundred years later. (620)

SERIES VII
[SINCERITY OF JEWISH PEOPLE]

452 *Sincerity of the Jews.* Lovingly and faithfully they hand on this book in which Moses declares that they have been ungrateful towards God throughout their lives, that he knows they will be still more so after his death, but that he calls heaven and earth to witness against them that he told them so often enough.

He declares that God will in the end grow angry with them and disperse them among the peoples of the earth, that as they angered him by worshipping gods who were not their gods, so he will provoke them by calling on a people that is not his people, and he wishes all his words to be preserved eternally and his book to be placed in the ark of the covenant to serve for ever as witness against them. Isaiah. Isaiah says the same thing, XXX. 8. (631)

SERIES VIII
[TRUE JEWS AND TRUE CHRISTIANS HAVE SAME RELIGION]

453 *To show that true Jews and true Christians have only one religion.*
The religion of the Jews seemed to consist essentially in the fatherhood of Abraham, circumcision, sacrifices, ceremonies, the Ark, the Temple, Jerusalem and finally the law and covenant of Moses.

I say that it consisted in none of these things, but only in the love of God, and that God rejected all the other things.

That God will not accept the fatherhood of Abraham: that the Jews will be punished like strangers by God if they offend him.

Deut. VIII. 19.:[1] 'If thou do at all forget the Lord thy God, and walk after other gods, I testify against you this day, that ye shall surely perish, as the nations which the Lord destroyeth before your face.'

That strangers will be received by God like Jews if they love him.

Is. LVI. 3: 'Neither let the son of the stranger speak saying, The Lord hath utterly separated me from his people. The sons of the stranger that join themselves to the Lord to serve him, and to love the name of the Lord, them will I bring to my holy mountain: their sacrifices shall be accepted, for mine house shall be called a house of prayer.'

That the true Jews considered their merit to come only from God and not from Abraham.

Is. LXIII. 16: 'Doubtless thou art our father, though Abraham be ignorant of us, and Israel acknowledge us not: thou, O Lord, art our father, our redeemer.'

Moses himself told them that God will not regard persons.

Deut. X. 17: God said he, 'regardeth not persons, nor taketh reward.'

The Sabbath was only a sign, Ex. XXXI. 13, and in memory of the exodus from Egypt, Deut. V. 15, and is therefore no longer necessary since Egypt must be forgotten.

Circumcision was only a sign. Gen. XVII. 11.

And that is why, when they were in the desert, they were not circumcised because they could not be confused with other peoples. And after the coming of Christ it is no longer necessary.

That the circumcision of the heart is commanded.

Deut. X. 16–17; Jer. IV. 4: 'Circumcise therefore the foreskin of your heart, and be no more stiff-necked. For the Lord your God is God of Gods, a mighty and a terrible, which regardeth not persons.'

That God said that he would one day perform it.

Deut. XXX. 6: 'God will circumcise thine heart, and the

1. Pascal mistakenly wrote 'IX'. In this, and following quotations, Pascal cuts and compresses the text considerably, but without indicating this in his MS.

heart of thy seed, to love the Lord thy God with all thine heart.'

That the uncircumcised in heart shall be judged.

Jer. IX. 26: 'For God will judge the uncircumcised and all the house of Israel, because they are uncircumcised in heart.'

That the outward is useless without the inward.

Joel. II. 13: '*Rend your heart*,' etc.

Is. LVIII. 3, 4, etc.

The love of God is commanded throughout Deuteronomy.

Deut. XXX. 19: 'I call heaven and earth to record this day against you, that I have set before you life and death. . . . Therefore choose life, that thou mayest love the Lord thy God, and that thou mayest obey his voice, for he is thy life.'

That the Jews, being without this love, will be rejected for their offences, and the heathen chosen in their place.

Hos. I. 10.

Deut. XXXII. 20: 'I will hide my face from them, at the sight of their later offences.[1] For they are a very froward generation, children in whom is no faith. They have moved me to jealousy with those which are not a people, with a foolish nation.'

Is. LXV.

That temporal goods are false and that the true good is to be united with God.

Ps. CXLIV. 15.

That the sacrifices of the Jews are displeasing to God. That their feasts were displeasing to God. Amos V. 21.

Is. LXVI. 15, I. 11 – Jer. VI. 20 – David, *miserere* [Ps. LI] – even on the part of the good.

Expectavi [Ps. XL]: Ps. L. 8, 9, 10, 11, 12, 13 and 14.

That he established them solely for their hardness of heart. Micah (admirably) VI.

I Sam. XV. 22 – Hos. VI. 6.

That the sacrifices of the heathen will be received by God. And God will take no more pleasure in the sacrifices of the Jews. Mal. I. 11.

1. Pascal has mistranslated: 'I will see what their end shall be.'

That God will make a new covenant through the Messiah and that the old will be rejected.

Jer. XXXI. 31.

Mandata non bona [Statutes that were not good] Ezekiel.[1]

That the former things will be forgotten.

Is. XLIII. 18, 19 – LXV. 17, 18.

That the Ark will be forgotten.

That the Temple will be rejected.

Jer. VII. 12, 13, 14.

That the sacrifices will be rejected and other pure sacrifices established.

Mal. I. 11.

That the order of Aaron's priesthood shall be condemned, and that of Melchizedek introduced by the Messiah.

Dixit dominus [Ps. CX].

That this priesthood shall be everlasting.

Ibid.

That Jerusalem will be condemned and Rome accepted.

Dixit dominus.

That the name of the Jews will be rejected and a new name given.

Is. LXV. 15.

That the last name will be better than that of the Jews and everlasting.

Is. LVI. 5.

That the Jews will be without prophets. Amos.[2]

Without kings, without princes, without sacrifices, without idols.

That the Jews will none the less always exist as a people.

Jer. XXXI. 36.   (610)

---

1. Ezek. XX. 25.
2. Amos VII. 9.

SERIES IX
[PARTICULARITY OF JEWISH PEOPLE]

454 I see Christianity founded on a previous religion, in which I find the following facts.

(I am not speaking here of the miracles of Moses, Christ and the apostles, because they do not at first appear convincing, and I want here only to bring as evidence all those foundations of Christianity which are beyond doubt and cannot be called in doubt by anyone whatever.)

It is certain that in certain parts of the world we can see a peculiar people, separated from the other peoples of the world, and this is called the Jewish people.

I see then makers of religions in several parts of the world and throughout the ages, but their morality fails to satisfy me and their proofs fail to give me pause. Thus I should have refused alike the Moslem religion, that of China, of the ancient Romans, and of the Egyptians solely because, none of them bearing the stamp of truth more than another, nor anything which forces me to choose it, reason cannot incline towards one rather than another.

But as I consider this shifting and odd variety of customs and beliefs in different ages, I find in one corner of the world a peculiar people, separated from all the other peoples of the earth, who are the most ancient of all and whose history is earlier by several centuries than the oldest histories we have.

I find then this great and numerous people, descended from one man, worshipping one God, and living according to a law which they claim to have received from his hand. They maintain that they are the only people in the world to whom God has revealed his mysteries; that all men are corrupt and in disgrace with God, that they have all been abandoned to their senses and their own minds; and that this is the reason for the strange aberrations and continual changes of religions and customs among them, whereas these people remain unshakeable in their conduct; but that God will not leave the other peoples for ever in darkness, that a Redeemer will come, for all; that they are in the world to proclaim him to men; that they have been expressly created to be the forerunners and heralds of this great coming, and to call all peoples to unite with them in looking forward to this Redeemer.

My encounter with this people amazes me and seems worthy of attention.

I consider this law which they boast of receiving from God, and I find it admirable. It is the first of all laws, so much so that even before the word 'law' was in use among the Greeks they had received it and had been observing it for nearly a thousand years without interruption. Therefore I find it strange that the first law in the world should also happen to be the most perfect, so that the greatest lawgivers borrowed their own laws from it, as can be seen from the law of the twelve tables in Athens, subsequently taken over by the Romans, and as it would be easy to prove if Josephus and others had not sufficiently treated this matter. (619)

455 *Prophecies*. The oath that David will always have successors. Jeremiah.[1] (717)

SERIES X
[PERPETUITY OF JEWISH PEOPLE]

456 These are facts: while philosophers are all split into different sects, there are in one corner of the world people who are the most ancient in the world, who declare that the whole world is in error, that God has revealed the truth to them, that it will always exist on earth. In fact all the other sects come to an end; this one still exists and for 4,000 years they have been declaring that they have it from their forefathers that man has fallen from communion with God into total estrangement from God, but that he has promised to redeem them, that this doctrine will always be on earth, that their law has a double meaning.

1. XXXIII. 22.

That for 1,600 years they had men whom they believed to be prophets foretelling the time and manner.

That 400 years later they were scattered everywhere, because Christ had to be proclaimed everywhere.

That Christ came in the manner and at the time foretold.

That since then the Jews have been scattered everywhere as a curse, but none the less survive. (618)

457   Hypothesis that the apostles were rogues.
The time clearly, the manner obscurely.
Five proofs of figurative things.
2,000 [years]: 1,600 prophets
                400 dispersed. (572)

SERIES XI
[PROOFS OF RELIGION]

458   *Contradictions.* Infinite wisdom and infinite folly of religion.
(588b)

459   Zeph. III. 9: 'For then will I turn to the people a pure language, that they may all call upon the name of the Lord, to serve him with one consent.'

Ezek. XXXVII. 25: 'and my servant David shall be their prince for ever.'

Exod. IV. 22: 'Israel is my son, even my first born.'
(713b)

460   The Christians' God is a God who makes the soul aware that he is its sole good: that in him alone can it find peace; that only in loving him can it find joy: and who at the same time fills it with loathing for the obstacles which hold it back and prevent it from loving God with all its might. Self-love and concupiscence, which hold it back, are intolerable. This God makes the soul aware of this underlying self-love which is destroying it, and which he alone can cure. (544)

461   The world exists for the exercise of mercy and judgement, not as if the men in it were created by the hands of God, but as if

they were God's enemies, granted by his grace enough light
to find their way back if they wish to seek and follow him,
and enough to punish them if they refuse to seek or follow
him.   (584)

462 The prophets foretold events and were not foretold. Then
came the saints, foretold but not foretelling. Christ both
foretold and foretelling.   (739)

463 It is a remarkable fact that no canonical author has ever used
nature to prove God. They all try to make people believe in
him. David, Solomon, etc., never said: 'There is no such thing
as a vacuum, therefore God exists.' They must have been clev-
erer than the cleverest of their successors, all of whom have
used proofs from nature. This is very noteworthy.   (243)

464 I will allow him no peace in either, so that with no place to
settle or rest. . . .   (419)

465 These children are amazed to see respect paid to their fellows.
                                                       (321)

466 If it is a sign of weakness to prove God from nature, do not
look down on Scripture: if it is a sign of strength to have
recognized these contradictions, respect Scripture for it. (428)

467 *Order.* After [the section on] corruption say: it is right that all
who are in this state should know it, whether they are
satisfied with it or not, but it is not right that all should see
redemption.   (449)

468 All things on earth show man's wretchedness and God's mercy,
man's helplessness without God and man's power with God.
                                                       (562)

469 (*Vileness.*) God has used the blindness of this people for the
benefit of the elect.   (577)

470 The vilest feature of man is the quest for glory, but it is just
this that most clearly shows his excellence. For whatever
possession he may own on earth, whatever health or essential
amenity he may enjoy, he is dissatisfied unless he enjoys the

good opinion of his fellows. He so highly values human reason that, however privileged he may be on earth, if he does not also enjoy a privileged position in human reason he is not happy. This is the finest position on earth, nothing can deflect him from this desire, and this is the most indelible quality in the human heart.

And those who most despise men, and put them on the same level as the beasts, still want to be admired and trusted by them, and contradict themselves by their own feelings, for their nature, which is stronger than anything, convinces them more strongly of man's greatness than reason convinces them of their vileness. (404)

471 For my part, I confess that as soon as the Christian religion reveals the principle that men are by nature corrupt and have fallen away from God, this opens one's eyes so that the mark of this truth is everywhere apparent: for nature is such that it points at every turn to a God who has been lost, both within man and without, and to a corrupt nature. (441)

472 *Greatness.* Religion is so great a thing that it is right that those who will not take the trouble to look for it, if it is obscure, should be deprived of it. What is there to complain about if it can be found just by looking? (574)

473 Interpretation of the words 'good' and 'evil'. (500)

474 When the creation of the world began to recede into the past, God provided a single contemporary historian, and charged an entire people with the custody of this book, so that this should be the most authentic history in the world and all men could learn from it something which it was so necessary for them to know and which could only be known from it. (622)

475 The veil which is drawn over these books for the Jews is also there for bad Christians, and for all who do not hate themselves. But how well-disposed we are to understand them and know Christ when we truly hate ourselves! (676)

476 I do not say that the closed *mem* is mystical. (688)

477 Pride is a counterweight and antidote for all forms of wretchedness. Here is a strange monster, and a very palpable aberration. Here he is, fallen from his place, looking anxiously for it. That is what all men do. Let us see who has found it. (406)

478 Without examining every particular kind of occupation it is sufficient to put them all under the heading of diversion. (137)

479 For the philosophers there are 280 kinds of sovereign good. (746)

480 In all religions sincerity is essential: true heathens, true Jews, true Christians. (590)

481 Against the history of China, the historians of Mexico, of the five suns, of which the last was only 800 years ago.[1]

Difference between a book accepted by a people and one which creates a people. (594)

482 PROOFS — 1. The Christian religion, by the fact of being established, by establishing itself so firmly and so gently, though so contrary to nature — 2. The holiness, sublimity and humility of a Christian soul — 3. The miracles of holy Scripture — 4. Jesus Christ in particular — 5. The apostles in particular — 6. Moses and the prophets in particular — 7. The Jewish people — 8. Prophecies — 9. Perpetuity: no religion enjoys perpetuity — 10. Doctrine, accounting for everything — 11. The holiness of this law — 12. By the order of the world.

Without any doubt after this, considering the nature of life and of this religion, we ought not to resist the inclination to follow it if our hearts are so inclined: and it is certain that there are no grounds for laughing at those who do follow it. (289)

1. Cf. Montaigne, *Essays*, III. 6.

SERIES XII
[PROPHECIES]

483   *Prophecies* (In Egypt, *Pugio Fidei*), p. 659,[1] *Talmud*:

'It is a tradition amongst us that at the coming of the Messiah the house of God, intended for the dispensation of his word, will be full of filth and uncleanness, and that the wisdom of the Scribes will be corrupt and rotten. Those who fear to sin will be condemned by the people, and treated as fools and madmen.'

Is. XLIX: 'Listen, O isles, unto me; and hearken ye people from far; the Lord hath called me from the womb; in the shadow of his hand hath he hid me: and he hath made my mouth like a sharp sword: and said unto me: "Thou art my servant, in whom I will be glorified." Then I said: "Lord, have I laboured in vain? have I spent my strength for nought? Yet surely my judgment is with the Lord, and my work with my God." And now saith the Lord, that formed me from the womb to be his servant, to bring Jacob and Israel again to him: "Thou shalt be glorious in the eyes of the Lord, and I shall be thy strength: it is a light thing that thou shouldest restore the tribes of Jacob; I will also give thee for a light to the Gentiles, that thou mayest be my salvation unto the ends of the earth." Thus saith the Lord to him who has humbled his soul, to him whom man despiseth, to him whom the Gentiles abhor, to a servant of rulers: "Kings and princes shall worship thee, because of the Lord that is faithful and he shall choose thee."

'Thus saith the Lord: "I have heard thee in a day of salvation and mercy, and I have given thee for a covenant of the people, to establish the earth, to cause to inherit the desolate heritages; that thou mayest say to the prisoners, 'Go forth,' to them that are in darkness, 'Show yourselves,' and come

---

1. The reference is to *Pugio Fidei*. Pascal has considerably modified the Biblical text, and the translation given is of what he actually wrote.

into possession of rich and fertile lands. They shall not hunger nor thirst; neither shall the heat nor sun smite them; for he that hath mercy on them shall lead them, even by the springs of living water shall he guide them, and he will make all the mountains a way before them. Behold, the peoples shall come from every part, from the East and from the West, from the North and from the South. Sing, O heavens, and be joyful, O earth, for it hath pleased the Lord to comfort his people, and he will have mercy upon his afflicted who hope in him."

'But Zion said: "The Lord hath forsaken me, and my Lord hath forgotten me." Can a woman forget her child, that she should not have compassion on the son of her womb? Yea, she may forget, yet will I not forget thee, O Zion; behold I have graven thee upon the palms of my hands; thy walls are continually before me. Those who shall build thee up again make haste, thy destroyers shall go forth of thee. Lift up thine eyes round about, and behold; all these gather themselves together and come to thee. As I live, thou shalt surely clothe thee with them all as with an ornament; for thy waste and desolate places, and the land of thy destruction shall be too narrow for the great number of thy inhabitants, and the children which thou shalt have in the barren years shall say: "The place is too strait, move out the boundaries, give place to us that we may dwell." Then shalt thou say in thine heart: "Who hath begotten me this abundance of children, seeing I had lost my children, and was barren, a captive, and removing to and fro? and who hath brought up these? Behold, I was left alone; these, where had they been?" Thus saith the Lord: "Behold, I have lifted up mine hand to the Gentiles, and set up my standard to the people, and they shall bring thy sons in their arms and on their breasts: kings shall be thy nursing fathers and queens thy nursing mothers: they shall bow down to thee with their face towards the earth, and lick up the dust of thy feet; and thou shalt know that I am the Lord and they shall not be ashamed that wait for me, for who shall take the prey from the strong and mighty? But even though the prey should be taken away, nothing shall hold me from saving thy children and destroying thine enemies, for all flesh shall know that I the Lord am thy saviour and thy redeemer, the mighty one of Jacob." '

Is. L: 'Thus saith the Lord: "What is this bill of divorcement by which I have put away the synagogue? and why have I delivered her into the hands of your enemies? Is it not for her ungodliness and iniquity that I have put her away?

' "For I came, and none received me: I called, and there was none to answer. Is my hand shortened at all that it cannot redeem?

' "That is why I shall show the marks of my wrath: I shall clothe the heavens with blackness and make sackcloth their covering.

' "The Lord hath given me the tongue of the learned, that I should know how to speak a word in season to him that is weary. He wakeneth mine ear to hear as the learned.

' "The Lord disclosed his will to me, and I was not rebellious.

' "I gave my back to the smiters and my cheeks to them that plucketh off the hair, I hid not my face from shame and spitting, but the Lord hath helped me, therefore have I not been confounded.

' "He is near that justifieth me: who is he that shall charge me with sin, for the Lord God himself is my protector?

' "All men shall pass away and be consumed by time; let those who fear the Lord hearken then to the words of his servant, let him that walketh in darkness put his trust in the Lord. But as for you, ye only kindle the wrath of the Lord upon you, ye walk in the light of the fire and in the sparks that ye have kindled. This ye have had of mine hand: ye shall lie down in sorrow." '

Is. LI: 'Hearken to me, ye that follow after righteousness, ye that seek the Lord. Look unto the rock whence ye are hewn, and to the hole of the pit whence ye are drawn, look unto Abraham your father, and unto Sarah that bore you. Behold he was alone and childless when I called him and blessed him and increased him. Behold how I have blessed Zion, and heaped favour and comfort upon her.

'Hearken unto me, O my people, and give ear unto me, for

a law shall proceed from me, and a judgment which shall be for a light to the Gentiles.'

Amos VIII. 9: (After enumerating all the sins of Israel, the prophet says that God has sworn to avenge them.)

'And it shall come to pass in that day, saith the Lord God, that I will cause the sun to go down at noon, and I will darken the earth in the clear day, and I will turn your feasts into mourning, and all your songs into lamentation, and I will bring up sackcloth upon all loins, and I will make it as the mourning of an only son, and the end thereof as a bitter day. For behold, the days come, saith the Lord God, that I will send a famine in the land, not a famine of bread nor a thirst of water, but of hearing the words of the Lord. And they shall wander from sea to sea, and from the north even to the east; they shall run to and fro to seek the word of the Lord, and shall not find it.

'In that day shall their fair virgins and young men faint for thirst, they that have followed the idols of Samaria, and have sworn by the God worshipped in Dan, and have followed the worship of Beersheba, even they shall fall, and never rise up again.'

Amos III. 2: 'You only have I known as my people of all the families of the earth.'

Dan. XII. 7: after writing about the whole extent of the Messiah's reign, says: 'All these things shall be finished when he shall have accomplished to scatter the people of Israel.'

Hag. II. 4: 'Ye who compare this second house with the glory of the first, and find it as nothing, yet now be strong, saith the Lord, O Zerubbabel, and Joshua, the high priest, and all ye people of the land, and work without cease. For I am with you, saith the Lord of hosts: according to the word that I covenanted with you when ye came out of Egypt, so my spirit remaineth among you. Fear ye not, for thus saith the Lord of hosts: "Yet once, it is a little while, and I will shake the heavens, and the earth, and the sea and the dry land [manner of speaking indicating a great and extraordinary change],[1] and I will shake all nations. And the desire of all nations shall come, and I will fill this house with glory," saith the Lord.

1. Pascal's comment.

' "The silver is mine and the gold is mine," saith the Lord [that is to say that it is not thus that I wish to be honoured; as it is written elsewhere: 'All the beasts of the field are mine: wherefore offer them to me in sacrifice?'];[1] "the glory of this latter temple shall be greater than that of the former," saith the Lord of hosts, "and in this place will I set up my house," saith the Lord.'

Deut. XVIII. 16: 'In Horeb, in the day of the assembly, saying: "Let us not hear again the voice of the Lord our God, neither let us see this great fire any more, that we die not." And the Lord said unto me: "They have well spoken that which they have spoken: I will raise them up a prophet from among their brethren, like unto thee, and I will put my words in his mouth; and he shall speak unto them all that I shall command him: and it shall come to pass that whosoever will not hearken unto my words which he shall speak in my name, I will require it of him." '

Gen. XLIX. 8: 'Judah, thou art he whom thy brethren shall praise: thy hand shall be in the neck of thine enemies: thy father's children shall bow down before thee. Judah is a lion's whelp, from the prey, my son, thou art gone up: he couched as a lion, and as a she-lion who shall rouse her up.

'The sceptre shall not depart from Judah, nor a lawgiver from between his feet, until Shiloh come, and unto him shall the gathering of the people be, to obey him.'   (726)

SERIES XIII
[PARTICULAR PROPHECIES]

484 *Predictions of particular things.* They were strangers in Egypt with no possession of their own in that country or anywhere else – (there was not the slightest sign of the kingship which came so long afterwards, nor of the supreme council of seventy judges, which they called the Sanhedrin, which was set up by Moses and went on up to the time of Christ. All these things were as far removed from their present state as they could be)

1. Pascal's comment.

– when Jacob on his death-bed blessed his twelve sons and told them they would enjoy possession of a great land, and in particular foretold to the family of Judah that the kings who should one day govern them would be of his race, and that all his brothers would be subject to him. (And that the Messiah who was to be the hope of the nations would be born of his line, and that the kingship would not be taken from Judah, nor the governor and lawgiver from his descendants, until the expected Messiah was born into his family.)

The same Jacob, disposing of this future land (and as if he were its master) gave to Joseph one more portion than the others.[1] 'I give you,' he said, 'one share more than your brothers.' And when he came to bless his two children, Ephraim and Manasseh, whom Joseph had presented to him with Manasseh the elder on his right and Ephraim the younger on his left, he crossed his arms, and, placing his right hand on Ephraim's head and his left on that of Manasseh, he blessed them like that. When Joseph pointed out to him that he was giving preference to the younger, he answered with remarkable firmness: 'I know, my son, I know it very well, but Ephraim will increase much more than Manasseh.' So true did this turn out to be that, since Ephraim alone was almost as fruitful as two entire families composing a whole kingdom, they were commonly called by his name alone. The same Joseph as he died charged his children to carry his bones with them when they went to this land where they only arrived 200 years later.

Moses, who wrote down all these things so long before they happened, himself distributed to each family its share of the land, before they arrived there, as if he were master over it. And finally declared that God should raise up from their nation and their race a prophet whom he prefigured, and proclaimed to them on God's behalf, with exact predictions, everything due to happen in the land into which they should enter after his death, the victories that God would give them, their ingratitude towards God, the punishments they would receive and the rest of their adventures.

He gave them judges to divide out the land. He prescribed

1. Gen. XLVIII. 22.

the whole form of political government they should observe, the cities of refuge they should build, etc. (711)

SERIES XIV
[DANIEL]

485   Dan. II. 27: 'The secret which the king hath demanded cannot all the wise men, the soothsayers shew unto the king.'

[This dream must have disturbed him deeply.][1]

'But there is a God in heaven that revealeth secrets, and maketh known to the king what shall be in the latter days.

'But, as for me, this secret is not revealed to me for my wisdom that I have, but this same God hath revealed it to me to make it known in thy presence.

'Thy dream then was this: "Thou, O king, sawest a great image. This great image, whose brightness was excellent, stood before thee: and the form thereof was terrible. This image's head was of fine gold, his breast and his arms of silver, his belly and his thighs of brass, his legs of iron, his feet part of iron and part of earth [clay].

' "Thou sawest till that a stone was cut without hands, which smote the image upon his feet that were of iron and clay, and brake them to pieces.

' "Then was the iron, the clay, the brass, the silver and the gold broken to pieces together, and became like chaff, and the wind carried them away, that no place was found for them, and the stone that smote the image became a great mountain, and filled the whole earth. This is the dream, and I will now tell the interpretation thereof before the king.

' "Thou, O king, art a king of kings, for the God of heaven hath given thee so great a power, that thou art feared by all peoples: thou art this head of gold which thou hast seen.

' "And after thee shall arise another kingdom inferior to thee, and another third kingdom of brass, which shall bear rule over all the earth.

1. Throughout this fragment Pascal's marginal comments are given in square brackets.

' "And the fourth kingdom shall be strong as iron, forasmuch as iron breaketh in pieces and pierceth all things, shall this kingdom break all these in pieces and bruise.

' "And whereas thou sawest the feet and toes, part of clay and part of iron, the kingdom shall be divided; but there shall be in it part of the strength of iron and part of the weakness of clay.

' "But even as iron is not mixed with clay, those who are shown by iron and clay shall not cleave one to another, though they mingle themselves with the seed of men.

' "And in the days of these kings shall God set up a kingdom which shall never be destroyed, and the kingdom shall not be left to other people, but it shall break in pieces and consume all these kingdoms, and it shall stand for ever. Forasmuch as thou sawest that the stone was cut out of the mountain without hands and brake into pieces the iron, the clay, the silver and the gold, God hath made known to the king what shall come to pass hereafter; and the dream is certain and the interpretation thereof sure."

'Then Nebuchadnezzar fell upon his face. . . .'

Dan. VIII: Daniel saw the fight between the ram and the goat, who conquered him and ruled over the earth. Then the goat's great horn was replaced by four others towards the four winds of heaven, and out of one of them came forth a little horn, which waxed towards the south, and towards the east, and towards the land of Israel, and it rose up against the host of heaven, and cast down some of the stars and stamped up on them. At the last it slew the prince, and by him the perpetual sacrifice was taken away and the sanctuary was cast down.

This is what Daniel saw. He asked what it meant and a voice cried out thus: 'Gabriel, make this man to understand the vision he hath had.' And Gabriel said:

'The ram which thou sawest is the king of the Medes and Persians, and the goat is the king of Greece, and the great horn that he had between his eyes is the first king of that kingdom.

'Now that horn being broken, whereas four others came in its place, four kingdoms shall come after him of this nation, but not in his power.

'And in the latter time of their kingdoms, when the transgressions are come to the full, a king shall arise, insolent and mighty, but not by his own power, and he shall prosper in all things, and he shall destroy the holy people and, succeeding in his undertakings with a false and crafty spirit, he shall slay many, and at the end shall stand up against the prince of princes, but he shall perish miserably, yet not by a violent hand.'
Dan. IX. 20:

'And while I was praying with my whole heart and confessing my sin and the sin of my people, and lying with my face to the ground before my God, Gabriel, whom I had seen in the vision at the beginning, came to me and touched me about the time of the evening oblation, and gave me understanding, saying, "Daniel, I am now come forth to give thee understanding of things, from the beginning of thy supplications. I am come to show thee what thou desirest, for thou art greatly beloved; therefore understand the matter and consider the vision. Seventy weeks are determined upon thy people and upon thy holy city, to finish the transgression, to make an end of sins, and to make reconciliation for iniquity, and to bring in everlasting righteousness, and to seal up the visions and the prophecy, and to anoint the most Holy. [After which this people will no more be thy people, nor this city the holy city – the time of wrath will be past, the years of grace will come for ever.]

' "Know therefore and understand that from the going forth of the commandment to restore and to build Jerusalem unto the Messiah, the prince, shall be seven weeks, and three score and two weeks [the Hebrews used to divide numbers and put the smaller one first: thus this 7 and 62 make 69 of the 70. That leaves the 70th; that is the last 7 years which he goes on to mention], the street and the walls shall be built again, even in times of trouble and affliction. And after three score and two weeks [following the first 7] the Messiah shall be slain [Christ will thus be slain after 69 weeks, that is in the last week] and the people of the prince that shall come shall destroy the city and the sanctuary, and the end thereof shall be with a flood and unto the end of the war desolations are determined.

'And he shall confirm the covenant with many for one week

[that is the 70th week remaining] and in the midst of the week [that is the last 3½ years] he shall cause the sacrifice and the oblation to cease, and for the overspreading of abominations he shall make it desolate, even until the consummation, and that determined shall be poured upon the desolate." '

Dan. XI.: 'The angel said to Daniel: "There shall stand up [after Cyrus under whom this was written] yet three kings in Persia [Cambyses, Smerdis, Darius] and the fourth [Xerxes] who shall come then shall be far richer and stronger and shall stir up all his peoples against the Greeks.

' "And a mighty king shall stand up [Alexander] that shall rule with great dominion, and do according to his desire, and when he shall stand up his kingdom shall be broken and shall be divided towards the four winds of heaven – [as he said before, ch. VII. 6 and VIII. 8] – and not to his posterity, nor according to his dominion which he ruled, for his kingdom shall be plucked up, even for others beside those. [The four principal successors].

' "And he [Ptolemy, son of Lagus] who comes after him to be king of the south [Egypt] shall be strong, but another [Seleucus, king of Syria] shall be strong above him, and his dominion shall be a great dominion. [Appian says he was the mightiest of Alexander's successors.]

' "And in the end of years they shall join themselves together, for the king's daughter of the south [Berenice, daughter of Ptolemy Philadelphus, son of the other Ptolemy] shall come to the king of the north [Antiochus Deus, king of Syria and Asia, nephew of Seleucus Lagidas] to make peace between these princes.

' "But she and her children shall not long retain power, for she and those that sent her and her children and her friends shall be put to death. [Berenice and her son were killed by Seleucus Callinicus.]

' "But out of a branch of her roots shall one stand up [Ptolemy Evergetes had the same father as Berenice] which shall come with a mighty army and shall enter into the land of the king of the north, and shall make it all subject unto him, and shall also carry captive into Egypt their gods, with their princes, their gold and their silver, and all their most precious spoils, and shall continue many years and the king of the north shall not be able to do aught against him. [If he had not been recalled to Egypt for domestic reasons he would have stripped Seleucus in a very different way, says Justin.]

'"So the king of the south shall return into his kingdom, but the sons of the other [Seleucus Ceraunus and Antiochus Magnus] shall be stirred up and shall assemble a multitude of great forces.

'"And their army shall come and shall spoil all: and the king of the south [Ptolemy Philopator] shall be stirred up and shall also assemble a great host and shall fight [against Antiochus Magnus] and shall conquer [at Raphia]. And his host shall be proud and his heart shall be lifted up [this Ptolemy profaned the Temple, according to Josephus], and he shall cut down many ten thousands, but he shall not be strengthened by it.

'"For the king of the north [Antiochus Magnus] shall return, and shall set forth a multitude greater than the former. [The young Ptolemy Epiphanes being king], and in those times there shall many stand up against the king of the south, even the robbers of thy people [apostates who had abandoned their religion to please Evergetes when he sent troops to Scopas] shall exalt themselves to establish the vision, but they shall fall. [Because Antiochus recaptured Scopas and defeated them.]

'"And the king of the north shall destroy the ramparts and the most fenced cities, and all the arms of the south shall not withstand.

'"And he will do in all things according to his own will and he shall stand in the land of Israel and it shall give in to him.

'"Then he shall set his face to take dominion over the whole kingdom of Egypt [despising the youth of Epiphanes, says Justin.]

'"And for this he shall make a covenant with him and shall give him his daughter. [Cleopatra, so that she should betray her husband. Appian says about this that, mistrusting his ability to master Egypt by force because of the Romans' protection, he decided to try guile.] He shall try to corrupt her, but she shall not stand on his side.

' "After this shall he turn his face unto the isles [that is, coastal towns] and shall take many [as Appian says.]

' "But a great prince shall stand against his conquests and shall cause the reproach offered by him to cease. [Scipio Africanus, who halted the progress of Antiochus Magnus because he was offending the Romans in the persons of their allies.]

' "He will return to his own kingdom, and shall perish, and be no more. [He was killed by his own people.]

' "Then shall stand up in his estate a tyrant, a raiser of taxes [Seleucus Philopator or Soter, son of Antiochus Magnus] in the glory of his kingdom [which is the people], but within few days he shall be destroyed, neither in anger nor in battle.

' "And in his estate shall stand up a vile person, to whom they shall not give the honour of the kingdom, but he shall come in skilfully and obtain the kingdom by flatteries.

' "All arms shall be broken before him. He shall overthrow them, also the prince of the covenant, for after the league made with him he shall work deceitfully, for he shall come up, and shall become strong with a small people, and shall enter peaceably even upon the fattest places of the province, and he shall do that which his fathers have not done; he shall scatter among them the spoils and he shall forecast great devices even for a time." '

(722)

SERIES XV

[ISAIAH AND JEREMIAH: LATIN TEXTS]

486 Is. I. 21. Good changed to evil and God's vengeance.

[There follow a number of Latin quotations from the Vulgate, of which the following are the references.]

Is. X. 1, XXVI. 20, XXVIII. 1.

Miracles: Is. XXXIII. 9: XXXIII. 10: XL. 17: XLI. 26: XLIII. 13: XLIV. 20, 21, 22, 23, 24: LIV. 8: LXIII. 12, 14, 16, 17: LXVI. 17.

Jer. II. 35: IV. 22, 23, 24, 25, 26: V. 4, 5, 6: V. 29, 30: VI. 16, 17, 18.

Trust in external sacraments: Jer. VII. 14, 15, 16.

The essential does not consist in external sacrifice: Jer. VII. 22, 23, 24.

Multiplicity of doctrines: Jer. XI. 13 : XI. 21 : XV. 2 : XVII. 9 (that is, who shall know all the evil in it, for it is already known that it is wicked).

Jer. XVII. 15, 17 : XXIII. 15, 17.   (682)

SERIES XVI
[PROPHECIES]

487 *During the lifetime of the Messiah.* A riddle. Ezek. XVII.

His precursor. Mal. III.

He will be born a child. Is. IX.

He will be born in the town of Bethlehem. Mic. V.

He will mainly appear in Jerusalem and will be born of the family of Judah and David.

He is to blind the wise and learned. Is. VI, Is. VIII – Is. XXIX – Is. LXI and preach good tidings to the poor and the meek, open the eyes of the blind, heal the sick – and lead into the light those who languish in darkness. Is. LXI.

He is to teach the way of perfection and be the teacher of the Gentiles. Is. LV; XLII. 1–7.

The prophecies are to be unintelligible to the ungodly. Dan. XII. – Hos. XIV. 9. but intelligible to those who are properly instructed.

The prophecies which represent him as poor represent him as ruler of the nations: Is. LII. 14; LIII, etc. Zech. IX. 9.

The prophecies which foretell the time only foretell him as ruler of the Gentiles and suffering, and not as in the clouds and a judge. And those which represent him thus as a judge and in glory do not indicate the time.

That he is to be the victim for the sins of the world. Is. XXXIX, LIII, etc.

He is to be the precious cornerstone. Is. XXVIII. 16.

He is to be the stone of stumbling and rock of offence. Is. VIII.

Jerusalem is to dash itself against this stone.

The builders are to reject it. Ps. CXVIII. 22.

God is to make this stone the head of the corner.

And the stone is to grow into a mighty mountain and fill all the earth. Dan. II.

That he is thus to be rejected, unrecognized, betrayed. Ps. CIX. 8. Sold. Zech. XI. 12: spat upon, buffeted, mocked, afflicted in countless ways, given gall to drink. Ps. LXIX. 21: pierced. Zech. XII. 10: his feet and hands pierced, slain and lots cast for his raiment. Ps. XXII.

That he would rise again. Ps. XV. the third day. Hos. VI. 2.

That he would ascend into heaven to sit on the right hand. Ps. CX.

That kings would take up arms against him. Ps. II.

That being on the right hand of the Father he would be victorious over his enemies.

That the kings of the earth and all the peoples will worship him. Is. LX.

That the Jews will continue to exist as a nation. Jeremiah.

That they will be wanderers without kings, etc. Hos. III.

Without prophets. Amos.

Awaiting salvation and not finding it. Is.

Vocation of the Gentiles through Jesus Christ. Is. LII. 15.

Is. LV – Is. LX – Ps. LXXI.

Hos. I. 9: 'Ye are not my people and I will not be your God, when ye are multiplied by dispersion. In the places where it is said they are not my people, I will call it my people.'   (727)

488 By killing him so that they should not accept him as the Messiah the Jews conferred on him the final sign that he was the Messiah.

And by continuing their refusal to acknowledge him they became unimpeachable witnesses.

And by killing him and continuing to deny him they fulfilled the prophecies.   (761)

SERIES XVII
[PROPHECIES]

489 *Captivity and lasting exile of the Jews.* Jer. XI. 11. I will bring evil
upon Judah which they shall not be able to escape.

Figures. Is. V: 'The Lord had a vineyard and he looked that
it should bring forth grapes, but it brought forth only wild
grapes. Thus I shall lay it waste and destroy it. The land shall
bring forth only thorns and I shall forbid the clouds to [rain]
upon it.

'For the vineyard of the Lord is the house of Israel, and the
men of Judah his pleasant plant. I looked for righteousness, but
behold iniquity.'

Is. VIII. 13: 'Sanctify the Lord and let him be your fear and
dread. Fear him only and he shall be to you for a sanctuary. But
he will be for a stone of stumbling and rock of offence to both
the houses of Israel.

'He shall be for a snare and a gin to the people of Jerusalem,
and many of them shall stumble against this stone and fall, and
be broken, and be snared and will perish there.

'Bind up the testimony and seal the law for my disciples.

'I will wait patiently upon the Lord that hideth his face from
the house of Jacob.'

Is. XXIX. 9: 'Stay yourselves and wonder, O people of
Israel, stagger and stumble, but not with wine, for the Lord
hath poured out upon you the spirit of deep sleep. He will
close your eyes, he will cover your prophets and your princes,
the seers.'

Dan. XII. The wicked shall not understand, but those who
have learned wisdom shall understand.

Hosea, last verse, last chapter, says after many temporal
benedictions: 'Who is wise and he shall understand these
things...?'

[Is. XXIX cont.] 'And the visions of all the prophets will
become unto you as a sealed book, which men deliver to one
that is learned that he may read it, and he saith: "I cannot read

it for it is sealed," and if it is given to those who cannot read, they will say: "I am not learned."

'Wherefore the Lord said: "Forasmuch as this people honour me with their lips, but have removed their heart far from me, and have only served me by the ways of men: [This is the reason and cause, for if they worshipped God in their hearts they would understand the prophecies.][1]

'"Therefore I shall add to all the rest and proceed to do a marvellous work among this people, even a marvellous work and a wonder. For the wisdom of their wise men shall perish and their understanding shall be hid."'

Prophecies, proof of divinity. Is. XLI: 'If ye are gods, come near, show us what shall happen, and we will incline our hearts unto your words. Tell us the former things and declare us things for to come.

'That we may know that ye are gods, do good or do evil if ye can. Let us behold it and reason together.

'Behold ye are of nothing, ye are only an abomination. . . .

'Who among you hath declared [by contemporary authors][2] the things that were done from the beginning and before time that we may say: "He is righteous." Yea, there is none that showeth, none that declareth things to come.'

Is. XLII: 'I am the Lord and my glory will I not give to another. Behold, the former things that have come to pass have I declared unto you and new things do I declare. Sing unto the Lord a new song from the end of the earth.'

XLIII. 8: 'Bring forth the blind people that have eyes and the deaf that have ears.

'Let all the nations be gathered together, who among them and their gods can tell of things past and things to come? Let them bring forth their witnesses that they may be justified, or let them hear and say: "It is truth."

'Ye are my witnesses, saith the Lord, and my servant whom I have chosen, that ye may know and believe me, and understand that I am he.

'I have declared, and have saved; I alone have done these

1. Pascal's comment.
2. Pascal's addition.

wonders before your eyes: therefore ye are my witnesses, saith the Lord, that I am God.

'For your sake have I brought down the hosts of Babylon. I am the Lord, your Holy One, the creator of Israel.

'It is I which maketh a way for you in the midst of the waters, and the sea and the mighty waters and which hath drowned and destroyed for ever the mighty enemies that stood against you.

'Remember ye not the former things, neither consider the things of old.

'Behold I will do a new thing: now it shall spring forth, shall ye not know it? I will even make a way in the wilderness and rivers in the desert.

'This people have I formed for myself, they shall show forth my praise, etc.

'I, even I, am he that blotteth out thy transgressions for mine own sake, and will not remember thy sins. For thy sake remember thine ingratitude and see if thou mayest be justified. Thy first father hath sinned and all thy teachers have transgressed against me.'

Is. XLIV: '"I am the first and I am the last," saith the Lord, "and who shall be like unto me? Let him declare the order of things since I appointed the ancient people and let him show the things that are coming.

'"Fear ye not. Have I not told you all these things? Ye are even my witnesses."'

Prediction of Cyrus. [Is. XLV. 4] 'For Jacob my servant's sake, and Israel mine elect, I have even called thee by thy name.'

Is. XLV. 21: 'Come and let us take counsel together. Who hath declared this from ancient time? Who hath told it from that time? Have not I, the Lord?'

Is. XLVI: 'Remember the former things of old, and know that there is none like me, declaring the end from the beginning and from ancient times the things that are not yet done, saying: My counsel shall stand and I will do all my pleasure.'

Is. XLII. 9: 'Behold, the former things are come to pass and new things do I declare: before they spring forth I tell ye of them.'

Is. XLVIII. 3: 'I have declared the former things from the

beginning: I did them suddenly and they came to pass. Because I know that thou art obstinate, and thy neck an iron sinew and thy brow brass, I have even from the beginning declared it unto thee. Before it came to pass I showed it to thee, lest thou shouldest say: "Mine idol hath done them and mine image hath commanded them."

'Thou hast seen all this, and will not ye declare it? I have showed thee new things from this time, even hidden things, and thou didst not know them. They are created now, and not from the beginning. I have hidden them from thee lest thou shouldest say: "Behold I knew them."

'Yea, thou heardest not: yea, thou knewest not: yea, from that time that thine ear was not opened. For I knew that thou wouldest deal very treacherously, and wast called a transgressor from the womb.'

Rejection of the Jews and conversion of the Gentiles. Is. LXV: 'I am sought of them that asked not for me. I am found of them that sought me not. I said: "Behold me, behold me," unto a nation that did not call upon my name.

'I have spread out my hands all the day unto a rebellious people, which walketh in a way that was not good, after their own thoughts; a people that provoketh me to anger continually before my face by its sins, that sacrificeth to idols, etc.

'These shall be scattered like smoke in the day of my wrath, etc.

'Your iniquities and the iniquities of your fathers together will I assemble and recompense even into your bosom.

'Thus saith the Lord: For my servants' sakes I will not destroy all Israel, but I will keep some of them, as the new wine is found in the cluster, and one saith: "Destroy it not, for a blessing is in it."

'And I will bring forth a seed out of Jacob and out of Judah an inheritor of my mountains; and mine elect shall inherit it, and my servants shall dwell there, and in my fields which shall be fat and wondrously abundant.

'But I will slay all the rest, because ye have forgotten your God and served strange gods. When I called ye did not answer;

when I spake ye did not hear, but did choose that wherein I delighted not.

'Therefore thus saith the Lord God: Behold, my servants shall eat, but ye shall be hungry. My servants shall rejoice, but ye shall be ashamed. My servants shall sing for joy of heart, but ye shall cry for sorrow of heart, and shall howl for vexation of spirit.

'And ye shall leave your name for a curse unto my chosen. For the Lord shall slay thee, and call his servants by another name, that he who blesseth himself in the earth shall bless himself in the God of truth, etc.

'Because the former troubles are forgotten.

'For, behold, I create new heavens and a new earth, and the former things shall not be remembered nor come into mind.

'But be ye glad and rejoice for ever in that which I create, for, behold, I create Jerusalem a rejoicing, and her people a joy, and I will rejoice in Jerusalem and joy in my people, and the voice of weeping shall be no more heard in her, nor the voice of crying.

'Before they call, I will answer; and while they are yet speaking I will hear. The wolf and the lamb shall feed together, and the lion shall eat straw like the bullock; and dust shall be the serpents' meat. They shall not hurt nor destroy in all my holy mountain.'

Is. LVI: 'Thus saith the Lord: Keep ye judgment and do justice, for my salvation is near to come and my righteousness to be revealed.

'Blessed is the man that doeth this, that keepeth the sabbath from polluting it, and keepeth his hand from doing any evil.

'Neither let the son of the stranger that hath joined himself to the Lord speak, saying: "The Lord will utterly separate me from his people."

'For thus saith the Lord: Whosoever keepeth my sabbath, and chooseth the things that please me, and taketh hold of my covenant, even unto him will I give in my house a place and a name better than of sons and daughters: I will give him an everlasting name that shall not be cut off.'

LIX. 9: 'For our iniquities is judgment far from us. We wait for light, but behold obscurity; for brightness, but we walk in darkness.

'We grope for the wall like the blind: we stumble at noonday as in the night: we are in desolate places like dead men.

'We roar all like bears, and mourn sore like doves. We look for judgment, but there is none: for salvation, but it is far from us.'

Is. LXVI. 18: 'For I know their works and their thoughts: it shall come, that I will gather all nations and tongues, and they shall see my glory.

'And I will set a sign among them: and I will send those that escape of them unto the nations, to Africa, to Lydia, to Italy, to Greece, and to the peoples that have not heard of my fame, neither have seen my glory. And they shall bring all your brethren.'

Rejection of the Temple. Jer. VII: 'Go ye into Shiloh, where I set my name at the first and see what I did to it for the wickedness of my people.

[For I have rejected it and made myself a temple in another place.][1]

'And now, because ye have done all these works, saith the Lord, therefore will I do unto this temple, which is called by my name, wherein ye trust, and unto the place which I gave to you and to your fathers, as I have done to Shiloh.

'And I will cast you out of my sight as I have cast out all your brethren, even the whole seed of Ephraim [cast out for ever.][2]

'Therefore pray not thou for this people.'

Jer. VII. 22: 'What can it profit ye to put burnt offering to sacrifice? For I spake not to your fathers, nor commanded them in the day that I brought them out of the land of Egypt, concerning burnt offerings or sacrifices. But this thing commanded I them, saying: "Obey my voice and walk ye in all the ways that I have commanded you, and I will be your God, and ye shall be my people."'

[It was not until they had sacrificed to the golden calves that

1. Pascal's comment.
2. Pascal's comment.

I commanded sacrifices so that an evil custom be put to good use.]¹

Jer. VII. 4: 'Trust ye not in lying words, saying: "The temple of the Lord, the temple of the Lord, the temple of the Lord are these."' (713)

SERIES XVIII

[PROPHECIES: THE JEWS AND CHRIST]

490 'We have no other king but Caesar.'² (721)

491 Corrupt nature.
Man does not act according to the reason which constitutes his being. (439)

492 Sincerity of the Jews.
Once the prophets ceased. Maccabees.
Since Christ. Massorah.
This book will be for a witness to you.
The defective final letters.
Sincere against their honour and dying for it.
This has no parallel in the world nor roots in nature. (630)

493 Prophecies fulfilled.
I Kings XIII. 2.
II Kings XXIII. 16.
Joshua VI. 26 – I Kings XVI. 34 – Deut. XXXIII.
Mal. I. II: The sacrifice of the Jews rejected and the sacrifice of the heathen (even outside Jerusalem) and in every place [accepted].
Before dying Moses foretold the calling of the Gentiles. Deut. XXXII. 21. And the rejection of the Jews.
Moses foretold what was to happen to each tribe. (714)

494 Jews witnesses of God. Is. XLIII. 9, XLIV. 8. (714)

495 They are clearly a people created expressly to serve as witness to the Messiah. Is. XLIII. 9, XLIV. 8. They hand down the books

1. Pascal's comment.
2. John XIX. 15.

and love them and do not understand them. And all this was foretold: that the judgments of God are entrusted to them, but as a sealed book. (641)

496 Harden their heart. How? By flattering their concupiscence and giving them hopes of satisfying it. (714)

497 *Prophecy.* Your name will be for a curse to my chosen people and I will give them another name. (714)

498 *Prophecy.* – Amos and Zechariah. They sold the just man and for this they shall nevermore be called.
Christ betrayed.
Egypt will be forgotten.
See Is. XLIII. 16, 17, 18, 19: Jer. XXIII. 6, 7.
Prophecy. – The Jews shall be scattered everywhere. Is. XXVII. 6.
New law. Jer. XXXI. 32.
The two glorious temples. Christ will come there. Hag. II. 7, 8, 9, 10. Malachi. Grotius.
Calling of the Gentiles. Joel II. 28. Hos. II. 24. Deut. XXXII. 21. Mal. I. 11. (715)

499 What man ever had greater glory?
The entire Jewish people foretells him before his coming. The Gentiles worship him after his coming.
Both the Gentile and Jewish peoples regard him as their centre.
And yet what man ever enjoyed such glory less?
For thirty of his thirty-three years he lives without showing himself. For three years he is treated as an impostor. The priests and rulers reject him. Those who are nearest and dearest to him despise him, finally he dies betrayed by one of his disciples, denied by another and forsaken by all.
What benefit then did he derive from such glory? No man ever had such great glory, no man ever suffered greater ignominy. All this glory has only been of use to us, to enable us to recognize him, and he had none of it for himself. (792)

SERIES XIX
[FIGURATIVE MEANINGS]

500　Fine to see with the eyes of faith the story of Herod, or Caesar.
(700)

501　*Figures*. To show that the Old Testament is – is only – figurative and that by temporal blessings the prophets meant other kinds of blessing:

　　1. It would be unworthy of God.

　　2. Their sayings express the clearest promise of temporal blessings and yet they say that their sayings are obscure, and that their meaning will not be understood. Hence it appears that this hidden meaning was not that which they openly declared, and consequently that they meant other sacrifices, another Redeemer etc. They say that it will not be understood before the time is accomplished. Jer. XXXIII ult.

　　The second proof is that their sayings are contradictory and cancel one another out. Thus, if we suppose that by the words 'law' and 'sacrifice' their meaning was simply that of Moses, there is a glaring and gross contradiction: therefore they meant something else, and sometimes contradict themselves in the same chapter.

　　Now to understand what an author means. . . .　　(659)

502　*Reasons for using figures*. They had to address a carnal people and make it the depository of a spiritual covenant.

　　To inspire faith in the Messiah there had to be previous prophecies and they had to be handed down by people above suspicion, universally known as conscientious, loyal and extraordinarily zealous.

　　For the successful accomplishment of all this, God chose this carnal people to whom he entrusted the prophecies foretelling the Messiah as saviour and dispenser of the carnal blessings dear to them.

　　And so they showed extraordinary enthusiasm for their prophets and handed on for all to see the books foretelling the

Messiah, assuring all nations that he must truly come in the manner foretold in the books which they held open for all to read. And so this people, disappointed by the poor and ignominious coming of the Messiah, became his cruellest enemies, with the result that of all people in the world they can least be suspected of favour towards us, and are the most scrupulous and zealous observers imaginable of the law and the prophets, which they maintain incorrupt.

Thus it is that those who rejected and crucified Christ, who was for them a cause of scandal, are the same who hand down the books which bear witness to him and say he will be rejected and a cause of scandal. Thus they showed he was the Messiah by refusing him, and he was proved as much by the righteous Jews who accepted him as by the unrighteous who rejected him, since both were foretold.

That is why the prophecies have a hidden spiritual meaning, to which the Jewish people were hostile, beneath the carnal meaning which they favoured. If the spiritual meaning had been revealed, they would have been incapable of taking it to their hearts, and, being unable to hand it on, they would have lacked the zeal to preserve their books and ceremonies; and, if they had taken these spiritual promises to their hearts and kept them free from corruption until the coming of the Messiah, their testimony would have had no validity, because they would have been on his side.

That is why it was a good thing that the spiritual meaning was concealed, but, on the other hand, if this meaning had been so well hidden that it did not show at all, it would have been no good as a proof of the Messiah. What then took place?

It was concealed beneath the temporal meaning in the great majority of passages, and clearly revealed in one or two, apart from the fact that the time and state of the world were foretold as clearly as noonday; and this spiritual meaning was so clearly explained in certain places that anyone unable to recognize it had to be suffering from the sort of blindness imposed on the spirit by the flesh when it takes control.

This then is how God acted. This meaning is concealed beneath another in countless places and revealed only on certain rare occasions, but yet in such a way that the places where it is hidden are ambiguous and capable of both interpretations, while those where it is revealed are without ambiguity and can only fit the spiritual meaning.

There was thus no reason for falling into error and only a people as carnal as the Jews could possibly go wrong.

For, when they were promised blessings, what prevented them from understanding this as true blessings but their cupidity, which made them interpret it as earthly blessings? But those whose only blessing lay in God related them to God alone.

For the will of man is divided between two principles: cupidity and charity. It is not that cupidity and faith in God are incompatible, nor that charity and earthly blessings never go together, but cupidity makes use of God and delights in the world while charity does just the opposite.

Now things are described in relation to ultimate purpose, and anything which frustrates us can be called an enemy. Thus creatures, though good, will be enemies of the righteous if they deflect them from God, and God himself is the enemy of those whose covetousness he hampers.

Thus, since the word 'enemy' depends on ultimate purpose, the righteous took it to mean their passions and the carnal people took it to mean the Babylonians, and so these terms were only obscure for the unrighteous.

And this is what Isaiah says: *Seal the law among my disciples*, and that Christ will be a stone of stumbling,[1] but 'Blessed is he whosoever shall not be offended in him.'[2]

The last verse of Hosea puts it perfectly: 'Who is wise and he shall understand these things? For the ways of the Lord are right and the just shall walk in them, but the transgressors shall fall therein.'   (571)

503   '... shall fall therein.' And yet this covenant made to blind some and enlighten others provided a sign in just those whom it blinded of the truth which the others had to know. For the visible blessings they received from God were so great and so

1. VIII. 16 and 14.
2. Matt. XI. 6.

divine that it was quite clear that he was capable of bestowing on them invisible blessings and a Messiah.

For nature is an image of grace, and visible miracles are images of invisible ones: *'That ye may know, I say unto thee, arise.'*[1]

Is. LI says that the Redemption will be like the crossing of the Red Sea.

God showed by the escape from Egypt and from the sea, by the defeat of kings, by the manna, by the whole line of Abraham that he was able to bring salvation and make bread come down from heaven, so that this hostile people is a figure and representation of the very Messiah whom they do not know. . . .

He thus taught us that all these things were only·figurative, and the meaning of 'truly free', 'true Israelite', 'true circumcision', 'true bread of heaven' . . . .

(Kirkerus – Usserius.[2])

Each man finds in these promises what lies in the depths of his own heart; either temporal or spiritual blessings, God or creatures; but with this difference, that those who are looking for creatures there find them indeed, but with many contradictions: they are forbidden to love them, bidden to worship and to love God alone (which comes to the same thing), and they find that the Messiah did not come for them; whereas those who are looking for God find him, without any contradictions, and find that they are bidden to love God alone and that a Messiah did come at the time foretold to bring them the blessings for which they ask.

Thus the Jews had miracles and prophecies which they saw fulfilled, and their law taught them that they should worship and love one God alone; it was also perpetual. Thus it bore all the marks of true religion, which indeed it was, but the teaching of the Jews must be distinguished from that of the Jewish law. Now the teaching of the Jews was not true, despite miracles, prophecies and perpetuity, because it lacked the further point concerning the worship and love of God alone. (675)

1. Mark 11. 10.
2. Conrad Kircher and J. Usher, seventeenth-century Old Testament scholars.

SERIES XX

[BELIEF. CLASSICAL QUOTATIONS]

504 They hide in the throng and call numbers to their aid. Tumult.
(260)

505 *Authority.* Hearsay is so far from being a criterion of belief that you should not believe anything until you have put yourself into the same state as if you had never heard it.

It is your own inner assent and the consistent voice of your reason rather than that of others which should make you believe.

Belief is so important.

A hundred contradictions might be true.

If antiquity was the criterion of belief, then the ancients had no criterion.

If general consent, if men had died . . . ?

Punishment of sinners: error.

False humility, pride.

Raise the curtain.

You are wasting your time, one must either believe, deny or doubt.

Are we then to have no criterion?

When animals do something we can judge whether they are doing it well; is there to be no criterion for judging men?

Denying, believing and doubting are to men what running is to horses.
(260)

506 *What he often sees causes him no surprise, even though he does not know how it comes about; but if something happens that he has never seen before he finds it sensational.* (Cicero)[1] (87)

Here is someone who with a great effort is going to say something very silly. (Terence)[2]

As though anything could be more unfortunate than a man ruled by his imagination. (Pliny)[3] (90)

---

1. *De Div.*, II. 27. The quotations in 506–8 are all at second hand from Montaigne.

2. *Heaut.*, II. v. 8. 3. II. 7.

507　It is by virtue of senatorial decrees and votes of the people that crimes are committed. (Seneca)[1]

Nothing is too absurd for some philosopher to have said it. (Cicero, de Div.)[2]

Pledged to certain fixed opinions they are compelled to defend what they do not approve. (Cicero)[3]

An excess of learning makes us suffer as much as an excess of anything else. (Seneca)[4]

What suits each man best is what is especially his own.[5]

Nature first of all imposed these bounds. (Georgics)[6]

It takes little learning to make a good mind.[7]

Something which is not disgraceful is no longer so when it earns popular approval.[8]

This is what suits me, you do as you ought. (Terence)[9]　　(363)

508　It is rare for anyone to pay enough respect to himself.[10]

So many gods rioting around one head.[11]

Nothing is more disgraceful than to assent before you know. (Cicero)[12]

I am not ashamed, as they are, to say I do not know what I do not know.[13]

They would have done better not to begin.[14]　　(364)

SERIES XXI

[TWO TYPES OF MIND]

509　Mask and disguise nature. No more king, pope, bishop, but august monarch, etc. . . . not Paris, but capital of the realm.

There are places where Paris must be called Paris, and others where it must be called capital of the realm.　　(49)

510　The more intelligent one is, the more men of originality one finds. Ordinary people find no difference between men.　　(7)

1. *Ep.*, xcv.　　2. II. lviii.　　3. *Tusc.*, II. ii.　　4. *Ep.*, cvi.
5. Cicero, *De Officiis*, I. xxxi.　　6. Virgil, *Georgics*, II. 20.
7. Seneca, *Ep.*, cvi.　　8. Cicero, *De Fin.*, xv.　　9. *Heaut.*, I. i. 28.
10. Quintilian, x. 7.　　11. Seneca, *Suas*, I. iv.　　12. *Acad.*, I. 12.
13. Cicero, *Tusc.*, I. xxv.　　　　14. Seneca, *Ep.*, lxxii.

511   Different kinds of right thinking, some in a particular order of things but not in others where they go quite astray.

Some draw correct conclusions from a small number of principles, and this is one kind of right thinking.

Others draw correct conclusions from things involving numerous principles.

For example, some have a good grasp of the properties of water, which involve few principles, but whose conclusions are so subtle that only an extremely accurate mind can reach them. These people might all the same not be great mathematicians, because mathematics comprises a large number of principles, and a mind may well be such that it can easily get right to the bottom of a few principles without being able to make the least advance in things involving many.

Thus there are two kinds of mind: one goes rapidly and deeply into the conclusions from principles, and this is the accurate mind. The other can grasp a large number of principles and keep them distinct, and this is the mathematical mind. The first is a powerful and precise mind, the second shows breadth of mind. Now it is quite possible to have one without the other, for a mind can be powerful and narrow, as well as broad and weak.   (2)

SERIES XXII

[MATHEMATICAL AND INTUITIVE MIND]

512   *Difference between the mathematical and the intuitive mind.* In the one principles are obvious, but remote from ordinary usage, so that from want of practice we have difficulty turning our heads that way; but once we do turn our heads the principles can be fully seen; and it would take a thoroughly unsound mind to draw false conclusions from principles so patent that they can hardly be missed.

But, with the intuitive mind, the principles are in ordinary usage and there for all to see. There is no need to turn our heads, or strain ourselves: it is only a question of good sight, but it must be good; for the principles are so intricate and numerous that it is almost impossible not to miss some. Now the omission of one principle can lead to error, and so one needs very clear sight to see all the principles as well as an accurate mind to avoid drawing false conclusions from known principles.

All mathematicians would therefore be intuitive if they had good sight, because they do not draw false conclusions from principles that they know. And intuitive minds would be mathematical if they could adapt their sight to the unfamiliar principles of mathematics.

Thus the reason why certain intuitive minds are not mathematical is that they are quite unable to apply themselves to the principles of mathematics, but the reason why mathematicians are not intuitive is that they cannot see what is in front of them: for, being accustomed to the clearcut, obvious principles of mathematics and to draw no conclusions until they have clearly seen and handled their principles, they become lost in matters requiring intuition, whose principles cannot be handled in this way. These principles can hardly be seen, they are perceived instinctively rather than seen, and it is with endless difficulty that they can be communicated to those who do not perceive them for themselves. These things are so delicate and numerous that it takes a sense of great delicacy and precision to perceive them and judge correctly and accurately from this perception: most often it is not possible to set it out logically as in mathematics, because the necessary principles are not ready to hand, and it would be an endless task to undertake. The thing must be seen all at once, at a glance, and not as a result of progressive reasoning, at least up to a point. Thus it is rare for mathematicians to be intuitive or the intuitive to be mathematicians, because mathematicians try to treat these intuitive matters mathematically, and make themselves ridiculous, by trying to begin with definitions followed by principles, which is not the way to proceed in this kind of reasoning. It is not that the mind does not do this, but it does so tacitly, naturally and artlessly, for it is beyond any man to express it and given to very few even to apprehend it. Intuitive minds, on the contrary, being thus accustomed to judge at a glance, are taken aback when presented with propositions of which they understand nothing (and of which the necessary preliminaries are definitions and principles so barren that they are not used to looking at them in such detail), and consequently feel repelled and disgusted.

But unsound minds are never either intuitive or mathematical.

Mathematicians who are merely mathematicians therefore reason soundly as long as everything is explained to them by definitions and principles, otherwise they are unsound and intolerable, because they reason soundly only from clearly defined principles.

And intuitive minds which are merely intuitive lack the patience to go right into the first principles of speculative and imaginative matters which they have never seen in practice and are quite outside ordinary experience. (1)

513 *Mathematics. Intuition.* True eloquence has no time for eloquence, true morality has no time for morality. In other words the morality of judgement has no time for the random morality of mind.

For judgement is what goes with instinct, just as knowledge goes with mind. Intuition falls to the lot of judgement, mathematics to that of the mind.

To have no time for philosophy is to be a true philosopher. (4)

514 The body is nourished gradually.

Ample food and little substance. (356)

SERIES XXIII

[VARIOUS]

515 *Misc.* – When words are repeated in an argument and one finds, on trying to correct them, that they are so apposite that it would spoil the work to change them, they must be left in: this is the sure sign. And this is blind envy working, and not realizing that in this passage such repetition is not a defect, because there is no general rule. (48)

516 *Pope.* – We like security: we like the pope to be infallible in matters of faith, and grave doctors to be so in moral questions so that we can feel reassured. (880)

517 If St Augustine were to appear today and enjoy as little
authority as his modern defenders he would not accomplish
anything. God has ruled his Church well by sending him
earlier, and endowed with authority. (869)

518 *Scepticism.* – Extreme intelligence is accused of being as foolish
as extreme lack of it; only moderation is good. The majority
have laid this down and attack anyone who deviates from it
towards any extreme whatever. I am not going to be awkward,
I readily consent to being put in the middle and refuse to be at
the bottom end, not because it is bottom but because it is the
end, for I should refuse just as much to be put at the top. It is
deserting humanity to desert the middle way.

The greatness of the human soul lies in knowing how to keep
this course; greatness does not mean going outside it, but rather
keeping within it. (378)

519 Nature does not. . . .

Nature has set us so exactly in the middle that if we alter one
side of the scales we alter the other as well. *Je faisons, zoa trekei.*[1]

This leads me to believe that there are certain mechanisms
in our head so arranged that we cannot touch one without
touching its opposite. (70)

520 I spent much of my life believing that there was such a thing
as justice, and in this I was not mistaken, for in so far as God
has chosen to reveal it to us there is such a thing. But I did not
take it in this way, and that is where I was wrong, for I thought
that our justice was essentially just, and that I had the means to
understand and judge it, but I found myself so often making
unsound judgements that I began to distrust myself and then
others. I saw that all countries and all men change. Thus, after
many changes of mind concerning true justice I realized that
our nature is nothing but continual change and I have never
changed since. And if I were to change I should be confirming
my opinion. The sceptic Arcesilaus who became a dogmatist
once more. (375)

1. 'Animals runs' in deliberately ungrammatical Greek.

521 It may be that there are such things as true proofs, but it is not certain.

Thus that only proves that it is not certain that everything is uncertain. To the greater glory of scepticism. (387)

522 How is it that this man so distressed at the death of his wife and his only son, deeply worried by some great feud, is not gloomy at the moment and is seen to be so free from all these painful and disturbing thoughts? There is no cause for surprise: he has just had a ball served to him and he must return it to his opponent. He is intent on catching it as it falls from the roof[1] so that he may win a point. How could you expect him to think of his personal affairs when he has this other business in hand? Here is a concern worthy of occupying this great soul and driving every other thought out of his mind! Here is this man, born to know the universe, to judge everything, to rule a whole state, wholly concerned with catching a hare. And if he will not stoop to that and wants always to be keyed up, the more fool he, because he will be trying to rise above man's estate and he is only a man when all is said, that is to say capable of little and of much, of all and nothing. He is neither angel nor beast, but man. (140)

523 A single thought is enough to occupy us: we cannot think of two things at once, which is just as well for us, according to the world, not according to God. (145)

524 We must judge divine commandments soberly, Father. Saint Paul in Malta. (853)

525 Montaigne is wrong. The only reason for following custom is that it is custom, not that it is reasonable or just, but the people follow it solely because they think it just. Otherwise they would not follow it any more, even though it were custom, because we are only ready to submit to reason or justice. But for that, custom would be regarded as tyranny, but the rule of reason and justice is no more tyrannical than that of pleasure. These are principles natural to men.

1. Method of serving in *jeu de paume*.

It would therefore be a good thing for us to obey laws and customs because they are laws (then we should never revolt, but we might be unwilling to submit, for we should always be searching for the right one): to know that there is no right and just law to be brought in, that we know nothing about it and should consequently only follow those already accepted. In this way we should never give them up. But the people are not amenable to this doctrine, and thus, believing that truth can be found and resides in laws and customs, they believe them and take their antiquity as a proof of their truth (and not just of their authority, without truth). Thus they obey them but are liable to revolt as soon as they are shown to be worth nothing, which can happen with all laws if they are looked at from a certain point of view. (325)

526 Evil is easy; it has countless forms, while good is almost unique. But a certain sort of evil is as hard to find as what is called good, and this particular evil is often on that account passed off as good. Indeed it takes as much extraordinary greatness of soul to attain such evil, as to attain good. (408)

527 We take examples to prove other things, and if we wanted to prove the examples we should take the other things as examples of the examples. For, since we always think the difficulty lies in what we are trying to prove, we find examples clearer and an aid to demonstration.

Thus, when we wish to prove a general fact, we must give the particular rule for a single case, but if we want to prove a particular case we must begin by the general rule. For what we are trying to prove always seems obscure and what we use for the proof seems clear; for when we put forward something to be proved, we first imagine that it must therefore be obscure, whereas the thing that is to prove it is clear, and thus we easily understand it. (40)

528 I have been embarrassed by such compliments as: I have given you a lot of trouble, I am afraid of boring you, I am afraid it may take too long. One is either persuasive or irritating. (57)

529 How difficult it is to propose something for someone else to

judge without affecting his judgement by the way we do it. If you say: 'I think it is excellent,' 'I think it is obscure,' or something like that, you either persuade his imagination to agree with you or irritate it, in the opposite sense. It is better to say nothing, and then he can judge according to what it really is, that is what it is then, and according to the way in which other circumstances over which we have no control have affected the issue. But at least we shall have added nothing, unless our silence also produces an effect, according to the twist or interpretation he may feel like giving to it, or according to what he may surmise from our gestures and expression, or tone of voice, depending on how skilful he is at reading faces. It is so difficult not to dislodge judgement from its natural basis, or rather this is so seldom firm and stable. (105)

530   All our reasoning comes down to surrendering to feeling.

But fancy is like and also unlike feeling, so that we cannot distinguish between these two opposites. One person says that my feeling is mere fancy, another that his fancy is feeling. We should have a rule. Reason is available but can be bent in any direction.

And so there is no rule. (274)

531   The things which we have most at heart, like hiding what few assets we have, often amount almost to nothing. It is a nothing which our imagination magnifies into a mountain: a different twist of the imagination easily makes us disclose it. (85)

532   *Scepticism.* I will write down my thoughts here as they come and in a perhaps not aimless confusion. This is the true order and it will always show my aim by its very disorder.

I should be honouring my subject too much if I treated it in order, since I am trying to show that it is incapable of it. (373)

533   We always picture Plato and Aristotle wearing long academic gowns, but they were ordinary decent people like anyone else, who enjoyed a laugh with their friends. And when they amused themselves by composing their *Laws* and *Politics* they did it for fun. It was the least philosophical and least serious part of their

lives: the most philosophical part was living simply and without fuss.

If they wrote about politics it was as if to lay down rules for a madhouse.

And if they pretended to treat it as something really important it was because they knew that the madmen they were talking to believed themselves to be kings and emperors. They humoured these beliefs in order to calm down their madness with as little harm as possible. (331)

534 Those who judge a work without any rule stand with regard to others as do those who have a watch with regard to those who have not. One man says: 'Two hours ago:' another says: 'It is only three quarters of an hour.' I look at my watch and tell the first: 'You must be bored,' and the second 'You hardly feel the time passing,' because it is an hour and a half ago. I take no notice of those who tell me that time must hang heavily on my hands and that I am judging it according to my own fancy.

They do not know that I am judging it by my watch. (5)

535 There are some vices which only keep hold on us through other ones, and if we take the trunk away they come off like the branches. (102)

536 God (and the apostles), foreseeing that the seeds of pride would give rise to heresies, and wishing to give them no opportunity to arise from the actual words, put into Scripture and the prayers of the Church contrary words and seeds to produce their fruit in due season.

Just as in morals he provides charity which produces fruits against concupiscence. (579)

537 When wickedness has reason on its side it becomes pleased with itself and displays reason in all its lustre.

When austerity or stern choice has failed to achieve true good and we have to go back to following nature, it then becomes pleased with itself at this reversal. (407)

538 The man who knows what his master wants will be more

heavily beaten because of what his knowledge enables him to do.

He that is righteous, let him be righteous still,[1] because of what his righteousness enables him to do.

From him who has been given most will most be demanded because of what this help enables him to do. (531)

539 There is a universal and essential difference between acts of will and all others.

The will is one of the chief organs of belief, not because it creates belief, but because things are true or false according to the aspect by which we judge them. When the will likes one aspect more than another, it deflects the mind from considering the qualities of the one it does not care to see. Thus the mind, keeping in step with the will, remains looking at the aspect preferred by the will and so judges by what it sees there. (99)

540 All the good maxims already exist in the world: we just fail to apply them.

For example, no one doubts that one should risk his life in defence of the common good, and many people do so, but not for religion.

Inequality must necessarily exist among men, it is true: but that once granted the door is open not only to the most absolute rule but to the most absolute tyranny.

It is necessary to relax the mind a little, but that opens the door to the greatest excesses.

Let us define the limits. There are no boundaries in things. Laws try to impose some, and the mind cannot bear it. (380)

541 Nature diversifies   Artifice imitates
    and imitates   and diversifies.   (120)

542 Thoughts come at random, and go at random. No device for holding on to them or for having them.

A thought has escaped: I was trying to write it down: instead I write that it has escaped me. (370)

543 *Digression.* Small turns, it is becoming. [?]

1. Rev. XXII. 11.

Do you hold it against me that I am very wary? The Fathers and. . . .

I picked them out later, because I did not. . . . (938)

544 *And there went out unto him all the land of Judaea and they of Jerusalem and were all baptized*[1] because of all the kinds and conditions of men who came there.

Stones can be children of Abraham.[2] (778)

545 'All that is in the world is lust of the flesh, lust of the eyes or pride of life.' *Libido sentiendi, libido sciendi, libido dominandi.*[3] Wretched is the cursed land consumed rather than watered by these three rivers of fire! Happy are those who are beside those rivers, neither immersed, nor carried away, but immovably steady beside these rivers, not standing but sitting, in a low and safe position. They will not rise thence before the light, but, after resting in peace, stretch out their hands to him who shall raise them to stand upright and steady in the porches of Jerusalem the blessed, where pride shall no more be able to fight against them and lay them low; and yet they weep, not at the sight of all the perishable things swept away by these torrents, but at the memory of their beloved home, the heavenly Jerusalem, which they constantly remember through the long years of their exile. (458)

546 The elect will not know their virtues nor the damned the gravity of their crimes. 'Lord, when saw we thee an hungred, or thirsty . . .?'[4] (515)

547 Jesus did not want devils or those who had not been called to bear him witness, but God and John the Baptist. (784)

548 If we turned from our ways God would heal and pardon us.
Lest they convert and be healed. (Isaiah)[5]
And their sins should be forgiven them. (Mark)[6] (779)

549 Jesus never condemned without a hearing.
To Judas: '*Friend, wherefore art thou come.*'[7] The same thing to the man who had no wedding garment.[8] (780)

---

1. Mark I. 5.   2. Cf. Matt. III. 9.   3. I John II. 16.
4. Matt. XXV. 37.   5. Is. VII. 10.   6. Mark IV. 12.
7. Matt. XXVI. 50.   8. Cf. Matt. XXII. 12.

550 'Pray lest ye enter into temptation.'[1] It is dangerous to be tempted. And those who are, are tempted because they do not pray.

'*And when thou art converted, strengthen the brethren,*' but first '*Jesus turned and looked upon Peter.*'[2]

St Peter asked permission to strike Malchus, and struck before hearing the answer. And Jesus answered afterwards.

The word 'Galilee' spoken by the crowd of the Jews as if by chance, when they accused Jesus before Pilate, gave Pilate a pretext to send him to Herod. Thus was accomplished the mystery according to which he was to be judged by both Jews and Gentiles. Apparent chance was the cause of the mystery being accomplished. (744)

551 Imagination magnifies small objects with fantastic exaggeration until they fill our soul, and with bold insolence cuts down great things to its own size, as when speaking of God. (84)

552 *He lit the earth with his lamp.*[3] There is little connexion between the weather and my mood. I have my fogs and fine weather inside me: whether my affairs prosper or not has indeed little to do with it. I sometimes struggle of my own accord against fortune. The glory of overcoming it makes me do so cheerfully whereas I sometimes show disgust when things go well. (107)

553 Write against those who probe science too deeply. Descartes. (76)

554 Power rules the world, not opinion, but it is opinion that exploits power.

It is power that makes opinion. To be easygoing can be a fine thing according to our opinion. Why? Because anyone who wants to dance the tightrope will be alone, and I can get together a stronger body of people to say there is nothing fine about it. (303)

1. Luke XXII. 40.
2. Luke XXII. 32 and 61. Pascal quotes the Vulgate, in which the word '*conversus*' is used in both verses.
3. *Odyssey*, XVIII. 136, quoted in Latin by Montaigne, *Essays*, II. 12.

555 Some people speak well but do not write well. It is because the place and the audience stimulate them and get more out of them than they could manage without such stimulus. (47)

556 When I was small I used to put my book away, and because it sometimes happened when I thought I had put it away, I was doubtful. . . .[1] (371)

557 Languages are ciphers in which letters are not changed into letters, but words into words, so that an unknown language can be deciphered. (45)

558 Diversity is as wide as all the tones of voice, ways of walking, coughing, blowing one's nose, sneezing. We first distinguish grapes from among fruits, then muscat grapes, then those from Condrieu, then from Desargues,[2] then the particular graft. Is that all? Has it ever produced two bunches alike, and has any bunch produced two grapes alike?

I have never judged anything in exactly the same way. I cannot judge a work while doing it. I must do as painters do and stand back, but not too far. How far then? Guess. . . . (114)

559 *Misc. Language.* Those who construct antitheses by forcing the use of words are like those who put in false windows for the sake of symmetry.

Their rule is not correct speech but correct figures of speech. (27)

560 *Jesus's sepulchre.* Jesus was dead but seen on the cross. He was dead and hidden in the sepulchre.
Jesus was buried only by saints.
Jesus performed no miracles in the sepulchre.
Only saints went into it.
It was there that Jesus took on a new life, not on the cross.
This is the supreme mystery of the Passion and Redemption.
Jesus teaches alive, dead, buried, risen again.
Jesus had nowhere on earth to rest except in the sepulchre.
His enemies only ceased tormenting him in the sepulchre. (552)

1. Meaning quite obscure.
2. A distinguished mathematician, friend of Pascal, who had property at Condrieu, near Lyon (1595–1662).

561 They say that eclipses are portents of disaster, because disasters are so common, and misfortune occurs often enough for these forecasts to be right, whereas if they said that eclipses were portents of good fortune they would often be wrong. They ascribe good fortune only to rare conjunctions of heavenly bodies and thus seldom guess wrong in their forecasts. (173)

562 There are only two kinds of men: the righteous who think they are sinners and the sinners who think they are righteous. (534)

563 *Heretics*. Ezekiel. All the heathen spoke ill of Israel, and so did the prophet. And the Israelites were far from justified in telling him: 'You talk like the heathen,' because his greatest strength came from the fact that the heathen talked like him. (886)

564 The true and only virtue is therefore to hate ourselves, for our concupiscence makes us hateful, and to seek for a being really worthy of love in order to love him. But as we cannot love what is outside us, we must love a being who is within us but is not our own self. And this is true for every single person. Now only the universal being is of this kind: the kingdom of God is within us, universal good is within us, and is both ourselves and not ourselves. (485)

565

Jesus Christ

Heathen | Mahomet

|ignorance of God| (591)

566 Everything turns out to the advantage of the elect.

Even the obscurities of Scripture, for they honour these because of the divinely clear parts, and everything turns out to the detriment of the others, even the clear parts, for they blaspheme against them because of the obscurities they cannot understand. (575)

567 We must not judge what the Pope is from a few words of the Fathers (as the Greeks said at a Council: important rules) but from the actions of the Church and the Fathers, and from the canons.

Unity and multiplicity, *two or three in one*[1] it is an error to exclude either, as do the papists who exclude multiplicity, or the Huguenots who exclude unity. (874)

568 It is not possible to have reasonable grounds for not believing in miracles. (815)

569 The Pope is head. Who else is known by all? Who else is recognized by all, with the power to infiltrate the whole body because he holds the main branch which infiltrates everywhere?

How easy it would have been for this to degenerate into tyranny! That is why Christ gave them this commandment: '*But ye shall not be so.*'[2] (872)

570 *Christ prefigured by Joseph.* Innocent, beloved of his father, sent by his father to see his brothers, is sold for twenty pieces of silver by his brothers. Through this he becomes their lord, their saviour, saviour of strangers and saviour of the world. None of this would have happened but for their plot to destroy him, the sale, and their rejection of him.

In prison Joseph, innocent between two criminals. Jesus on the cross between two thieves. He prophesies the salvation of one and the death of the other when to all appearances they are alike. Christ saves the elect and damns the reprobate for the same crime. Joseph only prophesies, Jesus acts. Joseph asks the man who will be saved to remember him when he comes in glory. And the man Jesus saves asks to be remembered when he comes into his kingdom. (768)

571 It is heresy always to interpret *omnes* as all. And a heresy not to interpret it sometimes as all, *drink ye all of this.*[3] The Huguenots are heretical in interpreting this as all. '*For that all have sinned.*'[4] The Huguenots are heretical in excepting the children of the faithful. We must therefore follow the Fathers and tradition to know when to do which, since there is a danger of heresy on each side. (775)

1. Cf. I Cor. XIV. 27–9.
2. Luke XXII. 26.
3. Matt. XXVI. 27.
4. Rom. V. 12.

572 *Misc.* – Manner of speaking.
    I (. . .) had intended to see to that. (54)

573 The Synagogue did not perish because it was figurative.
    But because it was only figurative it fell into slavery.

    The figure continued to exist until the coming of the truth so that the Church should always be visible either in the image which promised it or in the actual effect. (646)

574 'A miracle,' they say, 'would strengthen my faith.' They say so when they do not see one.

    There are reasons which from afar look as though they restrict our view, but when we come closer we begin to see beyond them. Nothing arrests the ready flow of our minds. There is no rule, we say, to which there is no exception, nor any truth so general that it does not present some defective aspect. It is enough that it should not be absolutely universal for us to feel enabled to apply the exception to the subject in hand, and to say, 'This is not always true, so there are cases when it is not so.' It only remains to show that this is one of them, and we shall be very clumsy or unlucky if we cannot find some loophole.

(263)

575 Extravagances of the Apocalyptics, Pre-Adamites, Millenarists, etc.

    Anyone wanting to base extravagant opinions on Scripture will, for example, base them on the following:

    It is written that 'this generation shall not pass till all these things shall be fulfilled.'[1] To that I reply that after this generation there shall come another and always another in succession.

    II Chron.[2] speaks of Solomon and the king as if they were two different people. I reply that they were in fact two. (651)

576 *Two contrary reasons.* We must begin with that, otherwise we cannot understand anything and everything is heretical. And even at the end of each truth we must add that we are bearing the opposite truth in mind. (567)

577 If we must never take any chances we ought not to do any-

1. Matt. XXIV. 34.
2. L 14.

thing for religion, for it is not certain. But how many chances we do take: sea voyages, battles. Therefore, I say, we should have to do nothing at all, for nothing is certain. And there is more certainty in religion than that we shall live to see tomorrow.

For it is not certain that we shall see tomorrow but it is certainly possible that we shall not. We cannot say the same of religion. It is not certain that it is true, but who would dare to say that it is certainly possible that it is not?

Now when we work for tomorrow and take chances we are behaving reasonably, for we ought to take chances, according to the rule of probability already demonstrated.

St Augustine saw that we take chances at sea, in battle, etc. – but he did not see the rule of probability which proves that we ought to. Montaigne saw that we are offended by a lame mind and that habit can do anything, but he did not see the reason for this.

All these people saw the effects but did not see the causes. In comparison with those who have discovered the causes they are like those who have only eyes compared to those who have minds. For the effects can, as it were, be felt by the senses but the causes can only be perceived by the mind. And, although these effects can be seen by the mind, this mind can be compared to that which sees the causes as the bodily senses may be compared to the mind. (234)

578 Eloquence is a depiction of thought, and thus those who add still more once they have done the painting are producing a picture instead of a portrait. (26)

579 Coach 'tipped up' or 'overturned' according to the intention.
'Spread' or 'pour' according to intention.[1]
M. le M[aître]'s defence of the man forced to become a Franciscan. (53)

580 Symmetry in what we see at a glance.
Based on the fact that there is no reason to do otherwise.
And based too on the human face,
Which is why we want symmetry only in breadth, not in height or depth. (28)

1. Examples of shades of meaning between similar French words.

581   Scaramouche who has only one thought in his head.

The doctor who goes on talking for a quarter of an hour when he has already said everything, because he is so eager to have his say.   (12)

582   Change figures, because of our weakness.   (669)

583   'Imagine how much I share your distress.'

The Cardinal had no wish for people to imagine what he felt.

'My mind is filled with anxiety': 'I am filled with anxiety' is better.   (56)

584   Eloquence which persuades gently, not imperiously, as a tyrant, not as a king.   (15)

585   There is a certain model of attractiveness and beauty consisting in a certain relation between our nature, weak or strong as it may be, and the thing which pleases us.

Everything that conforms to this model attracts us, be it a house, a song, a speech, verse, prose, a woman, birds, rivers, trees, rooms, clothes, etc.

Everything which does not conform to this model is displeasing to people of good taste.

And as there is an exact relation between a song and a house based on this good model, because both resemble a single model, though each in its own way, there is in the same way an exact relation between things based on bad models. It is not that there is only one bad model, because they are innumerable, but every bad sonnet, for example, whatever the false model it is based on, is exactly like a woman dressed according to that model.

Nothing gives a better idea of the absurdity of a bad sonnet than to consider its nature and its model and then to imagine a woman or a house conforming to that model.   (32)

586   *Poetic beauty*. Just as we talk of poetic beauty, so we should also talk of mathematical beauty and medicinal beauty. But we do not talk like that for the very good reason that we know what the object of mathematics is, namely proof; and what the object of medicine is, namely cure; but we do not know what constitutes the attraction which is the object of poetry. We do not

know what this natural model is that must be imitated, and for want of this knowledge we have inherited certain strange terms, 'golden age', 'marvel of our times', 'fatal', etc. And we call this jargon poetic beauty.

But anyone trying to imagine a woman dressed on that model, which consists in using big words for trivial things, will see a pretty young lady loaded with mirrors and chains, and that will make him laugh, because we know more about the nature of a woman's attractions than those of verse. But people who know nothing about it would admire her in this rig and there are many villages where she would be taken for the Queen. That is why we call sonnets on this model 'village queens'. (33)

587 Nobody is publicly accepted as an expert on poetry unless he displays the sign of poet, mathematician, etc., but universal men want no sign and make hardly any distinction between the crafts of poet and embroiderer.

Universal men are not called poets or mathematicians, etc. But they are all these things and judges of them too. No one could guess what they are, and they will talk about whatever was being talked about when they came in. One quality is not more noticeable in them than another, unless it becomes necessary to put it into practice, and then we remember it. For it is equally characteristic that they are not described as good speakers as long as no question of language arises, and that they are when it does.

It is therefore false praise to say of someone when he comes in that he is an expert on poetry and a bad sign if he is not consulted when it is a question of judging some verse. (34)

588 Faith is a gift of God. Do not imagine that we describe it as a gift of reason. Other religions do not say that about their faith. They offered nothing but reason as a way to faith, and yet it does not lead there. (279)

589 The devil disturbed the zeal of the Jews before Christ because he might have done them good, but not afterwards.

The Jewish people mocked by the Gentiles, the Christians persecuted. (704)

590 *Adam the figure of him that was to come.*[1] Six days to create one, six ages to create the other. The six days which Moses represents for the creation of Adam are only an image of the six ages for creating Christ and the Church. If Adam had not sinned and Christ had not come, there would have been only one covenant and one age of man, and creation would have been represented as accomplished at a single moment. (656)

591 *Lest, if they were subjected to terror instead of teaching, it should look like unjust rule.* St Aug. *Ep.* 48 or 49. Vol. IV. *Contra mendacium, ad Consentium.* (186)

SERIES XXIV
[VARIOUS]

592 If the Jews had all been converted by Christ we should only have suspect witnesses left. And if they had been wiped out we should have had none at all. (750)

593 The Jews reject him, but not all of them: the holy ones accept him and not the carnal ones, and far from telling against his glory this is the crowning touch to it. Their reason for doing so, and the only one to be found in all their writings, in the Talmud and the rabbis, is merely that Christ did not subdue the nations by force of arms. '*Gird thy sword, O most mighty.*'[2] Is that all they have to say? 'Christ was slain,' they say, 'he was defeated and did not subdue the heathen by force. He did not give us their spoils. He offers us no riches.' Is that all they have to say? That is what makes me love him. I would not want the man they envisage. It is clear that it is only sin that prevented them from accepting him, and by their rejection they have become unimpeachable witnesses, and, what is more, in doing so they are fulfilling the prophecies.

As a result of this people rejecting him this miracle took place.

1. Rom. v. 14.
2. Ps. XLV. 3.

The prophecies are the only lasting miracles which can be performed, but they are liable to be challenged.　　(760)

594　*Order.* General conduct of the world towards the Church. God wishing both to blind and to enlighten.

Since events have proved that these prophecies were divine, the rest of them ought to be believed, and thus we can see the order of the world in this way:

The miracles of Creation and the Flood being forgotten, God sent the law and miracles of Moses, and the prophets who prophesied particular things. And in order to prepare a lasting miracle he prepared prophecies and their fulfilment. But since the prophecies might be suspect, he wished to put them above suspicion, etc.　　(576)

595　Unless we know ourselves to be full of pride, ambition, concupiscence, weakness, wretchedness and unrighteousness, we are truly blind. And if someone knows all this and does not desire to be saved, what can be said of him?

How then can we have anything but respect for a religion which knows man's faults so well? What desire but that a religion which promises such desirable remedies should be true?　　(450)

596　Those who are unhappy to find themselves without faith show us that God does not enlighten them: but the others show us that there is a God who is blinding them.　　(202)

597　'The self is hateful. You cover it up, Mitton,[1] but that does not mean that you take it away. So you are still hateful.'

'Not so, because by being obliging to everyone as we are, we give them no more cause to hate us.'

'True enough if the only hateful thing about the self were the unpleasantness it caused us.

'But if I hate it because it is unjust that it should make itself the centre of everything, I shall go on hating it.

'In a word the self has two characteristics. It is unjust in itself for making itself centre of everything: it is a nuisance to others in that it tries to subjugate them, for each self is the enemy of

1. Daniel Mitton, a worldly gambler and friend of Pascal.

all the others and would like to tyrannize them. You take away the nuisance, but not the injustice.

'And thus, you do not make it pleasing to those who hate it for being unjust; you only make it pleasing to unjust people who no longer see it as their enemy. Thus you remain unjust, and can only please unjust people.' (455)

598 What spoils comparisons between the state of the Church in former times and its present situation is the fact that we usually regard St Athanasius, St Theresa and the rest as crowned with glory and years, judged almost divine before our time. Now that time has cleared things up, that is what it looks like, but at the time when he was being persecuted this great saint was just a man called Athanasius; and St Theresa just a woman. Elias was a man, subject to like passions as we are, as St Peter says,[1] to rid Christians of the false idea which makes us reject the example of the saints as bearing no relation to our state. 'They were saints,' we say, 'it is not the same for us.' What happened then in those days? St Athanasius was a man called Athanasius, accused of several crimes, condemned by such and such a council for such and such a crime. All the bishops agreed, and in the end the Pope. What were the dissentients told? That they were disturbing the peace, causing schism, etc.

Four kinds of person: zeal without knowledge, knowledge without zeal, neither knowledge nor zeal, both zeal and knowledge.

The first three condemn him, the last acquit him, are excommunicated by the Church, but yet save the Church.

Zeal, light. (868)

599 But is it *probable* that *probability* brings certainty?

Difference between peace and certainty of conscience. Truth alone brings certainty: the sincere quest for truth alone brings peace. (908)

600 The corruptness of reason can be seen in the number of different and extravagant customs. The truth had to appear so that man should stop living inside himself. (440)

1. Actually James v. 17.

601 The casuists submit decisions to corrupt reason and the choice of decisions to corrupt will, so that everything which is corrupt in man's nature plays a part in his conduct.   (907)

602 Anyone who wants can be made a priest, as under Jeroboam.

It is an appalling thing that the discipline of the Church today is represented as so excellent that any attempt to change it is treated as a crime. In former times discipline was invariably excellent, but we see that changes could be made without committing a sin, whereas in its present state no change may even be desired.

Men were indeed allowed to change the custom whereby the priesthood was conferred only with such circumspection that scarcely any proved worthy of it, but they are not now allowed to deplore the custom which produces so many unworthy ones.   (885)

603 Abraham took nothing for himself but only for his servants. Thus the righteous man takes nothing from the world or its applause for himself, but only for his passions, which he uses like a master, saying to one 'Go' and [to another] 'Come'.[1] *Thou shalt rule over thy desire.*[2] Thus mastered his passions become virtues; avarice, jealousy, anger, even God ascribes these to himself. And they are just as much virtues as mercy, pity, constancy, which are also passions. We must treat them like slaves, and give them food but prevent the soul feeding on it. For, when passions are in control they become vices, and then they give their food to the soul, which feeds on it and is poisoned.   (502)

604 *Church, Pope. Unity – Multiplicity.* If the Church is regarded as one, then the Pope, as its head, represents the whole: if it is regarded as multiple, then the Pope is only a part. The Fathers sometimes looked at it in one way and sometimes another, and thus spoke in different ways about the Pope.

St Cyprian, *Sacerdos Dei.*

But in laying down one of these two truths they did not exclude the other.

1. Matt. VIII. 9.   2. Gen. IV. 7.

Multiplicity which is not reduced to unity is confusion. Unity which does not depend on multiplicity is tyranny.

France is now almost the only place left where one is allowed to say that the council is above the Pope. (871)

605 Man is full of needs, and he only likes those people who can satisfy them all. 'He is a good mathematician,' you will say. But I am not concerned with mathematics: he would take me for a proposition. 'He is a good soldier.' He would take me for a place under siege. What I need then is an all-round good man[1] who can adapt himself to all my needs generally. (36)

606 A true friend is something so valuable, even for the greatest noblemen, that they ought to do all they can to have one to speak well of them and stand up for them in their absence. But they must choose carefully, for if all their efforts are spent on fools it will do them no good, however well they speak of them. And they will not even speak well of them if they find themselves on the weaker side, because they have no authority, and so they will run them down in order to be with the majority. (155)

607 *Figures.* Saviour, father, sacrificer, sacrifice, food, king, wise, lawgiver, afflicted, poor, destined to produce a people whom he should lead and feed, and bring into the land. (766)

608 *Christ. Offices.* He alone had to produce a great people, elect, holy and chosen, lead them, feed them, bring them into the place of rest and holiness, make them holy for God, make them the temple of God, reconcile them with God, save them from God's anger, redeem them from the bondage of sin which visibly reigns in man, give laws to this people, write these laws in their hearts, offer himself to God for them, sacrifice himself for them, be a spotless sacrifice, and himself the sacrificer, having himself to offer up his body and blood, and yet offer up bread and wine to God.

When he cometh into the world.[2]

'One stone upon another.'[3]

1. *Honnête homme* (Tr.). 2. Heb. x. 5. 3. Mark xiii. 2.

What came before, what came after. The Jews all surviving and wanderers. (766)

609 *Prophecies. Whom they have pierced.* (Zech. XII. 10).

That a Redeemer should come, who would crush the demon's head, who was to deliver his people from their sins, from *all their iniquities.*[1] That there should be a new covenant which would be everlasting, that there should be a new priesthood after the order of Melchisedech, which would be everlasting, that the Christ should be glorious, mighty, strong, and yet so wretched that he would not be recognized, that he would not be taken for what he is, but rejected and slain, that his people having denied him would no longer be his people, that the idolaters would accept him and resort to him, that he would leave Sion to reign in the centre of idolatry, that the Jews would still continue to exist for ever, that he should be of the tribe of Judah, where there would no longer be a king. (736)

610 (See the speeches of the Jansenist in Letters 2, 4, 5.[1] This is serious and elevated.)

I dislike a man who plays the fool as much as one who puts on airs. One would not make a friend of either.

One only consults the ear because one is lacking in heart. (30)

611 (After my Eighth Letter[2] I thought I had said enough in reply.)

His rule is allround excellence.[3]
Poet and not a man of allround excellence.[3]
Beauties of omission, of judgement. (30)

612 There can be no doubt that the soul is either mortal or immortal: this ought to make all the difference in ethics, and yet philosophers have drawn up their ethics independently of this question.

They debate to pass the time.

Plato, to dispose people towards Christianity. (219)

---

1. Ps. CXXX. 8.
2. References to the *Provincial Letters*.
3. *Honnêteté* and *honnête* (Tr.).

613　*Greatness, wretchedness.* The more enlightened we are the more greatness and vileness we discover in man.

The ordinary run of men.

Those who are superior.

Philosophers:

They surprise the ordinary run of men.

Christians: they surprise the philosophers.

Who then will be surprised to see that religion only gives profound knowledge of something which we recognize more clearly for being more enlightened?　　　　　　　　　　　(443)

614　*Figurative.* God used the Jews' concupiscence so that they should be of use to Christ (who brought the remedy for concupiscence).
(664)

615　*Figurative.* Nothing is so like charity as greed, and nothing is so unlike. Thus the Jews, rich with possessions to flatter their greed, were very like Christians and very much unlike them. And thus they had the two qualities they had to have: being very like the Messiah, in order to prefigure him, and being very unlike so that they should not be suspect witnesses.　　(663)

616　Concupiscence has become natural for us and has become second nature. Thus there are two natures in us, one good, the other bad. Where is God? Where you are not, and the kingdom of God is within you. Rabbis.　　　　　　　　　　(660)

617　Anyone who does not hate the self-love within him and the instinct which leads him to make himself into a God must be really blind. Who can fail to see that there is nothing so contrary to justice and truth? For it is false that we deserve this position and unjust and impossible to attain it, because everyone demands the same thing. We are thus born into an obviously unjust situation from which we cannot escape but from which we must escape.

However, no [other] religion has observed that this is a sin, that it is innate in us, or that we are obliged to resist it, let alone thought of providing a cure.　　　　　　　　　　(492)

618　If God exists we must love him alone and not transitory creatures. The argument of the ungodly in *Wisdom* is based solely on the assumption that God does not exist. 'Granted that,' they say, 'let us then delight in creatures.' It is a second-best. But if there were a God to love they would not have reached this conclusion, but quite the contrary. And this is what the wise conclude: 'God exists, so let us not delight in creatures.'

Thus everything which drives us to become attached to creatures is bad, since it prevents us from serving God, if we know him, or seeking him if we do not. Now we are full of concupiscence, therefore we are full of evil, therefore we ought to hate ourselves, and everything which drives us to become attached to anything but God alone.   (479)

619 All their principles are true, sceptics, stoics, atheists, etc. . . . but their conclusions are false, because the contrary principles are also true.   (394)

620 Man is obviously made for thinking. Therein lies all his dignity and his merit; and his whole duty is to think as he ought. Now the order of thought is to begin with ourselves, and with our author and our end.

Now what does the world think about? Never about that, but about dancing, playing the lute, singing, writing verse, tilting at the ring, etc., and fighting, becoming king, without thinking what it means to be a king or to be a man.   (146)

621 Civil war in man between reason and passions.
If there were only reason without passions.
If there were only passions without reason.
But since he has both he cannot be free from war, for he can only be at peace with the one if he is at war with the other.
Thus he is always torn by inner divisions and contradictions.
                                                               (412)

622 *Boredom.* Man finds nothing so intolerable as to be in a state of complete rest, without passions, without occupation, without diversion, without effort.

Then he faces his nullity, loneliness, inadequacy, dependence, helplessness, emptiness.

And at once there wells up from the depths of his soul boredom, gloom, depression, chagrin, resentment, despair.   (131)

623 If it is unnatural blindness to live without trying to find out what one is, it is a fearful blindness to lead an evil life while believing in God. (495)

624 *Prophecies.* That Christ shall be at his right hand while God subdues his enemies.[1]
   Therefore he will not subdue them himself. (731)

625 *Injustice.* It is extremely unjust that presumption should accompany necessity. (214)

626 *Seeking the true good.* For the ordinary run of men their good consists in fortune and external wealth or at least in diversion.
   The philosophers have shown how vain all this is and have defined it as best they could. (462)

627 Vanity is so firmly anchored in man's heart that a soldier, a rough, a cook or a porter will boast and expect admirers, and even philosophers want them; those who write against them want to enjoy the prestige of having written well, those who read them want the prestige of having read them, and perhaps I who write this want the same thing, perhaps my readers. . . .
(150)

628 *On our desire for the esteem of those around us.* Pride possesses us so naturally amidst all our miseries, errors, etc. We even die gladly provided people talk about it.
   Vanity: gambling, hunting, visits, theatre-going, false perpetuation of one's name. (153)

629 Man's dualism is so obvious that some people have thought we had two souls:
   Because a simple being seemed to them incapable of such great and sudden variations, from boundless presumption to appalling dejection. (417)

630 Man's nature is entirely natural, *wholly animal.*
   There is nothing that cannot be made natural. There is nothing natural that cannot be lost. (94)

1. Ps. cx.

631 It is good to be tired and weary from fruitlessly seeking the true good, so that one can stretch out one's arms to the Redeemer. (422)

632 Man's sensitivity to little things and insensitivity to the greatest things are marks of a strange disorder. (198)

633 Despite the sight of all the miseries which affect us and hold us by the throat we have an irrepressible instinct which bears us up. (411)

634 The most important thing in our lives is the choice of a trade, and chance decides it.

Custom makes masons, soldiers, roofers. 'He is an excellent roofer,' they say, and, speaking of soldiers: 'They are quite mad,' while others on the contrary say: 'There is nothing as great as war, everyone else is worthless.' From hearing people praise these trades in our childhood and running down all the others we make our choice. For we naturally love virtue and hate folly; the very words will decide, we only go wrong in applying them.

So great is the force of custom that where nature has merely created men, we create every kind and condition of men.

For some regions are full of masons, some of soldiers etc. There is no doubt that nature is not so uniform: it is custom then which does all this, for it coerces nature, but sometimes nature overcomes it and keeps man to his instincts despite all customs, good or bad. (97)

SERIES XXV
[HUMAN NATURE. STYLE. JESUITS ETC.]

635 We like seeing the mistake and passion of Cleobuline because she is unaware of it: she would be distasteful if she were not deceived.[1] (13)

636 'Prince' is pleasing to a king because it reduces his rank. (42)

1. In Mlle de Scudéry's novel Le Grand Cyrus (1649–53).

637 'Quench the brand of sedition': too flowery.
    'The restlessness of his genius': two bold words too many.
                                     (59)

638 When we are well we wonder how we should manage if we
were ill. When we are ill we take our medicine cheerfully; our
illness settles that problem for us. We no longer have the passions, and the desires for diversions and outings, which went
with good health and are incompatible with the exigencies of
our illness. Nature then inspires the passions and desires appropriate to our present state. It is only the fears that we owe to
ourselves, and not to nature, which disturb us by linking the
state in which we are with the passions of that in which we are
not.   (109)

639 Since nature makes us unhappy whatever our state, our desire^s
depict for us a happy state, because they link the state in which
we are with the pleasures of that in which we are not. Even if
we did attain these pleasures, that would not make us happy, because we should have new desires appropriate to this new state.
    This general proposition must be particularized.   (109b)

640 If people who are always optimistic when things are going
badly, and overjoyed when they turn out well, are not equally
distressed at misfortune, they may be suspected of being pleased
at failure; they are delighted to find excuses for optimism to
show that they care, and to conceal by simulated joy their real
joy at seeing the failure of their affairs.   (182)

641 Our nature consists in movement; absolute rest is death.   (129)

642 Mitton sees quite well that nature is corrupt and that men are
opposed to integrity, but he does not know why they can fly
no higher.   (448)

643 Fine deeds are most admirable when kept secret. When I see
some of them in history, as on p. 184,[1] they please me greatly;
but of course they were not completely secret because they
have become known, and, although everything possible was
done to keep them secret, the detail by which they came to

    1. In his edition of Montaigne, *Essays*, I. 14.

light spoils everything, for the finest thing about them was the attempt to keep them secret. (159)

644 Can it be anything but a complaisant world that makes you find things probable? Will you make us believe it is the truth, and that, if the fashion of duelling did not exist, you would find it probable that one may fight, looking at the thing in itself?[1]
(910)

645 Justice is what is established; thus all our established laws will necessarily be regarded as just without examination since they are established. (312)

646 *Feeling.* Memory and joy are feelings, and even mathematical propositions can become feelings, for reason makes feelings natural and natural feelings are eradicated by reason. (95)

647 *Honnête homme.* We must be able to say not that he is a mathematician, or a preacher, or eloquent, but that he is a man of all-round excellence [*honnête homme*]. This universal quality is the only one I like. If, on seeing someone, we remember his book, it is a bad sign. I should like no quality to be noticeable until it comes up and there is occasion to use it (*nothing in excess*) for fear that one particular quality may predominate and provide a label. I do not want people to think of him as a good speaker until the question of speaking well arises, but then they should think so. (35)

648 *Miracles.* People come to this conclusion by themselves, but you must give the reason for it.

It is tiresome to be the exception to the rule; we must even be strictly opposed to exceptions, but yet, as there certainly are exceptions to the rule, they must be judged strictly but fairly.
(833)

649 *Montaigne.* What is good in Montaigne can only be acquired with difficulty. What is bad in him, I mean apart from morals, could have been corrected in a moment if someone had warned

1. Reference to the Jesuit doctrine of probabilism, attacked in the *Provincial Letters*, for which this and similar fragments were drafts.

him that he was making too much of things and talking too much about himself. (65)

650 Have you never met people who, in protest at your lack of regard for them, boast of the distinguished people who think well of them? My answer would be: 'Show me the merits by which you captivated these people and I will think well of you too.' (333)

651 Memory is necessary for all the operations of reason. (369)

652 When some passion or effect is described in a natural style, we find within ourselves the truth of what we hear, without knowing it was there. We are consequently inclined to like the person who made us feel it, for he has shown us not his wealth but our own, and this kindness makes him agreeable to us; besides, the common fact of our understanding is bound to move us to like him. (14)

653 *Probability.* Anyone can add to it, no one can take away. (913)

654 You never accuse me of falsehood concerning Escobar,[1] because he is well known. (939)

655 Talk about humility gives occasion for pride to the proud and humility to the humble. Similarly, sceptical arguments allow the positive to be positive. Few speak humbly of humility, chastely of chastity, dubiously of scepticism. We are nothing but lies, duplicity, contradiction, and we hide and disguise ourselves from ourselves. (377)

656 As I write down my thought it sometimes escapes me, but that reminds me of my weakness, which I am always forgetting, and teaches me as much as my forgotten thought, for I care only about knowing that I am nothing. (372)

657 Pity for the unfortunate does not run counter to concupiscence; on the contrary, we are very glad to show such evidence of friendship and thus win a reputation for sympathy without giving anything in return. (452)

1. Jesuit moral theologian.

658   *Conversation.* Big words about religion: 'I deny it.'
     Conversation. Scepticism helps religion.   (391)

659   Must one kill to destroy evildoers?
     That is making two evildoers in place of one. *Overcome evil with good*[1] (St Augustine).   (911)

660   *Spongia solis.*[2] When we see the same effect always occurring, we conclude that it is necessarily so by nature, like the fact that it will dawn tomorrow etc., but nature often gives us the lie and does not obey its own rules.   (91)

661   The mind naturally believes and the will naturally loves, so that when there are no true objects for them they necessarily become attached to false ones.   (81)

662   Grace will always be in the world and nature too, so that in a way it is natural. Thus there will always be Pelagians and always Catholics, and always strife.
     Because our birth creates the former and the grace of our re-birth the latter.   (521)

663   Nature constantly begins the same things over again, years, days, hours, spaces too. And numbers run end to end, one after another. This makes something in a way infinite and eternal. It is not that any of this is really infinite and eternal, but these finite entities multiply infinitely. Thus only number, which multiplies them, seems to me to be infinite.   (121)

664   Man is properly speaking *wholly animal.*   (94b)

665   An empire based on opinion and imagination reigns for a time, and such an empire is mild and voluntary. That of force reigns for ever. Thus opinion is like the queen of the world, but force is its tyrant.   (311)

666   Anyone condemned by Escobar is really condemned.   (932)

667   *Eloquence.* There must be elements both pleasing and real, but what is pleasing must itself be drawn from what is true.   (25)

1. Rom. XII. 21.
2. Either sunspots or a kind of phosphorescent mineral.

668 Each man is everything to himself, for with his death everything is dead for him. That is why each of us thinks he is everything to everyone. We must not judge nature by ourselves, but by its own standards. (457)

669 In every dialogue and address we must be able to say to those who take offence: 'What are you complaining about?' (188)

670 Great wit, bad character. (46)

671 If you want people to think well of you, do not speak well of yourself. (44)

672 We not only look at things from different points of view, but with different eyes; we do not care to find them alike. (124)

673 'He no longer loves the person he loved ten years ago.' I quite believe it: she is not the same any more, nor is he. He was young and so was she; now she is quite different. Perhaps he would still love her as she used to be then. (123)

674 We do not keep ourselves virtuous by our own power, but by the counterbalance of two opposing vices, just as we stay upright between two contrary winds. Take one of these vices away and we fall into the other. (359)

675 *Style.* When we see a natural style we are quite amazed and delighted, because we expected to see an author and find a man, whereas people of good taste who think they will find a man when they see a book are quite surprised to find an author. *You have spoken more as a poet than a man.*[1]

Those people do honour to nature who tell her that she can talk of anything, even theology. (29)

676 The world must be really blind if it believes you. (937)

677 The Pope hates and fears scholars who are not vowed to his obedience. (873)

678 Man is neither angel nor beast, and it is unfortunately the case that anyone trying to act the angel acts the beast. (358)

1. Petronius, xc.

679 *Provincial Letters.* Those who love the Church complain when they see morals corrupted, but at least the laws survive. But these people corrupt the laws. The model is spoilt. (894)

680 *Montaigne.* Montaigne's faults are great. Lewd words: that is no good, despite Mlle de Gournay. Credulous: 'people without eyes.' Ignorant: 'squaring the circle, bigger world.' His views on deliberate homicide, on death. He inspires indifference regarding salvation: 'without fear or repentance'. As his book was not written to encourage piety, he was under no obligation to do so, but we are always under an obligation not to discourage it. One may excuse his somewhat free and licentious views on certain situations in life (pp. 730,331) but his completely pagan views on death are inexcusable; for all hope of piety must be abandoned if we are not at least willing to die as Christians. Now, throughout his book he thinks only of dying a death of cowardly ease. (63)

681 I do not admire the excess of a virtue like courage unless I see at the same time an excess of the opposite virtue, as in Epaminondas, who possessed extreme courage and extreme kindness. Otherwise it is not rising to the heights but falling down. We show greatness, not by being at one extreme, but by touching both at once and occupying all the space in between.

But perhaps it is only a sudden flash of the soul from one extreme to the other; perhaps greatness only ever lies in a single point, as in a glowing ember? Maybe, but at least that shows how agile the soul is, even if it does not show its range. (353)

682 *Infinite movement.* Infinite movement, ubiquitous point, moment of rest. Infinite without quantity, indivisible and infinite. (232)

683 *Order.* Why should I choose to divide my ethics into four rather than six? Why should I define virtue as four, or two, or one? Why as *desist and resist*[1] rather than 'follow nature' or 'discharge your private business without injustice', like Plato, or anything else?

1. *Abstine et sustine*, Epictetus's maxim.

'But,' you will say, 'there everything is summed up in a word.' – 'Yes, but that is no good unless you explain it.' And when you come to explain it, as soon as you open up this precept which contains all the others, out they all come in the original confusion that you wanted to avoid. Thus when they are all enclosed in one they are concealed and useless, as if they were in a box, and they only come to light in their natural confusion. Nature has laid them all down, without enclosing one inside another.   (20)

684 *Order.* Nature has made all her truths self-contained. Our art encloses some truths inside others, but this is not natural. Each has its own place.   (21)

685 *Glory.* Animals do not admire each other. A horse does not admire its companion. It is not that they will not race against each other, but this is of no consequence, for, back in the stable, the one who is heavier and clumsier does not on that account give up his oats to the other, as men want others to do to them. With them virtue is its own reward.   (401)

686 When they say that heat is merely the movement of certain globules and light the *conatus recedendi* [centrifugal force] that we feel, we are amazed. What! is pleasure nothing but a ballet of spirits? We had such a different conception of it, and these feelings seem so far removed from those other ones, which, we say, are the same as those with which we are comparing them. The feeling of fire, the warmth which affects us in quite a different way from touch, the reception of sound and light, all seem mysterious to us. And yet it is as straightforward as throwing a stone. It is true that the smallness of the spirits entering the pores touches other nerves, but they are still nerves.   (368)

687 I had spent a long time studying abstract sciences, and I was put off them by seeing how little one could communicate about them. When I began the study of man I saw that these abstract sciences are not proper to man, and that I was straying further from my true condition by going into them than were others by being ignorant of them. I forgave others for not knowing

much about them, but I thought I should at least find many companions in my study of man, since it is his true and proper study. I was wrong. Even fewer people study man than mathematics. It is only because they do not know how to study man that people look into all the rest. But is it not so that man ought not even to have this knowledge and that it is better for him not to know himself if he wants to be happy?   (144)

688   What is the self?

A man goes to the window to see the people passing by; if I pass by, can I say he went there to see me? No, for he is not thinking of me in particular. But what about a person who loves someone for the sake of her beauty; does he love *her*? No, for smallpox, which will destroy beauty without destroying the person, will put an end to his love for her.

And if someone loves me for my judgement or my memory, do they love me? *me*, myself? No, for I could lose these qualities without losing my self. Where then is this self, if it is neither in the body nor the soul? And how can one love the body or the soul except for the sake of such qualities, which are not what makes up the self, since they are perishable? Would we love the substance of a person's soul, in the abstract, whatever qualities might be in it? That is not possible, and it would be wrong. Therefore we never love anyone, but only qualities.

Let us then stop scoffing at those who win honour through their appointments and offices, for we never love anyone except for borrowed qualities.   (323)

689   It is not in Montaigne but in myself that I find everything I see there.   (64)

690   May God not impute our sins to us, that is all the consequences and results of our sins, which are appalling; even of our slightest faults, if we are prepared to follow them up mercilessly.   (506)

691   Scepticism is right. For, after all, men before Christ did not know where they stood, nor whether they were great or small. And those who said either one or the other knew nothing about it and were guessing irrationally, at random. Indeed they were always wrong for excluding one or the other.

What therefore ye ignorantly seek religion declares unto you.[1]

(432)

692 *Montalte.*[2] Lax views are so popular that it is strange that theirs give offence. It is because they have exceeded all bounds. Moreover, plenty of people see the truth but cannot attain it, but there are few who do not know that the purity of religion is contrary to our corruption. Ridiculous to say that an eternal reward is offered for morals *à la* Escobar. (915)

693 The easiest conditions to live in from the world's point of view are the hardest from that of God; and vice versa. Nothing is so hard from the world's point of view as the religious life, while nothing is easier from that of God. Nothing is easier than to enjoy high office or great wealth in a worldly way, nothing harder than to live such a life in God's way, without taking interest or pleasure in it. (906)

694 *Order.* I could easily have treated this discourse in this kind of order: show the vanity of all kinds of conditions, show the vanity of ordinary lives, and then the vanity of philosophers' lives, whether sceptical or Stoic, but the order would not have been kept. I know something about it and how few people understand it. No human science can keep it. St Thomas did not keep it. Mathematics keeps it, but it goes so far as to be useless. (61)

695 Original sin is folly in the eyes of men, but it is put forward as such. You should therefore not reproach me for the unreasonable nature of this doctrine, because I put it forward as being unreasonable. But this folly is wiser than all men's wisdom, *it is wiser than men.*[3] For without it, what are we to say man is? His whole state depends on this imperceptible point. How could he have become aware of it through his reason, seeing that it is something contrary to reason and that his reason, far from discovering it by its own methods, draws away when presented with it? (445)

1. An adaptation of Acts XVII. 23.
2. Louis de Montalte was Pascal's pseudonym for the *Prov. Letters.*
3. I Cor. I. 25.

696 Let no one say that I have said nothing new; the arrangement
of the material is new. In playing tennis both players use the
same ball, but one plays it better.

I would just as soon be told that I have used old words. As
if the same thoughts did not form a different argument by being
differently arranged, just as the same words make different
thoughts when arranged differently!　(22)

697 Those who lead disorderly lives tell those who are normal that
it is they who deviate from nature, and think they are following
nature themselves; just as those who are on board ship think
that the people on shore are moving away. Language is the same
everywhere: we need a fixed point to judge it. The harbour is
the judge of those aboard ship, but where are we going to find
a harbour in morals?　(383)

698 *Nature copies itself.* Nature copies itself. A seed cast on good
ground bears fruit, a principle cast into a good mind bears fruit.
Numbers copy space, though so different by nature.
Everything is made and directed by the same master.
Root, branches, fruit: principles, consequences.　(119)

699 When everything is moving at once, nothing appears to be
moving, as on board ship. When everyone is moving towards
depravity, no one seems to be moving, but if someone stops
he shows up the others who are rushing on, by acting as a fixed
point.　(382)

700 *Generals.* It is not enough for them to introduce such behaviour
into our temples. They not only want to be tolerated in the
Church, but, as if they had become the strongest party, want to
drive out those who do not belong to them.

Mohatra.[1] It is not for a theologian to be astonished by it.
Who could have told your generals that the time was so near
when they would provide the universal Church with such
behaviour, and call the rejection of such perversions an act of
war? *Those so great plagues called they peace.*[2]　(934)

---

1. Contract denounced in *Prov.*, VIII.
2. Wisdom XIV. 22.

701 When we want to correct someone usefully and show him he is wrong, we must see from what point of view he is approaching the matter, for it is usually right from that point of view, and we must admit this, but show him the point of view from which it is wrong. This will please him, because he will see that he was not wrong but merely failed to see every aspect of the question. Now, no one is annoyed at not seeing everything, but no one wants to be wrong; the reason for that may be that man is not by nature able to see everything, and by nature cannot be wrong from the point of view he adopts, as sense impressions are always true. (9)

702 *Grace.* Movements of grace, hardness of heart, external circumstances. (507)

703 *Glory.* Romans III. 27, glory is excluded. By what law? That of works? No, but by faith. Faith, therefore, is not in our power as are the works of the law, and it is given to us in a different way. (516)

704 *Venice.*[1] What good will it do you, except that princes need it and peoples have a horror of it? If they had asked you and implored the assistance of Christian princes in obtaining it, you might have justified this attempt. But that for fifty years princes have spent themselves on it in vain and it took such an urgent need to obtain it. . . . (954)

705 Great and small are liable to the same accidents, the same annoyance, the same passion, but one is at the top of the wheel and the other near its centre, and thus less shaken by the same movements. (180)

706 *Bind and loose.* God did not wish to grant absolution without the Church. As she has a part in the offence, he wants her to have a part in the pardon. He associates her with this power as kings associate their parliaments, but, if she absolves or if she binds without God, she is no longer the Church. It is the same with the parliament, for, though the king has granted pardon

1. The Jesuits had after fifty years banishment been allowed to return there.

to someone, it must be ratified, but, if parliament ratifies without the king or refuses to ratify on the king's orders, it is no longer the king's parliament but a rebellious body.   (870)

707 They cannot enjoy perpetuity, and they seek universality. For this they make the whole Church corrupt so that they can be saints.   (898)

708 *Popes.* Kings dispose of their kingdoms, but popes cannot dispose of theirs.   (877)

709 We know so little about ourselves that many people think they are going to die when they are quite well, and many think they are quite well when they are on the point of death, not sensing the approach of fever or the abscess ready to form.   (175)

710 *Language.* The mind must not be led off on to something else except for relaxation, but at the right time; give it relaxation when it is due and not otherwise. Relaxation at the wrong time wearies it and wearying it at the wrong time relaxes it, for we just give everything up. Malicious concupiscence takes such delight in producing the very opposite of what people want to get from us without giving us any pleasure, the coin for which we will give people all they want.   (24)

711 *Strength.* Why do we follow the majority? Is it because they are more right? No, but they are stronger.

Why do we follow ancient laws and opinions? Is it because they are the soundest? No, but they are unique and leave us no basis for disagreement.   (301)

712 Someone told me one day that he felt full of joy and confidence when he had been to confession. Someone else told me that he was still afraid. My reaction was that one good man could be made by putting these two together, for each of them lacked something in not sharing the feelings of the other. The same thing often happens in other connexions.   (530)

713 It is not solely absolution that remits sins in the sacrament of penance, but contrition, which is not genuine unless it desires the sacrament.

Likewise it is not the nuptial benediction which takes away the sin from procreation, but the desire to procreate children for God, which is only genuine in marriage.

And as a contrite person without the sacrament is better fitted to receive absolution than an impenitent person with the sacrament, so the daughters of Lot,[1] for example, who only wanted to have children, were purer without marriage than married people with no desire for children. (923)

714 *Pope.* There is some contradiction, for, on the one hand, they say that tradition must be followed, and would not dare to disown it, while on the other they say what they like. We shall always believe the former, since it would also be contrary to their wish not to believe it. (944)

715 Chief talent regulating all the others. (118)

716 Fear death when there is no danger, and not when there is, for one must be a man. (215)

717 Rivers are moving roads which take us where we want to go. (17)

718 The prophecies were ambiguous; they are so no longer. (830)

719 'Yet I have left me seven thousand.'[2] I love these worshippers who are unknown to the world, and even to the prophets. (788)

720 *Universal.* Ethics and language are particular, but also universal, branches of knowledge. (912)

721 *Probability.* The ardour of the saints in seeking out the truth was pointless if the probable is safe.

The fear of the saints who always followed the safest course. St Teresa who always followed her confessor. (917)

722 *Probable.* Let us see if we are sincerely seeking God by making some comparisons with things we care about.

It is probable that this meat will not poison me.

It is probable that I shall not lose my case by not lobbying.

1. Gen. XIX. 30.
2. I Kings XIX. 18.

Probable. Even if it were true that serious authors and reasons were sufficient, I say that they are neither serious nor reasonable.

Why! A husband can take advantage of his wife, according to Molina! Is the reason he gives reasonable and is the contrary reason of Lessius reasonable either?

Do you dare then to trifle with the king's edicts, as when you say that going into a field and waiting for someone is not duelling?

That the Church has indeed forbidden duelling but not going for a walk?

Likewise usury but not. . . .

And simony but not. . . .

And revenge but not. . . .

And sodomy but not. . . .

And the *quam primum*[1] but not. . . .   (922)

723 *Two infinites. Mean.* When we read too quickly or too slowly we do not understand anything.   (69)

724 The extent of a man's virtue ought not to be measured by his efforts but by his usual behaviour.   (352)

725 Sinners without penance, righteous without charity, a God without power over men's wills, predestination without mystery.   (884b)

726 *Pope.* God does not perform miracles in the ordinary conduct of his Church. It would be a strange miracle if infallibility resided in one man, but that it should be in the many seems so natural that God's conduct is hidden beneath nature, as in all his other works.   (876)

727 They make the exception into the rule. In olden times, was not absolution given before penance? Do so in the spirit of an exception. But you make the exception into a rule with no exceptions, so that you do not even want the rule to be exceptional any more.   (904)

728 All the false beauties we criticize in Cicero find admirers, and many of them.

Miracles, St Thomas, Vol. III, book viii, ch. xx.   (31)

1. 'As soon as possible', i.e. the obligation to confess mortal sin.

729 *Casuists.* Considerable alms, reasonable penance.

Although we cannot define what is exactly right, we can easily see what is not. It is absurd of the casuists to think that they can interpret it as they do.

People who become accustomed to think and to speak ill. Their great numbers, far from indicating their perfection, indicate the contrary.

The humility of one is the pride of many. (931)

SERIES XXVI
[SOURCES OF ERROR]

730 CC *Thou being a man makest thyself God.*
Is it not written: 'Ye are Gods . . . and the Scripture cannot be broken.[1]
CC *This sickness is not unto death but life.*
'Lazarus sleepeth.' Then he said: 'Lazarus is dead.'[2] (754)

731 These people are heartless.
We should not make friends of them. (196)

732 Poet and not man of all-round excellence [*honnête homme*]. (38)

733 The Church has always been attacked by contrary errors, but perhaps never before at the same time, as now. If she is suffering more because of the multiplicity of errors, she has the advantage that they cancel themselves out.

She complains of both, but much more of the Calvinists, because of their schism.

It is certain that many on the two opposing sides are mistaken. They must be disabused.

Faith embraces many apparently contradictory truths, 'a time to weep and a time to laugh,'[3] etc., 'answer, answer not.'[4]

The origin of this is the union of two natures in Christ.

And also the two worlds. The creation of a new heaven and a new earth. New life, new death.

1. John x. 33–5. 2. John xi. 4, 11, 14.
3. Eccl. iii. 4. 4. Prov. xxvi. 4, 5.

Everything duplicated and the same names remaining.

And finally the two men who are in the righteous. For they are the two worlds, and a member and image of Christ. Thus all the names fit them: righteous sinners; living dead; dead living; reprobate elect, etc.

There are, then, a great number of truths, both of faith and morals, which seem repugnant but all exist in admirable order.

The source of all heresies is the exclusion of certain of these truths.

And the source of all the objections levelled at us by heretics is their ignorance of certain of our truths.

It usually happens that, being unable to imagine the connexion between two opposing truths, and thinking that the acceptance of the one entails the exclusion of the other, they hold on to one and exclude the other, and think that we are doing just the opposite. Now this exclusion is the cause of their heresy, and ignorance of the fact that we hold the other causes their objections.

First example. Jesus Christ is God and man. The Arians, unable to combine two things which they believe to be incompatible, say that he is man, and in this are Catholic, but they deny that he is God, and in that they are heretical. They claim that we deny his humanity, and in that they are ignorant.

Second example. On the subject of the Blessed Sacrament. We believe that, the substance of bread being changed and transsubstantiated into that of Our Lord's body, Jesus Christ is really present in it: that is one of the truths. Another is that this sacrament also prefigures that of the Cross, and glory, and is a commemoration of both. Here we have the Catholic faith embracing two apparently opposing truths.

Modern heresy, unable to conceive that this sacrament contains at once the presence and the figuration of Jesus Christ, and is both a sacrifice and a commemoration of a sacrifice, believes that one of these truths cannot be admitted without thereby excluding the other.

They fix on the single point that the sacrament is figurative, and in this they are not heretical. They think that we exclude this truth, and hence raise so many objections about passages in the Fathers which attest it. Finally they deny the real presence and in this they are heretical.

Third example. Indulgences.

That is why the shortest way to prevent heresy is to teach all truths, and the surest way of refuting it is to proclaim them all.

For what will the heretics say?

To know if a given opinion is that of a Father. . . .   (862)

734   *Title.* How is it we believe so many liars who say they have seen miracles and do not believe any of those who say they have secrets to make man immortal or rejuvenate him?

After considering what makes us trust impostors claiming to have cures, to the extent that we often put our lives into their hands, it seemed to me that the real reason is that some of them are genuine, for there could not possibly be so many false ones, enjoying so much credit, unless some of them were genuine. If there had never been a cure for any ill, and all ills had been incurable, men could not possibly have imagined that they could provide any, still less could so many others have given credence to those who boasted of having such cures. Similarly, if a man boasted that he could prevent death, no one would believe him, because there is no example of that happening. But as numerous cures have been found genuine, to the knowledge of even the greatest men, this has inclined men to be more trusting; from the fact that this was known to be possible, it was concluded that it actually is. For the people normally argue like this: 'Something is possible, therefore it is.' Because a thing cannot be denied in general, certain particular effects being genuine, the people, unable to distinguish which of the particular effects are genuine, believe in them all. Similarly, the reason we believe in so many false effects of the moon is that there are some genuine ones, like the tides of the sea. It is the same with prophecies, miracles, divination by dreams, spells, etc., for, if none of this had ever been genuine, none of it would ever have been believed. Thus instead of concluding that there are no true miracles because there are so many false ones, we must on the contrary say that there certainly are true miracles since there are so many false ones, and that false ones are only there because true ones exist. The same argument must be applied to religion, for men could not possibly have imagined so many false religions unless there were a true one. The objection to that is that savages have a religion; but the answer is that they have heard about it, as can be seen from the flood, circumcision, St Andrew's cross, etc.

(817)

735 After considering how it is that there are so many false miracles, false revelations, spells, etc., it seemed to me that the real reason is that some are true, for there could not possibly be so many false miracles if there were not some true ones, or so many false religions if there were not a true one. For if there had never been any of this, it is virtually impossible for men to have imagined it, and still more impossible that so many others would have believed it. But as some very great things have been genuine, and have thus been believed by great men, they made such an impression that almost everyone has become capable of believing in the false ones as well. Thus, instead of concluding that there are no true miracles because there are so many false ones, we must on the contrary say that there are only false ones because true ones exist. Similarly there are only false religions because a true one exists. The objection to that is that savages have a religion, but it is because they have heard of the true one, as can be seen from St Andrew's cross, the flood, circumcision, etc. The reason for this is that man's mind, being so conditioned by the truth, consequently becomes receptive to all the falsehoods of this. . . .

(818)

736 When we are accustomed to use the wrong reasons to prove natural phenomena, we are no longer ready to accept the right ones when they are discovered. The example given concerned the circulation of the blood, to explain why the vein swells below the ligature.

(96)

737 We are usually convinced more easily by reasons we have found ourselves than by those which have occurred to others.

(10)

738 Liancourt's story of the pike and the frog.[1] They always behave

1. Apparently a reference to fights observed between these two creatures.

like this, and never otherwise, nor show any other sign of intelligence. (341)

739 Truth is so obscured nowadays and lies so well established that unless we love the truth we shall never recognize it. (864)

740 Weaklings are those who know the truth, but maintain it only as far as it is in their interest to do so, and apart from that forsake it. (583)

741 The adding-machine produces effects closer to thought than anything done by the animals, but it does nothing to justify the assertion that it has a will like the animals. (340)

742 Even if people's interests are not affected by what they say, it must not be definitely concluded that they are not lying for there are some people who lie simply for the sake of lying. (108)

743 There is some pleasure in being on board a ship battered by storms when one is certain of not perishing. The persecutions buffeting the Church are like this. (859)

744 When we do not know the truth about something, it is a good thing that there should be some common error on which men's minds can fix, as, for example, the attribution to the moon of changes of seasons, progress of diseases, etc. For man's chief malady is restless curiosity about things he cannot know, and it is not so bad for him to be wrong as so vainly curious. (18)

745 The style of Epictetus, Montaigne and Salomon de Tultie[1] is the commonest, which is most persuasive, stays longest in the memory and is most often quoted, because it consists entirely of thoughts deriving from everyday conversations. For instance, when people speak of the commonly received error that the moon is the cause of everything, they never fail to say that Salomon de Tultie says that, when we do not know the truth about something, it is a good thing that there should be some common error . . . (which is the thought on the other side). (18b)

1. Anagram of Louis de Montalte, Pascal's pseudonym in the *Prov. Letters*.

746 On the fact that neither Josephus, nor Tacitus, nor other historians, spoke of Jesus Christ.

Far from telling against him, this is on the contrary in his
favour. For it is certain that Jesus Christ existed, that his religion
made a great stir, and so it is obvious that they simply concealed
it on purpose, or that they spoke about it and that it was
suppressed or changed. (787)

747 On the fact that the Christian religion is not unique.

Far from being a reason for believing it not to be the true
religion, it is on the contrary what proves it to be so. (589)

748 *Objection.* Those who hope for salvation are happy in that
respect, but this is counterbalanced by their fear of hell.

Reply. Who has more cause to fear hell, someone who does
not know whether there is a hell, but is certain to be damned if
there is, or someone who is completely convinced that there is a
hell, and hopes to be saved if there is? (239)

749 How warped is the judgement by which there is nobody who
does not put himself above the rest of the world, and who does
not prefer his own good, and continuing happiness and survival
to that of the rest of the world! (456)

750 Cromwell was about to ravage the whole of Christendom; the
royal family was lost and his own set for ever in power, but for
a little grain of sand getting into his bladder. Even Rome was
about to tremble beneath him. But, with this bit of gravel once
there, he died, his family fell into disgrace, peace reigned and
the king was restored. (176)

751 Those who are accustomed to judge by feeling have no understanding of matters involving reasoning. For they want to go
right to the bottom of things at a glance, and are not accustomed to look for principles. The others, on the contrary, who
are accustomed to reason from principles, have no understanding of matters involving feeling, because they look for principles and are unable to see things at a glance. (3)

752 Two sorts of people make everything equal, for example holi-
days and working days, Christians and priests, all the sins

amongst themselves. And from this some people conclude that what is bad for priests is also bad for Christians, while others conclude that what is not bad for Christians is permissible for priests. (866)

753 When Augustus learned that among the children under two put to death by Herod was his own son, he said that it was better to be Herod's pig than his son. (Macrobius, *Saturnalia*, lib. ii, ch. IV.) (179)

754 First degree: to be blamed for doing badly or praised for doing well.

Second degree: to be neither praised nor blamed. (501)

755 *He maketh a vain god.*[1]
Disgust. (258)

756 *Thought.* All man's dignity consists in thought, but what is this thought? How silly it is!

Thought, then, is admirable and incomparable by its very nature. It must have had strange faults to have become worthy of contempt, but it does have such faults that nothing is more ridiculous. How great it is by its nature, how vile by its faults! (365)

757 *Draining away.* It is an appalling thing to feel all one possesses drain away. (212)

758 *Light. Darkness.* There would be too much darkness if there were no visible signs of the truth. One admirable sign of it is that it has always resided in a visible Church and congregation. There would be too much light if there were only one opinion in the Church. That which has always existed is the true one, for the true one has always been there, but no false one has always been there. (857)

759 Thought constitutes man's greatness. (346)

760 *Objection.* Scripture is obviously full of things not dictated by the Holy Spirit.
Reply. Therefore they do not harm the faith.

1. Wisdom XV. 8.

Objection. But the Church has decided that it is all by the Holy Spirit.

Reply. I have two things to answer: 1. the Church has never decided that; 2. even if she had so decided, it could be maintained. (568)

761 Many minds are not sound. (568)

762 Dionysius has charity; he was in the right place. (568)

763 Do you think the prophecies quoted in the Gospels were put there to make you believe? No, to discourage you from believing. (633)

764 All the major forms of diversion are dangerous for the Christian life, but among all those which the world has invented none is more to be feared than the theatre. It represents passions so naturally and delicately that it arouses and engenders them in our heart, especially that of love; above all when it is represented as very chaste and virtuous. For the more innocent it seems to innocent souls, the more liable they are to be touched by it; its violence appeals to our self-esteem, which at once conceives the desire to produce the same effects which we see so well represented. At the same time our conscience is conditioned by the irreproachable sentiments to be seen there, which remove the fear of pure souls, who imagine that purity is not offended by loving with a love which seems to them so prudent.

Thus we leave the theatre with hearts so full of all the beauty and sweetness of love, and our mind so convinced of its innocence, that we are quite prepared to receive our first impressions of it, or rather to seek the opportunity of arousing them in someone else's heart, so that we may enjoy the same pleasures and sacrifices as those which we have seen so well depicted in the theatre.[1] (11)

765 If lightning struck low-lying places, etc., poets and people who can only argue about things of this kind would be without proofs. (39)

1. Though included in the *Copy*, this fragment is now generally accepted as being by Mme de Sablé (1599–1678), a close friend of Port Royal.

766 There are many people who hear a sermon in the same way as they hear Vespers. (8)

767 As the ranks of duke, king and magistrate are real and necessary (because power governs all things) they exist at all times and in all places, but, since it is mere whim that makes it this or that person, there is no consistency about it, it is liable to variation, etc. (306)

768 The commands of reason are much more imperative than those of any master, for if we disobey the one we are unhappy, but if we disobey the other we are foolish. (345)

769 *'Stand ye in the ways, and see, and ask for the old paths, and walk therein.' But they said: 'We will not walk therein.'*[1] *'But we will walk after our own devices.'*[2] They said to the nations of the world: 'Come unto us, follow the opinions of these new authors. Natural reason will be our guide. We also shall be like other nations, who all follow their natural light.'

Philosophers and all the religions and sects in the world have taken natural reason for their guide. Christians alone have been obliged to take their rules from outside themselves and to acquaint themselves with those which Christ left for us with those of old, to be handed down again to the faithful. Such constraint irks these good Fathers. They want to be as free as other people to follow the imagination of their hearts. In vain we cry out to them as the prophets of old said to the Jews: 'Go into the midst of the Church, ask for the old paths and walk therein.' They have answered like the Jews: 'We will not walk therein, but will walk after the devices of our own hearts.' And they said: 'We also shall be like all the nations.'[3] (903)

SERIES XXVII
[DIVERSION. DRAFT PREFACES]

770 Fewer men have been made continent by the example of Alexander's chastity than intemperate by that of his drunkenness.

1. Jer. VI. 16.   2. Jer. XVIII. 12.   3. I Sam. VIII. 20.

There is no shame in not being as virtuous as he, and it seems excusable to be no more vicious. We feel that our vices are somewhat out of the ordinary when we find ourselves practising the vices of such great men, yet we do not notice that in this respect they are just ordinary men. We take after them in the very particular in which they take after the people. For however exalted they may be, they still have some point of contact with the humblest of men. They are not hanging in mid-air quite detached from our society. No, indeed, if they are greater than we, it is because their heads are higher up, but their feet are as low down as ours. They are all on the same level and rest on the same ground. At that end they are just as lowly as we are, as the least of us, as children, as beasts.   (103)

771 Continual eloquence is tedious.

Princes and kings sometimes play; they are not always on their thrones. They get bored there. Greatness needs to be laid aside to be appreciated, continuity in anything is tedious. It is pleasant to be cold so that one can get warm.

Nature acts progressively. To and fro, it comes and goes, then goes further, then half as far, then further than ever. VVv.

The tides of the sea go vVvvVvv; the sun seems to do the same.   (355)

772 You are rude: 'Excuse me, please.' But for the apology I should not have noticed that there was any offence.

'With respect. . . .' There is nothing wrong but the apology.
                    (58)

773 Only the contest appeals to us, not the victory.

We like to watch animals fighting, but not the victor falling upon the vanquished. What did we want to see but the final victory? And once it has happened we have had enough. It is the same with gaming, with the pursuit of truth. We like to see the clash of opinions in debate, but do we want to contemplate the truth once it is found? Not at all. If we are to enjoy it, we must see it arising from the debate. It is the same with passions; there is some pleasure in seeing the collision of two opposites, but when one asserts its mastery it becomes mere brutality.

We never go after things in themselves, but the pursuit of things. Thus in the theatre scenes of unclouded happiness are no good, any more than extreme and hopeless misery, or brutal love affairs, or harsh cruelty. (135)

774 Against those who, trusting in the mercy of God, remain indifferent, without performing good works.

Since the twin sources of our sins are pride and sloth, God has revealed to us two of his attributes to cure them: his mercy and his justice. The proper function of justice is to bring pride low, however holy the works (*enter not into judgement . . .*[1]); the proper function of mercy is to combat sloth by encouraging good works according to this passage: 'The goodness of God leadeth thee to repentance,'[2] and this other one about the Ninevites: 'Let us repent, for who can tell if God will turn away from his fierce anger?'[3] Thus, his mercy, far from justifying slackness, is the very quality which formally combats it. Consequently, instead of saying: 'If God were not merciful, we should have to make every effort towards virtue,' we should on the contrary say that it is because God is merciful that we must make every effort. (497)

775 Against those who misuse passages of Scripture and make the most of any they find which seem to favour their error.

The chapter for Vespers, for Passion Sunday, the prayer for the king.

Explanation of the words: 'He that is not with me is against me,'[4] and these: 'For he that is not against us is on our part.'[5] If anyone says: 'I am neither for nor against,' we ought to reply: . . . (899)

776 The history of the Church should properly be called the history of truth. (858)

777 One of the antiphons for Christmas Vespers: *Unto the upright there ariseth light in the darkness.*[6] (847)

778 Men are not taught how to be gentlemen [*honnête*] but are

1. Ps. CXLIII. 2.   2. Rom. III. 4.   3. Jonah III. 9.   4. Matt. XII. 30.
5. Mark IX. 40.   6. Ps. CXII. 4.

taught everything else. And they are never so proud of anything as of being gentlemen. They are only proud of knowing the one thing they have never been taught. (68)

779 Children, who are scared of the face they have daubed, are just children, but how can someone who is so weak as a child become really strong when grown up? Only our imagination changes. Everything that grows progressively better also declines progressively. Nothing that was once weak can ever be absolutely strong. It is no good saying: 'He has grown, he has changed'; he is still the same. (88)

780 *Preface to the first part.* Discuss those who have dealt with self-knowledge; Charron's depressing and tedious divisions; Montaigne's muddle; the fact that he certainly felt the defects of a rigid method; that he avoided them by jumping from one subject to another; that he wanted to cut a good figure.

What a foolish idea to paint his own portrait! And at that, not casually or against his principles, as anyone may make a slip, but according to his own principles and as his prime and basic intention. For talking nonsense by accident, or through some weakness, is a common trouble, but what is intolerable is to talk nonsense deliberately, and such nonsense as this.... (62)

781 *Preface to the second part.* Discuss those who have dealt with this subject.

I marvel at the boldness with which these people presume to speak of God.

In addressing their arguments to unbelievers, their first chapter is the proof of the existence of God from the works of nature. Their enterprise would cause me no surprise if they were addressing their arguments to the faithful, for those with living faith in their hearts can certainly see at once that everything which exists is entirely the work of the God they worship. But for those in whom this light has gone out and in whom we are trying to rekindle it, people deprived of faith and grace, examining with such light as they have everything they see in nature that might lead them to this knowledge, but finding only obscurity and darkness; to tell them, I say, that they have only to look at the least thing around them and they will see in it God plainly revealed; to give them no other proof of this great and weighty matter than the course of the moon and the planets; to claim to have completed the proof with such an argument; this is giving them cause to think that the proofs of our religion are indeed feeble, and reason and experience tell me that nothing is more likely to bring it into contempt in their eyes. This is not how Scripture speaks, with its better knowledge of the things of God. On the contrary it says that God is a hidden God, and that since nature was corrupted he has left men to their blindness, from which they can escape only through Jesus Christ, without whom all communication with God is broken off. *Neither knoweth any man the Father save the Son, and he to whomsoever the Son will reveal him.*[1]

This is what Scripture shows us when it says in so many places that those who seek God shall find him. This is not the light of which we speak as of the noonday sun. We do not say that those who seek the sun at noon or water in the sea will find it, and so it necessarily follows that the evidence of God in nature is not of this kind. It tells us elsewhere: *Verily thou art a God that hidest thyself.*[2]   (242)

782   How many beings unknown to earlier philosophers have telescopes revealed to us! We boldly took Scripture to task over its great numbers of stars, saying: 'There are only 1,022 of them; we know.'

There is grass on earth; we can see it. – From the moon it could not be seen. – And on this grass there are hairs, and in these hairs little creatures, but beyond that there is nothing – Presumptuous man!

Compounds are made up of elements, but elements are not. – Presumptuous man, here is a subtle point!

We must not say that things exist which we cannot see. – Then we must talk like other people but not think like them.   (266)

783   When we try to pursue virtues to either extreme, vices appear

1. Matt. XI. 27.
2. Is. XLV. 15.

and imperceptibly slip into the same paths, imperceptible at the infinitesimal end of the scale and in masses at the infinite end, so that we get lost amid the vices and can no longer see the virtues. We take issue even with perfection. (357)

784 Different arrangements of words make different meanings, and different arrangements of meanings produce different effects. (23)

785 *Fear not little flock.*[1] *In fear and trembling.*[2]
Why then? Fear not provided you fear?
Fear not, provided you are afraid, but if you are not afraid, be fearful.
Whosoever shall receive me, receiveth not me, but him that sent me.[3]
No man knoweth . . . neither the Son.[4]
A bright cloud overshadowed them.[5]
St John was to turn the hearts of the fathers towards the children, and Jesus Christ to bring divisions between them. With no contradiction. (776)

786 If there is ever a time when one ought to profess two opposites it is when one is accused of leaving one out. Both Jesuits and Jansenists are therefore wrong to conceal them; but the Jansenists more so, because the Jesuits have been better at professing both. (865)

787 M. de Condren. 'There is no comparison,' he says, 'between the union of saints and that of the Blessed Trinity.'
Jesus Christ says just the opposite. (943)

788 Man's dignity consisted, in his innocence, in making use of creatures and being their master, but today in separating himself from them and submitting to them. (486)

789 *Meanings.* The same meaning changes according to the words expressing it. Meanings are given dignity by words instead of conferring it upon them. We must look for examples. (50)

790 I believe that Joshua was the first of God's people to bear that name, just as Jesus Christ was the last. (627)

1. Luke XII. 32. 2. Phil. II. 12. 3. Mark IX. 37. 4. Mark XIII. 32.
5. Matt. XVII. 5.

791 *General and particular effects.* The semi-Pelagians are wrong to assert as a general truth what is only a particular one, and the Calvinists in asserting as a particular truth what is a general one, as I see it. (777)

SERIES XXVIII

[SUPERIORITY OF CHRISTIANITY. HUMAN BEHAVIOUR]

792 I maintain that, if everyone knew what others said about him, there would not be four friends in the world; this is evident from the quarrels caused by occasional indiscreet disclosures.

(101)

793 I therefore reject all other religions.

Thus I find an answer to all objections.

It is right that so pure a God should disclose himself only to those whose hearts are purified.

Therefore this religion attracts me and I find it already sufficiently justified by so divine a morality, but I find more in it than that.

I find as a matter of fact that as far back as human memory goes there has existed a people more ancient than any other people.

Men are constantly being told that they are totally corrupt, but that a redeemer will come.

It is not just one man who says this but countless men, and a whole people, prophesying and saying this expressly for four thousand years; for four hundred years the books are dispersed.

The more I look into them the more truth I find: a whole people foretelling him before his coming, a whole people worshipping him after his coming; what went before and came after; the synagogue which went before him; the number of wretched Jews, without prophets, coming after him, who, being all hostile, are admirable witnesses of the truth of the prophecies in which their wretchedness and blindness are foretold; finally the Jews without idols or king.

The fearful darkness of the Jews foretold. *Thou shalt grope at noonday.*[1] *A book which men deliver to one that is learned . . . and he saith: I cannot read.*[2]

While the sceptre is still in the hands of the first foreign usurper.

The rumour of Christ's coming.

I marvel at an original and august religion, wholly divine in its authority, its longevity, its perpetuity, its morality, its conduct, its doctrine, its effects.

Thus I stretch out my arms to my Saviour, who, after being foretold for four thousand years, came on earth to die and suffer for me at the time and in the circumstances foretold. By his grace I peaceably await death, in the hope of being eternally united to him, and meanwhile I live joyfully, whether in the blessings which he is pleased to bestow on me or in the afflictions he sends me for my own good and taught me how to endure by his example.

(737)

794   It is amusing to think that there are people in the world who have renounced all the laws of God and nature only to invent laws for themselves, which they scrupulously obey, as, for example, Mahomet's soldiers, thieves and heretics, and likewise logicians.

It would seem that their licence should be without bounds or barriers, considering the number of just and sensible ones they have transgressed.

(393)

795   Sneezing absorbs all the functions of the soul just as much as the [sexual] act, but we do not draw from it the same conclusions against the greatness of man, because it is involuntary; although we bring it about, we do so involuntarily. It is not for the sake of the thing in itself but for another end, and is therefore not a sign of man's weakness, or his subjection to this act.

There is no shame in man giving in to pain, but it is shameful for him to give in to pleasure. This is not because pain comes to us from outside, whilst we seek pleasure, for we may seek pain and deliberately give in to it without this sort of abasement.

1. Deut. XXVIII. 29.   2. Is. XXIX. 11.

Why then is it to reason's credit to give in to the effect of pain, and to its shame to give in to that of pleasure? It is because it is not pain that tempts and attracts us; it is we ourselves who voluntarily choose it and allow it to get the better of us, so that we are masters of the occasion, and in this it is man giving in to himself. But in pleasure it is man who gives in to pleasure. Now, glory only comes from mastery and control, shame only from subjection. (160)

796 God
created all things for himself,
provided power of pain and blessing for himself.
    You can apply this either to God or to yourself.
    If to God, the Gospel is the rule.
    If to yourself, you are taking the place of God,
    Since God is surrounded by people full of charity, who ask of him the blessings of charity which are in his power, thus
    Know yourself, then, and know that you are a mere king of concupiscence and follow the paths of concupiscence. (314)

797 King and tyrant.
    I too will have thoughts at the back of my mind.
    I will beware of every journey.
    Size of establishment, respect for establishment.
    The pleasure of the great is the ability to make people happy.
    The proper function of wealth is to be freely given.
    The proper function of everything must be sought. The proper function of power is to protect.
    When force attacks masquerade, when a private soldier takes the square cap of a Chief Justice and flings it out of the window. (310)

798 *Martial's epigrams.* Men like malice, not against those with only one eye or in distress but against those who are happy and arrogant. Otherwise we go wrong, for concupiscence is the origin of all our impulses, and humanity.

We must please those who have humane and tender feelings. The story of the two one-eyed men is no good, because it does not console them and simply adds a little lustre to the author.

Nothing written simply for the author's benefit is any good. *He will strip off ambitious ornaments.*[1]   (41)

SERIES XXIX

[RELATIVITY OF HUMAN VALUES. THE BIBLE AND ITS TRUTH]

799 Genesis XVII[.7]: *And I will establish my covenant between me and thee for an everlasting covenant, to be a God unto thee.*
[9] *Thou shalt keep my covenant therefore.*   (612)

800 Scripture has provided passages to bring comfort to every condition and fear to every condition.

Nature seems to have done the same thing through the two natural, moral infinites. For we shall always have higher and lower, more able and less able, more exalted and more wretched, to humble our pride and exalt our abasement.   (532)

801 *Enchantment*[2] – *They have slept their sleep*[3] – *The fashion of this world.*[4]
Eucharist. Thou shalt eat bread.[5] – *Our daily bread.*[6]
His enemies shall lick the dust.[7] Sinners lick the dust, that is, love earthly pleasures.

The Old Testament contained figures of the joy to come, and the New the means of attaining it.

The figures were of joy, the means of penance, and yet the paschal lamb was eaten *with bitter herbs.*[8]

Whilst that I alone escape.[9] Before his death, Jesus was almost alone in martyrdom.   (666)

802 Time heals pain and quarrels because we change. We are no longer the same persons; neither the offender nor the offended are themselves any more. It is as if one angered a nation and came back to see them after two generations. They are still Frenchmen, but not the same ones.   (122)

---

1. Horace, *Ars Poetica*, 447.   2. Wisdom IV. 12.   3. Ps. LXXVI. 5.
4. I Cor. VII. 31.   5. Deut. VIII. 9.   6. Luke XI. 3.   7. Ps. LXXII. 9.
8. Ex. XII. 8.   9. Ps. CXLI. 10.

803 If we dreamed the same thing every night, it would affect us as much as the objects we see every day. And if an artisan was sure of dreaming for twelve hours every night that he was king, I believe he would be almost as happy as a king who dreamed for twelve hours every night that he was an artisan.

If we dreamed every night that we were being pursued by enemies and troubled by these distressing apparitions, and spent every day doing something different, as one does on a journey, we should suffer almost as much as if it were true, and would dread going to sleep as we dread waking up when we are afraid of really encountering some misfortune. And this would in fact cause almost as much pain as reality.

But because dreams are all different, and there is variety even within each one, what we see in them affects us much less than what we see when we are awake, because of the continuity. This, however, is not so continuous and even that it does not change too, though less abruptly, except on rare occasions, as on a journey, when we say: 'It seems like a dream.' For life is a dream, but somewhat less changeable.   (386)

804 Are we to say that men recognized original sin because they said that justice had left the earth? *Call no man happy until he is dead.*[1] Does that mean that they knew that eternal and absolute happiness begins at death?   (447)

805 By knowing each man's ruling passion, we can be sure of pleasing him, and yet each has fancies contrary to his own good, in the very idea he has of good, and this oddity is disconcerting.
                    (106)

806 We are not satisfied with the life we have in ourselves and our own being. We want to lead an imaginary life in the eyes of others, and so we try to make an impression. We strive constantly to embellish and preserve our imaginary being, and neglect the real one. And if we are calm, or generous, or loyal, we are anxious to have it known so that we can attach these virtues to our other existence; we prefer to detach them from our real self so as to unite them with the other. We would

1. Ovid, *Metam.*, III. 135.

cheerfully be cowards if that would acquire us a reputation for bravery. How clear a sign of the nullity of our own being that we are not satisfied with one without the other and often exchange one for the other! For anyone who would not die to save his honour would be infamous. (147)

807 John VIII[.30]

Many believed on him.

Then said Jesus: 'If ye continue in my word, then are ye my disciples indeed, and the truth shall make you free.'

They answered him: 'We be Abraham's seed, and were never in bondage to any man.'

There is a lot of difference between disciples and true disciples. We can recognize them by telling them that the truth will make them free. For they reply that they are free and that it is in their power to leave the devil's bondage. They are, indeed, disciples, but not true disciples. (519)

808 There are three ways to believe: reason, habit, inspiration. Christianity, which alone has reason, does not admit as its true children those who believe without inspiration. It is not that it excludes reason and habit, quite the contrary, but we must open our mind to the proofs, confirm ourselves in it through habit, while offering ourselves through humiliations to inspiration, which alone can produce the real and salutary effect. *Lest the Cross of Christ be made of none effect.*[1] (245)

809 Incomprehensible that God should exist and incomprehensible that he should not; that the soul should be joined to the body, that we should have no soul; that the world should be created, that it should not; that original sin should exist and that it should not. (230)

810 *What will become of men who despise little things and do not believe great ones?* (193)

811 The two oldest books in the world are those of Moses and Job, one a Jew and the other a heathen; both regarding Christ as their common centre and object; Moses recounting God's

1. I Cor. I. 17.

promises to Abraham, Jacob, etc., and his prophecies, and Job:
Oh that my words. . . . For I know that my Redeemer liveth.[1]

(741)

812 The style of the Gospels is remarkable in so many ways; among
others for never putting in any invective against the execution-
ers and enemies of Christ. For there is none in any of the historians against Judas, Pilate or any of the Jews.

If this restraint of the Evangelists had been put on, together
with many other features of such fine character, and if they had
only put it on in order to draw attention to it, not daring to
remark on it themselves, they would not have failed to acquire
friends to make such remarks for their benefit. But, since they
acted as they did without affectation and quite disinterestedly,
they did not cause anyone to remark on it. And I believe that
many of these things have never been remarked on before. That
shows how coolly the thing was done. (798)

813 We never do evil so fully and cheerfully as when we do it out
of conscience. (895)

814 We pervert our feelings just as we pervert our minds.

Our minds and feelings are trained by the company we keep,
and perverted by the company we keep. Thus good or bad
company trains or perverts respectively. It is therefore very
important to be able to make the right choice so that we train
rather than pervert. And we cannot make this choice unless it
is already trained, and not perverted. This is thus a vicious circle
from which anyone is lucky to escape. (6)

815 Ordinary people have the ability not to think about things they
do not want to think about. 'Do not think about the passages
concerning the Messiah,' said the Jew to his son. Our own people
often behave like this, and this is how false religions are preserved, and even the true one as far as many people are concerned.

But there are some without this ability to stop themselves
thinking, who think all the more for being forbidden to do so.
These people rid themselves of false religions, and even of the
true one, unless they find solid arguments for them. (259)

1. Job XIX. 23–5.

816 'I should soon have given up a life of pleasure,' they say, 'if I had faith.' But I tell you: 'You would soon have faith if you gave up a life of pleasure. Now it is up to you to begin. If I could give you faith, I would. But I cannot, nor can I test the truth of what you say, but you can easily give up your pleasure and test whether I am telling the truth.' (240)

817 There is no denying it; one must admit that there is something astonishing about Christianity. 'It is because you were born in it,' they will say. Far from it; I stiffen myself against it for that very reason, for fear of being corrupted by prejudice. But, though I was born in it, I cannot help finding it astonishing. (615)

818 Victory over death. 'What shall it profit a man if he shall gain the whole world, and lose his own soul? For whosoever will save his life shall lose it.'[1]

'I am not come to destroy the law but to fulfil.'[2]

Lambs did not take away the sins of the world, but I am 'the lamb that taketh away the sins of the world.'[3]

'Moses gave you not that bread from heaven.'[4]

Moses did not bring you out of captivity and 'make you free indeed.'[5] (782)

819 The prophecies of particular events are mixed in with those concerning the Messiah, so that the prophecies of the Messiah should not lack proof and particular prophecies should not be unfulfilled. (712)

820 There are two ways of persuading men of the truths of our religion; one by the power of reason, the other by the authority of the speaker.

We do not use the latter but the former. We do not say: 'You must believe that because Scripture, which says it, is divine,' but we say that it must be believed for such and such a reason. But these are feeble arguments, because reason can be bent in any direction. (561)

1. Mark VIII. 36, 35. 2. Matt. v. 17. 3. John I. 29. 4. John VI. 32. 5. John VIII. 36.

SERIES XXX
[HABIT AND CONVERSION]

821 For we must make no mistake about ourselves: we are as much automaton as mind. As a result, demonstration is not the only instrument for convincing us. How few things can be demonstrated! Proofs only convince the mind; habit provides the strongest proofs and those that are most believed. It inclines the automaton, which leads the mind unconsciously along with it. Who ever proved that it will dawn tomorrow, and that we shall die? And what is more widely believed? It is, then, habit that convinces us and makes so many Christians. It is habit that makes Turks, heathen, trades, soldiers, etc. (The faith received at baptism is the advantage Christians have over heathen.) In short, we must resort to habit once the mind has seen where the truth lies, in order to steep and stain ourselves in that belief which constantly eludes us, for it is too much trouble to have the proofs always present before us. We must acquire an easier belief, which is that of habit. With no violence, art or argument it makes us believe things, and so inclines all our faculties to this belief that our soul falls naturally into it. When we believe only by the strength of our conviction and the automaton is inclined to believe the opposite, that is not enough. We must therefore make both parts of us believe: the mind by reasons, which need to be seen only once in a lifetime, and the automaton by habit, and not allowing it any inclination to the contrary: *Incline my heart.*[1]

Reason works slowly, looking so often at so many principles, which must always be present, that it is constantly nodding or straying because all its principles are not present. Feeling does not work like that, but works instantly, and is always ready. We must then put our faith in feeling, or it will always be vacillating.   (252)

432 We should feel sorry for both, but we should feel sorry for the former out of affection and the latter out of contempt.

1. Ps. cxix. 36.

One must belong to the religion they despise in order not to despise them.

That is not good form.

That shows that there is nothing to be said to them, not out of contempt, but because they have no common sense. God must touch them.

People of that kind are academics, scholars, and that is the nastiest kind of man I know.

You will convert me.

I do not take that view out of bigotry, but because of the way man's heart is made; not out of zealous piety and detachment, but on purely human grounds and for motives of self-interest and self-love.

It is quite certain that there is no good without the knowledge of God; that the closer one comes, the happier one is, and that ultimate happiness is to know him with certainty; that the further away one goes, the more unhappy one is, and that ultimate unhappiness would be to be certain of the opposite [to him].

Doubt is then an unhappy state, but there is an indispensable duty to seek in our doubt, and thus anyone who doubts and does not seek is at once unhappy and in the wrong. If, in addition, he is cheerful and presumptuous, I can find no words to describe so extravagant a creature.

Is it not enough that miracles should be performed in one place, and that Providence should be manifest in one people?

Yet it is certain that man is so unnatural that in his heart are the seeds of joy at this.

Is it something to be said with joy? It is then something that ought to be said with gloom.

A fine reason to rejoice and proudly boast like this: 'Let us therefore rejoice; let us live without fear or anxiety and wait for death, since it is all uncertain and then we shall see what will happen to us.' I do not see the logic of this.

It is good form not to be complacent, and compassionate to show complaisance for others.

Is it brave of a dying man to go in his weakness and agony to confront a powerful and eternal God?

How happy I should be if I were in such a state and someone took pity on my foolishness, and was kind enough to save me from it in spite of myself!

What joy, to look forward to nothing but helpless misery! What comfort, to have no hope of a comforter!

But if we cannot touch them, they will not be without their use.

But the very people who seem most opposed to the glory of religion will not be without their use for others in this respect.

We shall base our first argument on the fact that there is something supernatural about this, for such blindness is not natural. And if their folly makes them run so counter to their own good, the horror of such a deplorable example and so pitiful a folly will help to keep others from it.

Are they so firm as to be insensitive to everything that affects them? Try them with the loss of their wealth or honour. What? It is magic! (194b, c)

822 *History of China.* I only believe histories whose witnesses are ready to be put to death.

Which is the more credible of the two, Moses or China?

There is no question of the broad view. I tell you that there is enough here to blind and to enlighten.

With this one word I destroy all your arguments. 'But China obscures the issue,' you say. And I reply: 'China obscures the issue but there is light to be found. Look for it.'

Thus all you say serves one of these purposes without telling against the other. So it helps and does not harm.

We must look at this in detail, then. We must put the evidence on the table. (593)

823 An heir finds the deeds to his house. Will he say, perhaps, that they are false, and not bother to examine them? (217)

824 The law obliged men to have what it did not give: grace gives what it obliges men to have. (522)

825 Apparent refutation [?]

God giveth grace to the humble:[1] *did he then not give them humility?*

1. James iv.6. and I Pet. v.5.

His own received him not:[1] *as many as did not receive him, were they not his own?* (901)

SERIES XXXI

[FIGURATIVE LANGUAGE IN BIBLE. HUMAN RELATIONS]

826 *And look that thou make them after the pattern which was showed thee in the mount.*[2]

The Jewish religion, then, was formed on the pattern of the Messianic truth, and the Messianic truth was recognized by the Jewish religion, which prefigured it.

Among the Jews the truth was only figurative; in heaven it is revealed.

In the Church it is concealed and recognized by its relationship to the figurative.

The figure was drawn from the truth.

And the truth was recognized from the figure. (673)

827 St Paul himself says that people will forbid marriage,[3] and speaks of it himself in I Cor. [VII. 29] in words which are a trap. For, if a prophet had said one thing and St Paul had then said another, he would have been denounced. (673)

828 The bonds securing men's mutual respect are generally bonds of necessity, for there must be differences of degree, since all men want to be on top and all cannot be, but some can.

Imagine, then, that we can see them beginning to take shape. It is quite certain that men will fight until the stronger oppresses the weaker, and there is finally one party on top. But, once this has been settled, then the masters, who do not want the war to go on, ordain that the power which is in their hands shall pass down by whatever means they like; some entrust it to popular suffrage, others to hereditary succession, etc.

And that is where imagination begins to play its part. Until

1. John I. II.
2. Ex. XXV. 40.
3. I Tim. IV. 3.

then pure power did it, now it is power, maintained by imagination in a certain faction, in France the nobles, in Switzerland commoners, etc.

So these bonds securing respect for a particular person are bonds of imagination. (304)

829 These great mental efforts on which the soul occasionally lights are not things on which it dwells; it only jumps there for a moment, not for ever, as on the throne. (351)

SECTION THREE

MIRACLES

SERIES XXXII

[OPINION OF SAINT-CYRAN]

830 These are the main points I want to put to the Abbé de Saint-Cyran.[1] But, as I have no copy of them, I must ask him to be good enough to return this paper together with his answers.

1. Whether it is necessary, for an effect to be miraculous, that it should be beyond the powers of men, devils and all natural creation?

[Theologians say that miracles are supernatural either in substance, *quoad substantiam*, as when two bodies interpenetrate, or when a single body is in two places at the same time; or supernatural in the manner in which they are produced, *quoad modum*, as when they are produced by means not naturally capable of producing them: as when Jesus Christ healed the eyes of the blind man with mud, and Peter's mother-in-law by bending over her, and the woman afflicted with the issue of blood through her touching the hem of his garment. And most of the miracles he performed for us in the Gospels are of this latter kind. So too is the curing of a fever or some other illness either instantaneously or more completely than nature could achieve, through touching a relic or invoking the name of God. Thus the view of the person putting forward these difficulties is correct and in conformity with that of all theologians, even those of the present day.]

2. Whether it is not sufficient for it to be beyond the natural powers of the means employed? My view is that any effect is miraculous when it exceeds the natural powers of the means employed. Thus I call it miraculous when illness is cured by touching a sacred relic, when a man possessed is healed by invoking the name of Jesus, etc., because the effects exceed the natural powers of the words used to invoke God or the natural

1. Martin de Barcos, nephew of the famous St Cyran, Jansenius's friend. His answers to Pascal are given in square brackets.

powers of a relic, neither of which can heal the sick nor drive out devils. But I do not call it a miracle to drive out devils by the devil's art, for in using the devil's art to drive out devils the effect does not exceed the natural powers of the means employed. Thus it seemed to me that the true definition of miracles is the one I have just given.

[What the devil is able to do is not a miracle, any more than what an animal is able to do, even though man is unable to do it himself.]

3. Whether St Thomas is not opposed to this definition, and considers that for an effect to be miraculous it must exceed the powers of all natural creation?

[St Thomas holds the same opinion as the others, although he divides the second kind of miracles into two categories: miracles as regards their subject (*quoad subjectum*) and miracles as regards the natural order (*quoad ordinem naturae*). He says that the former are those which nature can produce absolutely, but not in a given subject; for instance, it can produce life, but not in a dead body; and that the latter are those which it can produce in a given subject, but not so promptly by a given means; for instance, curing in a moment and at a single touch a fever or sickness, though it is not actually incurable.]

4. Whether declared and acknowledged heretics can perform true miracles to confirm an error?

[True miracles can never be performed by anyone, Catholic or heretic, holy or wicked, to confirm an error, because God would thereby be affirming and setting the stamp of his approval upon error like a false witness, or, rather, a false judge. This is an attested and constant fact.]

5. Whether known and declared heretics can perform such miracles as curing illnesses which are not actually incurable; whether, for example, they can cure a fever to confirm an erroneous proposition? Father Lingendes preaches that they can.

(No answer given to this question.)

6. Whether known and declared heretics can perform miracles which are beyond all natural creation by invoking the name of God or by a sacred relic?

[They can do so to confirm a truth, and history affords examples of this.]

7. Whether secret heretics, who, while not separated from the Church yet remain in error, and do not declare themselves against the Church, the better to seduce the faithful and strengthen their own hand, [can perform] miracles going beyond all natural creation by invoking the name of Jesus or by a sacred relic, or even whether they can perform such as merely go beyond human powers, like the immediate cure of sicknesses which are not actually incurable?

[Secret heretics have no more power to work miracles than declared ones, since nothing is hidden from God, sole author and worker of miracles, of whatever kind they may be, provided they are true miracles.]

8. Whether miracles performed by the name of God, or the intermediary of divine things, are not the marks of the true Church, and whether all Catholics have not asserted this against heretics?

[All Catholics agree on this, especially Jesuit authors; one has only to read Bellarmine. Even when heretics have performed miracles, an occasional if rare occurrence, these miracles were signs of the Church, because they were only performed to confirm the truth taught by the Church and not the heretics' error.]

9. Whether it has ever happened that heretics performed miracles, and of what kind?

[There are very few attested cases, but those which are related are only miraculous *quoad modum*, that is to say, natural effects miraculously produced in a way outside the natural order.]

10. Whether the man in the Gospel who drove out devils in the name of Jesus, and of whom Jesus said 'he who is not against us is for us', was the friend or enemy of Christ, and what do interpreters of the Gospel say about it? I ask this because Father Lingendes preached that this man was opposed to Christ.

[The Gospel sufficiently attests that he was not opposed to Christ, and the Fathers and nearly all the Jesuit authors maintain this.]

11. Whether Antichrist will work wonders in his own name or in that of Jesus Christ?

[As he will not come in the name of Jesus Christ, but in his own name, according to the Gospel, he will likewise perform no miracles in Christ's name, but in his own, and against Christ, to destroy the faith and his Church. For this reason they will not be true miracles.]

12. Whether the oracles were miraculous?

[Miracles of the heathen and idols have been no more miraculous than the other works of devils and magicians.]

(Appx XIII.)

831 The second miracle may presuppose the first; the first cannot presuppose the second. (810)

SERIES XXXIII
[RULES FOR MIRACLES]

832 5. *Miracles. Beginning.* Miracles distinguish between doctrines and doctrine distinguishes between miracles.

There are false ones and true ones. There must be some sign by which they can be recognized, otherwise they would be useless.

Now they are not useless, but, on the contrary, fundamental.

Now the rule we are given must be such as to leave intact the proof afforded by true miracles of the truth, which is the main purpose of miracles.

Moses has given two rules: that the prophecy does not come to pass (Deut. XVIII), and that the miracles do not lead to idolatry (Deut. XIII); and Jesus Christ gives one.

If doctrine determines miracles, miracles are useless for doctrine.

If miracles determine. . . .

Objections to the rule. Distinctions of time, one rule in Moses' time, another now. (803)

833 Any religion is false which in its faith does not worship one God

as the principle of all things and in morals does not love one God as object of all things. (487)

834 *Reasons for not believing.*

John XII. 37: *But though he had done so many miracles before them, yet they believed not on him, that the saying of Esaias the prophet might be fulfilled.* ... *He hath blinded their eyes. These things said Esaias when he saw his glory and spake of him.*

For the Jews require a sign and the Greeks seek after wisdom, but we preach Christ crucified.[1]

But full of signs and full of wisdom.

But you preach Christ not crucified and a religion without miracles and without wisdom.

The reason men do not believe in true miracles is lack of charity. John [x. 26]: *But ye believe not because ye are not of my sheep.*

The reason they believe in false ones is lack of charity. II Thess. II [10–11].

Foundation of religion. This is miracles. What, then, does God speak against miracles, against the foundations of our faith in him?

If there is a God, faith in God had to exist on earth. Now Christ's miracles were not foretold by Antichrist, but Antichrist's miracles were foretold by Christ. Thus, if Jesus Christ was not the Messiah, he would certainly have led men into error, but Antichrist can certainly not lead them into error.

When Christ foretold the miracles of Antichrist, did he think he was destroying faith in his own miracles?

There is no reason for believing in Antichrist which is not a reason for believing in Christ, but there are reasons for believing in Christ which are not reasons for believing in the other.

Moses foretold Jesus Christ and bade men to follow him; Jesus Christ foretold Antichrist and forbade men to follow him.

It was impossible in Moses' time to keep faith in Antichrist, who was then unknown, but it is very easy in Antichrist's time to believe in Jesus Christ who is already known. (826)

1. I Cor. I. 22, followed by Pascal's Latin comment.

835 The prophecies, even the miracles and proofs of our religion, are not of such a kind that they can be said to be absolutely convincing, but they are at the same time such that it cannot be said to be unreasonable to believe in them. There is thus evidence and obscurity, to enlighten some and obfuscate others. But the evidence is such as to exceed, or at least equal, the evidence to the contrary, so that it cannot be reason that decides us against following it, and can therefore only be concupiscence and wickedness of heart. Thus, there is enough evidence to condemn and not enough to convince, so that it should be apparent that those who follow it are prompted to do so by grace and not by reason, and those who evade it are prompted by concupiscence and not by reason.

Disciples indeed,[1] *An Israelite indeed,*[2] *Free indeed,*[3] *Meat indeed.*[4] I presume one believes in miracles. (564)

836 You corrupt religion either for the benefit of your friends or against your enemies; you deal with it as you please. (855)

837 If there were no false miracles there would be certainty.

If there were no rule for distinguishing between them, miracles would be useless and there would be no reason to believe.

Now, humanly speaking, there is no such thing as human certainty, only reason. (823)

838 The Jews, who were called to subdue nations and kings, have been slaves to sin, and Christians, whose vocation was to serve and be subjects, are free children. (671)

839 Judges XIII. 23: 'If the Lord were pleased to kill us, he would not have . . . shewed us all these things.'

Hezekiah, Sennacherib.[5]

Jeremiah, Ananias the false prophet dies in the seventh month.[6]

II Macc. III: the temple about to be sacked, rescued miraculously. II Macc. xv.

I Kings XVII: The widow to Elijah who had raised her son: By this I know thy word is truth!

---

1. John VIII. 31.   2. I. 47.   3. VIII. 36.   4. VI. 55.
5. II Kings XIX.   6. Jer. XXVIII. 15-17.

I Kings XVIII: Elijah with the prophets of Baal.

Never in any dispute about the true God or the truth of religion has a miracle taken place on the side of error and not on that of truth. (827)

840 This is not the home of truth; it wanders unrecognized among men. God has covered it with a veil that keeps it from being recognized by those who do not hear his voice. The field is clear for blasphemy, even against truths which are at the least quite obvious. If the truths of the Gospels are proclaimed, contrary truths are proclaimed too and the issues so clouded that people cannot distinguish between them. We are asked: 'What have you got to make people believe in you rather than the others? What wonders do you perform? You have nothing but words, and so have we. If you had miracles, well and good.' It is a fact that doctrine should be supported by miracles, and this is abused in order to blaspheme against doctrine. And if miracles take place, we are told that miracles are not enough without doctrine, and this is another fact which enables them to blaspheme against miracles.

Jesus healed the man blind from birth and performed numerous miracles on the sabbath day, thereby blinding the Pharisees, who said that miracles must be judged by doctrine.

'We have Moses; as for this fellow, we know not from whence he is.'[1]

It is a marvellous thing that you do not know whence he is, and yet he performs such miracles.

Jesus spoke neither against God nor against Moses.

Antichrist, and the false prophets foretold by both Testaments, will speak openly against God and against Jesus Christ.

'He who is not against. . . .' Anyone who is a secret enemy would not be allowed by God to perform miracles openly.

Never in any public dispute, with both parties claiming to be on the side of God, Christ and the Church, do miracles occur on the side of the false Christians and not on the other side.

John X. 20: 'He hath a devil,' others said: 'Can a devil open the eyes of the blind?'

1. John IX. 29.

The proofs drawn from Scripture by Jesus and the Apostles are not conclusive, for they only say that Moses said that a prophet would come, but this does not prove that he was the one, and that was the whole question. These passages serve therefore only to show that there is nothing against Scripture in this, and that no inconsistency is apparent, but not that there is agreement. Now this is sufficient; no inconsistency, together with miracles.

God and men have reciprocal duties. This word must be forgiven: *What I ought to have done;*[1] 'Accuse me,' says the Lord in Is. 1.[2]

God must fulfil his promises, etc.

Men owe it to God to accept the religion he sends them.

God owes it to men not to lead them into error.

Now, they would be led into error if the workers of miracles proclaimed a doctrine not visibly false in the light of common sense, and if a greater worker of miracles had not already warned them not to believe such men.

Thus, if the Church were divided and the Arians, for example, who claimed, like the Catholics, to base themselves on Scripture, had performed miracles, and the Catholics had not, people would have been led into error.

For, just as someone who proclaims God's secrets is not worthy to be believed on his own private authority (which is why unbelievers have their doubts), so if someone shows he is in communion with God by raising the dead, foretelling the future, parting the sea, healing the sick, every unbeliever will give in. The unbelief of Pharaoh and the Pharisees results from supernatural hardening of heart.

There is therefore no difficulty when miracles and a doctrine above suspicion are found together on the same side, but when miracles and a suspect doctrine are found on the same side, we must then see which is the clearer. Jesus was suspect.

Bar-Jesus blinded.[3] God's power overcomes that of his enemies.

1. Is. v. 4, *quod debui* in Vulgate.
2. Is. I. 18, *arguite me* in Vulgate.
3. Acts XIII. 11.

The Jewish exorcists set upon by devils, who said: 'Jesus I know and Paul I know, but who are ye?'[1]

Miracles exist for the sake of doctrine and not doctrine for the sake of miracles.

If miracles are true, can any doctrine be made to convince? No, because that will not happen.

But though an angel. . . .[2]

Rule: Doctrine must be judged by miracles, miracles must be judged by doctrine.

All this is true, but there is no contradiction.

For the times must be distinguished.

How glad you are to know the general rules! You think this will enable you to stir up trouble and bring everything to nought! You will be prevented from doing so, Father. Truth is one and firm.

God's duty makes it impossible for a man who hides his evil doctrine and reveals only what is sound, professedly conforming to God and the Church, to perform miracles in order that a false and subtle doctrine should be imperceptibly instilled. That cannot be.

Still less that God, who knows men's hearts, should perform miracles for the benefit of such a man.   (843)

841   Jesus says that the Scriptures bear witness to him, but he does not show in what respect.

Even the prophecies could not prove Jesus Christ in his lifetime, so no one would have been guilty for not believing in him before his death, if miracles had not been sufficient without doctrine. Now those who did not believe in him while he was still alive were sinners, as he says himself, and had no excuse. They must therefore have seen some proof which they resisted. Now they did not have Scripture, but only his miracles. Therefore these are sufficient when not in conflict with doctrine, and must be believed.

John VII. 40: Dispute among the Jews as among Christians today.

1. Acts XIX. 15.
2. Gal. I. 8.

Some believe in Jesus Christ, others do not believe because of the prophecies saying he was to be born in Bethlehem.

They should have been more careful to see whether he was not in fact from there, for, as his miracles were convincing, they should have made very sure of the alleged contradictions between his doctrine and Scripture, and the obscurity was no excuse, but blinded them.

Thus those who refuse to believe in present-day miracles on the grounds of some alleged farfetched contradiction have no excuse.

The people who believed in him on the strength of his miracles were told by the Pharisees: 'This people who knoweth not the law are cursed. Have any of the rulers or the Pharisees believed on him? For we know that out of Galilee ariseth no prophet.' Nicodemus answered: 'Doth our law judge any man before it hear him?' (829)

842 Our religion is wise and foolish: wise, because it is the most learned and most strongly based on miracles, prophecies, etc., foolish, because it is not all this which makes people belong to it. This is a good enough reason for condemning those who do not belong, but not for making those who do belong believe. What makes them believe is the Cross. *Lest the Cross of Christ should be made of none effect.*[1]

And so St Paul, who came with wisdom and signs, said that he came with neither wisdom nor signs, for he came to convert, but those who come only to convince may say they come with wisdom and signs. (588)

843 There is a lot of difference between not being for Christ and saying so, and not being for Christ and pretending to be. The former can perform miracles, but not the latter, for it is clear in the case of the former that they are against the truth but not in that of the others, and so the miracles are clearer. (836)

844 It is so obvious that we must love one God alone that there is no need of miracles to prove it. (837)

1. I Cor. I. 17.

845 A fine state for the Church to be in when it has no support left
but God! (861)

846 Jesus proved he was the Messiah, but never by proving his
doctrine from Scripture or the prophecies, but always by
miracles.

He proved by a miracle that he could forgive sins.

'Rejoice not in your miracles,' said Jesus, 'but because your
names are written in heaven.'[1]

'If they hear not Moses, neither will they be persuaded
though one rose from the dead.'[2]

Nicodemus recognized by his miracles that his doctrine was
from God. '*Rabbi, we know that thou art a teacher come from God,
for no man can do these miracles that thou doest except God be with
him.*'[3] He does not judge miracles by doctrine, but doctrine by
miracles.

The Jews had a doctrine of God, as we have one of Christ, and
it was confirmed by miracles. They were told not to believe in
all workers of miracles, and moreover instructed to refer to the
high priests and follow their directions. And so all the reasons
we have for refusing to believe in miracle workers applied to
them as regards their prophets. They were, however, very much
to be blamed for rejecting the prophets, because of their
miracles, and Christ also, and would have incurred no blame if
they had not seen the miracles. '*If I had not done the works ...
they had not had sin.*'[4]

Therefore all faith rests on miracles.

Prophecy is not called miraculous; as when St John speaks
of Jesus' first miracle at Cana, then of his words to the woman
of Samaria, to whom he disclosed all her secret life, and then of
how he healed the son of a nobleman. St John calls this last
'the second sign'.[5] (808)

847 By pointing out the truth we can make people believe it, but
the injustice of our masters is not corrected by being pointed
out; we can ensure awareness by pointing out falsehood, but we
cannot ensure a purse by pointing out injustice. (893)

1. Luke X. 20. 2. Luke XVI. 31. 3. John III. 2. 4. John XV. 24.
5. John II and IV. 54.

848 Miracles and truth are necessary because the whole man must be convinced in body and soul. (806)

849 Charity is not a figurative precept. It is a horrible thing to say that Christ, who came to replace figures by the truth, came only to set up the figure of charity in place of the reality that was there before.

'If the light be darkness, what will the darkness be?'[1] (665)

850 There is a lot of difference between tempting and leading into error. God tempts but does not lead into error. To tempt is to provide opportunities for us to do certain things if we do not love God, but putting us under no necessity to do so. To lead into error is to compel a man necessarily to conclude and follow a falsehood. (821)

851 *If thou be the Christ, tell us plainly.*
The works that I do in my Father's name, they bear witness of me.
But ye believe not because ye are not of my sheep.
My sheep hear my voice.[2]
John VI. 30: *What sign showest thou then, that we may see and believe thee? (They do not say: What doctrine dost thou preach?)*[3]

For no man can do these miracles that thou doest except God be with him.[4]
II Macc. XIV. 15: *God who always helpeth his portion with manifestations of his presence.*
Luke XI. 16: *And others, tempting him, sought of him a sign from heaven.*
An evil and adulterous generation seeketh after a sign, and there shall be no sign given it.[5]
[Mark] VIII. 12: *And he sighed deeply in his spirit, and saith: Why doth this generation seek after a sign?*
They asked for a sign with evil intent. *And he could there do no mighty work.*[6] And yet he promises them the sign of Jonah, the great and incomparable sign of his resurrection.

1. Cf. Matt. VI. 23. 2. John X. 24.
3. Pascal's Latin comment. 4. John III. 2.
5. Matt. XII. 39. 6. Mark VI. 5.

Except ye see signs and wonders, ye will not believe.[1] He does not blame them for not believing unless there are miracles, but for not believing unless they see for themselves.

Antichrist. *With all lying wonders,* says St Paul (II Thess. 11. 9), *after the working of Satan, And with all deceivableness of unrighteousness in them that perish; because they received not the love of the truth, that they might be saved. And for this cause God shall send them strong delusion, that they should believe a lie.* As in the passage of Moses: *For the Lord proveth you to know whether ye love the Lord.*[2]

Behold I have told you before.[3] (842)

852 In the Old Testament when you are turned away from God, in the New Testament when you are turned away from Jesus Christ:

These are the occasions for withholding faith in the miracles thus indicated; no other cases must be allowed.

Does it follow that they were entitled to withhold belief in all the prophets who came to them? No; they would have sinned in not rejecting those who denied God, and they would have sinned too in rejecting those who did not deny God.

As soon as we see a miracle, then, we must either submit or have peculiar indications to the contrary. We must see whether they deny God, or Christ, or the Church. (835)

853 Reproach Mitton for remaining unmoved at God's reproaches. (192)

854 'Though ye believe not me, believe the miracles.'[4] He refers to them, as it were, as something more powerful.

The Jews as well as the Christians had been told not always to believe the prophets; but none the less, the scribes and Pharisees made much of his miracles, trying to prove them to be either false or the work of the devil, for they could not help being convinced if they once recognized them as coming from God.

Today we need not trouble to make this distinction, and yet it is perfectly easy to make. Those who deny neither God nor Christ perform no miracles open to doubt.

1. John IV. 48.   2. Deut. XIII.   3.   3. Matt. XXIV. 25.
4. Cf. John X. 38.

There is no man which shall do a miracle in my name, that can lightly speak evil of me.[1]

But we do not have to make such a distinction. Here is a sacred relic, here is a thorn from the crown of the saviour of the world, over whom the prince of this world has no power, performing miracles by the very power of this blood shed for us. Here is God himself choosing this house, there to blaze forth his power.

It is not men performing this miracle by some unknown and dubious virtue, obliging us to draw difficult distinctions. It is God himself, the instrument of the Passion of his only son, who, being in many places, chooses this one and draws men in from every side to receive this miraculous relief for their flagging spirits. (839)

855 John VI. 26: *Not because ye saw the miracles, but because ye were filled.* Those who follow Christ because of his miracles honour his power in all the miracles it produces, but those who, professing to follow him for his miracles, really follow him only because he consoles them and fills them with the good things of the world dishonour his miracles when they threaten their own convenience.

John IX. 16: *This man is not of God because he keepeth not the sabbath day. Others said: How can a man that is a sinner do such miracles?* Which is the clearer?

('This is the house of God, for he works extraordinary miracles there.'

Others: 'This is not the house of God, for they do not believe there that the Five Propositions are in Jansenius.' Which is the clearer?)

'*What sayest thou of him?*' He said: '*He is a prophet.... If this man were not of God, he could do nothing.*' (834)

856 *Disputes.* Abel, Cain / Moses, magicians / Elijah, false prophets / Jeremiah, Ananias / Micah, false prophets / Jesus Christ, Pharisees / Saint Paul, Bar-Jesus / Apostles, exorcists / Christians, infidels / Catholics, heretics / Elijah, Enoch, Antichrist.

The truth always prevails in miracles. The two crosses. (828)

1. Mark IX. 39.

857 Jer. XXIII. 32: the miracles of the false prophets; in the Hebrew and in Vatable[1] we find 'lightness'.

'Miracle' does not always mean miracles. In I Sam. XIV. 15 'miracle' means 'trembling' and reads thus in Hebrew. Likewise Job XXXIII. 7, very obviously, and again Is. XXI. 4 and Jer. XLIV. 22.

'*Portentum*' means 'graven image', Jer. L. 38, and reads thus in the Hebrew and Vatable.

Is. VIII. 18: Christ says that he and his disciples will be for signs and wonders. (819)

858 The Church has three kinds of enemies: the Jews, who have never been part of its body, the heretics who have withdrawn from it, and bad Christians who rend it from within. These three different kinds of opponent usually attack it in different ways, but here they are attacking it in the same way.

As they are all without miracles, while the Church has always had miracles to show against them, they all have the same interest in shrugging them off, and have all used the pretext that doctrine must not be judged by miracles but miracles by doctrine. Among those who listened to Christ there were two sides: those who followed his doctrine for the sake of his miracles and the others who said. . . . There were two sides in Calvin's time, and now there are the Jesuits. . . . (840)

SERIES XXXIV
[MIRACLES FOR PORT ROYAL AGAINST JESUITS]

859 Unjust persecutors of those whom God visibly protects.

If they reproach you for your excesses, 'they are talking like heretics.'

If they say that the grace of Christ distinguishes between us, 'they are heretics.'

If miracles take place, 'this is a sign of their heresy.'

Ezekiel. They say: 'Here are the Lord's people speaking like this.' Hezekiah.

---

1. The great sixteenth-century Hebraist. The Authorized Version in every case follows Pascal's interpretation of these passages.

Reverend Fathers, all this happened figuratively. Other religions pass away, this one does not pass away.

Miracles are more important than you think. They were used to found the Church and will be used to continue it until Antichrist, until the end. The two witnesses.

The synagogue was figurative, and thus did not pass away, and merely figurative, and thus did pass away. It was a figure containing the truth, and thus it lasted until it no longer had the truth in it.

We are told: 'Believe in the Church,' but we are not told: 'Believe in miracles,' because the latter is natural but not the former. One needed a precept but not the other.

In the Old Testament, as in the New, miracles are performed by associating figures with them; salvation or something of no use, except to show that we must submit to creatures; figure of the sacraments. (852)

860 Either men have always spoken of the true God, or the true God has spoken to men. (807)

861 The two foundations; one inward, the other outward; grace, miracles; both supernatural. (805)

862 The unhappy people who have obliged me to speak of the fundamentals of religion. (883)

863 Montaigne against miracles.
Montaigne for miracles. (814)

864 Sinners purified without penance, the righteous sanctified without charity, all Christians without the grace of Christ, God with no power over the wills of men, predestination without mystery, redemption without certainty. (884)

865 Miracles are no longer necessary because we have already had them. But when tradition is not listened to any more, when the Pope is The only guide proposed, and he has been taken unawares, and when, with the true source of truth, that is tradition, excluded and the Pope, its trustee, prejudiced, truth is no longer free to appear, then men no longer speak of truth, and truth must itself speak to men. This is what happened in Arius's time.

Miracles under Diocletian
and under Arius. (832)

866 *Perpetuity.* Is your character based on Escobar?
Perhaps you have reasons for not condemning them.
It is enough that you should learn what I tell you about it. (−)

867 Would the Pope be dishonoured for being enlightened by God
and tradition? Is it not dishonouring him to separate him from
this holy alliance? (875)

868 Tertullian: *The Church will never be reformed.* (890)

869 To make a man a saint, grace is certainly needed, and anyone
who doubts this does not know what a saint, or a man, really is.
(508)

870 Heretics have always attacked these three signs that they lack.
(845)

871 Perpetuity – Molina – Novelty. (844b)

872 *Miracles.* How I hate those who profess to doubt miracles!
Montaigne talks about them as he should in these two passages. The one shows how prudent he is, and yet in the other
he believes, and laughs at those who do not.
However that may be, the Church is left without proof if
they are right. (813)

873 God either confounded false miracles or foretold them. In
either case he rose above what is supernatural from our point
of view, and raised us above it ourselves. (824)

874 The Church teaches and God inspires, and both infallibly. The
work of the Church serves only to prepare either for grace or
condemnation. What it does is enough to condemn, but not to
inspire. (881)

875 *Every kingdom divided against itself,* for Jesus was working against
the devil, and destroying his power over men's hearts in order
to bring in the kingdom of God, and exorcism prefigured this;
thus he adds *with the finger of God . . . the kingdom of God is come
upon you.*[1]

1. Luke XI. 17-20.

If the devil were in favour of the doctrine that destroys him, he will be divided against himself, as Jesus said.

If God were in favour of the doctrine that destroys his Church, he would be divided. (820)

876 'When a strong man armed keepeth his palace, his goods are in peace. . . .'[1] (300)

877 Will *Yes and No* be accepted in faith as well as in morals, if it is so inseparable in deeds?

When St Xavier performs miracles?

Unjust judges, do not draw up laws on the spur of the moment; judge according to those already established, and established by yourselves.

Woe unto you that decree unrighteous decrees![2]

In order to weaken your opponents you disarm the whole Church.

Woe unto you that decree. . . .

St Hilary. Wretched men who force us to speak of miracles.

Continual miracles false.

If they say they submit to the Pope, 'it is hypocrisy.'

If they are ready to sign all his constitutions, 'that is not enough.'

If they say our salvation depends on God, 'they are heretics.'

If they say one must not kill for an apple, 'they are attacking Catholic morality.'

If miracles are performed among them, 'this is not a sign of holiness, but, on the contrary, grounds for suspecting heresy.'

The way in which the Church has survived is that the truth has never been challenged, or if it has, there was always the Pope, or else the Church itself. (849)

878 *First Objection:* 'Angel from heaven . . . !'[3]

'Truth must not be judged by miracles, but miracles by truth.

'Therefore miracles are useless.'

Now they are of use and truth must not be opposed.

Therefore what Father Lingendes said, that 'God will not allow a miracle to lead men into error. . . .'

1. Luke XI. 21.   2 Is. X. I.   3. Gal. I. 8.

When there are parties in dispute within the same Church, miracles are decisive.

Second objection:

'But Antichrist will work signs and wonders.'

Pharaoh's magicians did not lead men into error.

Thus we cannot say to Christ concerning Antichrist: 'You have led me into error,' for Antichrist will work his wonders against Christ, and they cannot therefore lead to error.

Either God will not allow false miracles or he will bring about greater ones.

Christ has existed from the beginning of the world: that carries more weight than all the miracles of Antichrist.

If within the same Church miracles took place on the side of those in error, this would lead to error.

The schism is obvious, the miracle is obvious, but schism is a clearer sign of error than a miracle is of truth: therefore the miracle cannot lead to error.

But apart from schism error is not as obvious as a miracle; therefore the miracle would lead to error.

Where is thy God?[1] Miracles reveal him, like a flash of lightning.   (849)

879   Men are by nature roofers, or any other trade, except when in their own room.   (138)

880   The Five Propositions were once ambiguous, but are not so any more.   (831)

881   That the Five Propositions were condemned was no miracle, for no attack was being made against the truth, but the Sorbonne, and the Bull.

Those who love God with all their hearts cannot possibly fail to recognize the Church, plain as it is.

Those who do not love God cannot possibly be convinced of the Church.

Miracles carry such weight that God had to warn men not to think about them in opposition to him, clear though it is that God exists.

1. Ps. XLII. 3.

Otherwise they might have caused trouble.

And thus so far are passages like Deut. XIII from telling against the authority of miracles, that nothing could more clearly indicate their power.

Likewise with Antichrist: 'Insomuch that if it were possible they shall deceive the very elect.'[1]   (850)

882   *Atheists.* What grounds have they for saying that no one can rise from the dead? Which is harder, to be born or to rise again? That what has never been should be, or that what has been should be once more? Is it harder to come into existence than to come back? Habit makes us find the one easy, while lack of habit makes us find the other impossible.

Popular way to judge!

Why can a virgin not bear a child? Does not a hen produce eggs without a cock? What distinguishes them outwardly from the others? And how do we know that a hen cannot form the germ just as well as a cock?   (222)

883   There is such a discrepancy between his imagined merit and his stupidity that it is incredible that he should so grossly mis-judge himself.   (946)

884   After so many signs of piety they still suffer persecution, which is the clearest sign of piety.   (860)

885   It is a good thing that they should commit injustices, in case it might appear that the Molinists have acted justly; and so they must not be spared. They are fit to commit them.   (936)

886   'Sceptic' for 'obstinate'.   (51)

887   Descartes useless and uncertain.   (78)

888   Only those who are not courtiers use the word 'courtier', the same with 'pedant' and 'provincial', and I am ready to wager that it was the printer who put it into the title of *Letters to a Provincial.*   (52)

889   *Thoughts. With all these I sought for rest.*[2]

1. Matt. XXIV. 24.
2. Ecclesiasticus XXIV. 7.

If our state were really happy, we should not need to take our minds off it in order to make ourselves happy. (165)

890 Men are wholly occupied in pursuing their good, but they cannot justify their claim to possession nor have they the strength to make possession secure. It is the same with knowledge and pleasures. We possess neither truth nor good. (436b)

891 *Miracle.* This is an effect exceeding the natural powers of the means employed. And non-miracle is an effect not exceeding the natural powers of the means employed. Thus those who heal by invoking the devil are not performing a miracle, because that does not exceed the devil's natural powers, but. . . . (804)

892 Abraham, Gideon: sign above revelation.

The Jews blinded themselves by judging miracles by Scripture.

God has never abandoned his true worshippers.

I prefer to follow Jesus Christ rather than anyone else because he has miracles, prophecy, doctrine, perpetuity, etc.

Donatists: no miracles, which compels us to say it is the devil.

The more we particularize God, Christ, the Church. . . (822)

893 *Scriptural Blindness.*

Scripture, said the Jews, tells us that it is not known whence the Christ will come (John VII. 27); Scripture says (John XII. 34) 'that Christ abideth for ever' and this man says he will die. Thus, says St John: 'though he had done so many miracles before them, yet they believed not on him, that the saying of Esaias might be fulfilled. . . . He hath blinded their eyes.' (573)

894 The three signs of religion; perpetuity, godly life, miracles.

They destroy perpetuity by probability, godly life by their morality, miracles by destroying either their authenticity or their importance.

If they are to be believed, the Church will have no use for perpetuity, godliness or miracles.

Heretics too deny them, or deny their importance, but we should have to be lacking in sincerity to deny them, or out of our mind to deny their importance. (844)

895　Our religion is adapted to all sorts of minds. The first go no further than the institution, and our religion is such that its mere institution is enough to prove its truth. Others go as far back as the Apostles. The best instructed go as far back as the beginning of the world. Angels see it still better, and from a greater distance. (285)

896　My God, what stupid arguments! Would God have created the world in order to damn it? Would he ask so much of such feeble people? Scepticism is the cure for this disease, and will put this vanity in its place. (390)

897　*Humbling your heart.* (St Paul)[1]: this is the Christian character. '*Albe vous a nommé, je ne vous connais plus*' (Corneille)[2]: this is the character of inhumanity. The character of humanity is the opposite. (533)

898　Those who wrote that in Latin, talk French.

Once the harm had been done by putting them into French, some good should have been done by condemning them.

There is only one heresy explained in different ways in the Schools and in the world. (933)

899　No one has ever incurred martyrdom for miracles he claims to have seen; for, in the case of those which the Turks believe by tradition, human folly might perhaps go as far as martyrdom, but not for those actually seen. (884)

900　The Jansenists resemble the heretics in their moral reforms, but you resemble them in the harm you do. (887)

901　Miracles distinguish between things that are in doubt, between Jewish and heathen peoples, Jews and Christians, Catholics and heretics, slandered and slanderers, between the two crosses.[3]

But miracles would be no use to the heretics, for the Church, given authority by the miracles which have already engaged our belief, tells us that they lack the true faith. There can be no doubt that they do lack it, since the Church's first miracles pre-

1. Cf. Rom. XII. 16.
2. 'Alba has nominated you, I no longer know you,' *Horace*, II. iii.
3. Of Christ on the one hand and the thieves on the other.

clude faith in theirs. Thus miracle is set against miracle, and the first and greatest are on the Church's side. (841)

902   These women are astonished to be told that they are on the road to perdition, that their confessors are leading them to Geneva, and giving them the idea that Jesus is not present in the Eucharist, or on the right hand of the Father. They know that it is all false, and therefore offer themselves to God like this: *See if there be any wicked way in me.*[1] What happens next? This place is said to be the devil's temple; God makes it his own temple. It is said that the children should be taken away from there; God heals them there. It is said to be the arsenal of hell; God makes it the sanctuary of his grace. Finally it is threatened with all the wrath and vengeance of heaven; God loads them with his favours. One would have to be out of one's mind to conclude from this that they are on the road to perdition.

No doubt St Athanasius had the same signs as we have. (841)

903   *Story of the man born blind.* What does St Paul say? Is he constantly referring back to the prophecies? No, but to his miracle.

What does Jesus say? Does he refer back to the prophecies? No, he had not yet fulfilled them by his death, but he says: '*If I had not done . . .*[2] Believe in my works.

Two supernatural foundations of our wholly supernatural religion, one visible, the other invisible.

Miracles with grace, miracles without grace.

The synagogue, treated with love as figurative of the Church, and with hate as being merely figurative, was restored when about to collapse, when it stood well with God, and was thus figurative.

Miracles prove God's power over our hearts by that which he exercises over our bodies.

The Church has never approved a miracle among heretics.

Miracles, mainstay of religion. They distinguished the Jews, they have distinguished Christians, saints, the innocent, the true believers.

A miracle among schismatics is not so much to be feared, for

1. Ps. CXXXIX. 24.
2. John XV. 24.

the schism, being more obvious than the miracle, is an obvious sign of their error. But when there is no schism, and error is in dispute, a miracle makes the distinction.

If I had not done the works which none other man did.[1]

These unhappy people who have obliged me to speak of miracles!

Abraham, Gideon.

Confirm faith by miracles.

Judith. God speaks at last during the ultimate oppressions.

If the cooling off of charity leaves the Church with almost no true worshippers, miracles will stir them up.

They are the supreme effects of grace.

If a miracle took place among the Jesuits. . . .

When a miracle confounds the expectations of those in whose presence it occurs, and there is a discrepancy between the state of their faith and the miraculous instrument, it ought to induce them to change, but. . . . Otherwise there would be as much reason for saying that if the Eucharist brought a dead man to life one should become a Calvinist, as that one should remain a Catholic. But when it fulfils their expectations, and those who hoped that God would bless the remedies see themselves cured without remedies. . . .

Unbelievers.

No sign has ever occurred on the devil's side without a more powerful sign on God's side, unless, at least, such an occurrence had been foretold. (851)

904 The insane idea you have of your Company's importance is what has made you institute these atrocious methods. It is perfectly obvious that this is what made you adopt that of calumny, since you brand my slightest deceptions as atrocious, while excusing them in yourselves, because you regard me as an individual and yourselves as the *Imago*.[2]

It is quite clear that what you praise is folly fit for fairy-tales, like the privilege of not being damned.

1. John xv. 24.
2. Reference to *Imago Primi Seculi S. J.* (1640). See Fifth *Prov. Letter.*

Is it encouraging your children to condemn them when they serve the Church?

It is a device of the devil for diverting elsewhere the arms with which these people were attacking heresies.

You are bad politicians. (927)

905 *Scepticism.* Everything here is partly true, partly false. Essential truth is not like that, but is wholly pure and wholly true. Such mixture destroys it and reduces it to nothing. Nothing is purely true, and so nothing is true in the sense of pure truth. You will say that it is true that homicide is wrong. Yes, for we know very well what is evil and false. But what will you say is good? Chastity? I say it is not, for the whole world would come to an end. Marriage? No, continence is better. Not killing? No, for this would provoke atrocious disorders, and the wicked would kill all the good. Killing? No, for that destroys nature. We only possess the true and the good in part, mixed up with the bad and the false. (385)

906 *Probability.* They have some true principles, but they abuse them. Now abuse of truths should be punished as heavily as the introduction of lies.

As if there were two hells, one for sins against charity, the other for sins against justice. (916)

907 Aperitive quality of a key, attractive quality of a hook. (55)

908 Superstition and concupiscence.

Scruples, wrong desires.

Wrong fear.

Fear: not that which comes from believing in God, but from doubting whether or not he exists. The right fear comes from faith, false fear from doubt; the right fear is linked with hope, because it is born of faith and one hopes in the God in whom one believes; the wrong fear is linked with despair, because one fears the God in whom one has not put one's faith. Some fear to lose him, others to find him. (262)

909 People who break their word, without faith, without honour, without truth, deceitful of heart, deceitful of tongue, resembling, as an earlier criticism put it, the amphibious creature

in the story which remained ambiguously neither flesh nor fowl.

'Port-Royal is as good as Voltigerode.'[1]

Looked at from this angle, your procedure is as just as it is unjust from the point of view of Christian piety.

It is important for kings and princes to be esteemed for their piety, and for this they must go to you for confession. (924)

910 Figures denoting the universality of the redemption, like the sun shining on all, show nothing but universality, but figures denoting exclusions, like the Jews chosen to the exclusion of the Gentiles, show exclusion. (781)

911 'Jesus Christ redeemer of all.' – 'Yes, for he made his offer as a man redeeming all those wishing to come to him. If some die on the way, that is their misfortune; for his part, he offered them redemption.'

'That is all right in this example, where the one who redeems and the one who prevents death are two different people, but not for Christ, who does both.' – 'No, for Christ as redeemer is perhaps not master of all, and so, as far as in him lies, he is redeemer of all.' (781)

912 When you say that Christ did not die for all men, you are abusing a weakness of men, who at once apply this exception to themselves, and this encourages despair, instead of turning them away from it to encourage hope.

For in this way one accustoms oneself to inward virtues by outward habits. (781)

1. A German abbey which the Jesuits had tried to acquire.

SECTION FOUR

FRAGMENTS NOT FOUND IN THE *COPY*

A. THE MEMORIAL

(A piece of parchment recording the decisive experience of 1654 was found sewn into Pascal's clothing after his death, and it seems that he carried it with him at all times.)

913　The year of grace 1654.

Monday, 23 November, feast of Saint Clement, Pope and Martyr, and of others in the Martyrology.

Eve of Saint Chrysogonus, Martyr and others.

From about half past ten in the evening until half past midnight.

Fire

'God of Abraham, God of Isaac, God of Jacob,'[1] not of philosophers and scholars.

Certainty, certainty, heartfelt, joy, peace.

God of Jesus Christ.

God of Jesus Christ.

My God and your God.[2]

'Thy God shall be my God.'[3]

The world forgotten, and everything except God.

He can only be found by the ways taught in the Gospels.

Greatness of the human soul.

'O righteous Father, the world had not known thee, but I have known thee.'[4]

Joy, joy, joy, tears of joy.

I have cut myself off from him.

They have forsaken me, the fountain of living waters.[5]

'My God wilt thou forsake me?'[6]

Let me not be cut off from him for ever!

'And this is life eternal, that they might know thee, the only true God, and Jesus Christ whom thou hast sent.'[7]

Jesus Christ.

Jesus Christ.

1. Ex. III. 6.　2. John XX. 17.　3. Ruth I. 16.　4. John XVII. 25.
5. Jer. II. 13.　6. Cf. Matt. XXVII. 46.　7. John XVII. 3.

I have cut myself off from him, shunned him, denied him, crucified him.

Let me never be cut off from him!

He can only be kept by the ways taught in the Gospel.

Sweet and total renunciation.

Total submission to Jesus Christ and my director.

Everlasting joy in return for one day's effort on earth.

I will not forget thy word.[1] Amen.

B. FRAGMENTS IN THE *RECUEIL ORIGINAL*

(The fragments which follow include some which were not given to the copyist because they were considered too private, (e.g. *The Mystery of Jesus*), a large number of drafts for the *Provincial Letters*, and a few intended for other works, as well as a certain number apparently omitted from inadvertence. They are all to be found in the collection of Pascal's papers known as the *Recueil Original*.)

914 Every time the Jesuits take the Pope unawares, the whole of Christendom becomes guilty of perjury.

The Pope is very liable to be taken unawares, because he is so busy and trusts the Jesuits so much, and the Jesuits are perfectly capable of taking people unawares for the sake of spreading calumny. (882)

915 'Hearing the rumour about the Feuillants, I went off to see him,' said my old friend, 'talking of piety, he thought that I had some feeling for it.'

'And that I might easily be a Feuillant.'

'And that I might profitably write something against innovators, especially just now.'

'We have recently gone against our general chapter, which laid down that we should sign the Bull.'

'That he wished that God might inspire me.'

'Father, ought one to sign?' (902b)

1. Ps. CXIX. 16.

916   If they do not give up probability, their good maxims are no more holy than their evil ones, for they are based on human authority. And so, if they are more just, they will be more reasonable but not more holy: they take after the wild stem on to which they are grafted.

If what I say does not help to enlighten you, it will help to enlighten the people.

If these are silent, stones will speak.

Silence is the worst form of persecution. The saints have never kept silent. It is true that one needs a vocation, but it is not decrees in Council that must tell us whether we are called, it is the need to speak. Now that Rome has spoken, condemning the truth, as it is thought, now that they have written this and the books saying the opposite have been censured, then the more unjustly we are censured and the more forcibly they try to gag us, the louder we must cry out, until there comes a pope who will hear both sides, and consult ancient precedent so that justice can be done.

Thus good popes will still find the Church protesting.

The Inquisition and the Society: twin scourges of the truth.

'Why do you not accuse them of Arianism, for they said that Jesus Christ is God? Perhaps they do not mean that he is so by nature, as it is written: *Ye are gods!*[1]

If my letters are condemned in Rome, what I condemn in them is condemned in heaven.

I appeal to your tribunal, Lord Jesus.[2]

You are corruptible yourselves.

When I saw myself condemned, I was afraid that I had written badly, but the example of so many pious writings makes me think the opposite. No one is allowed to write well any more.

The Inquisition is so corrupt or ignorant.

'We ought to obey God rather than men.'[3]

I am not afraid of anything, I do not hope for anything. The bishops are not like that. Port Royal is afraid, and it is a bad policy to separate them, for they will no longer be afraid, but will make people more afraid of them.

1. John x. 34. 2. Quoted from a letter of St Bernard.
3. Acts v. 29.

I am not even afraid of your censures: mere words, unless they are based on those of tradition.

Do you censure everything? Even my respect? No? Tell me what then, otherwise you will achieve nothing, unless you point out what is wrong and why it is wrong. And that is something that they will have great difficulty in doing.

Probability. They have given a funny explanation of safety, for, after laying down that all their paths are safe, they no longer call safe what leads to heaven, with no danger of failing to arrive, but what leads there, with no danger of straying from this path.

(920)

917　The Christian's hope of possessing an infinite good is mingled with actual enjoyment as well as with fear, for, unlike people hoping for a kingdom of which they will have no part because they are subjects, Christians hope for holiness, and to be freed from unrighteousness, and some part of this is already theirs.

(540)

918　The rivers of Babylon flow, and fall, and carry away.

O holy Sion, where everything stands firm and nothing falls!

We must sit by these rivers, not under or in them, but above, not standing upright, but sitting down, so that we remain humble by sitting, and safe by remaining above, but we shall stand upright in the porches of Jerusalem.

Let us see if this pleasure is firm or transitory; if it passes away it is a river of Babylon.[1]

(459)

The Mystery of Jesus

919　Jesus suffers in his passion the torments inflicted upon him by men, but in his agony he suffers the torments which he inflicts on himself. *He was troubled.*[2] This punishment is inflicted by no human, but an almighty hand, and only he that is almighty can bear it.

Jesus seeks some comfort at least from his three dearest friends, and they sleep: he asks them to bear with him a while,

---

1. This fragment is a paraphrase of a meditation on Ps. CXXVII by St Augustine.
2. John XI. 33. Reflexive in Vulgate Latin.

and they abandon him with complete indifference, and with so little pity that it did not keep them awake even for a single moment. And so Jesus was abandoned to face the wrath of God alone.

Jesus is alone on earth, not merely with no one to feel and share his agony, but with no one even to know of it. Heaven and he are the only ones to know.

Jesus is in a garden, not of delight, like the first Adam, who there fell and took with him all mankind, but of agony, where he has saved himself and all mankind.

He suffers this anguish and abandonment in the horror of the night.

I believe that this is the only occasion on which Jesus ever complained. But then he complained as though he could no longer contain his overflowing grief: 'My soul is exceeding sorrowful, even unto death.'[1]

Jesus seeks companionship and solace from men.

It seems to me that this is unique in his whole life, but he finds none, for his disciples are asleep.

Jesus will be in agony until the end of the world. There must be no sleeping during that time.

Jesus, totally abandoned, even by the friends he had chosen to watch with him, is vexed when he finds them asleep because of the dangers to which they are exposing not him but themselves, and he warns them for their own safety and their own good, with warm affection in the face of their ingratitude. And warns them: 'The spirit is willing but the flesh is weak.'[2]

Jesus finding them asleep again, undeterred by consideration either for him or for themselves, is kind enough not to wake them up and lets them take their rest.

Jesus prays, uncertain of the will of the Father, and is afraid of death. But once he knows what it is, he goes to meet it and offer himself up. *Let us be going.*[3] *He went forth.* (John) [XVIII. 4.]

Jesus asked of men and was not heard.

Jesus brought about the salvation of his disciples while they slept. He has done this for each of the righteous while they

1. Matt. XXVI. 38.   2. Matt. XXVI. 41.
3. Matt. XXVI. 46.

slept, in nothingness before their birth and in their sins after their birth.

He prays only once that the cup might pass from him, even then submitting himself to God's will, and twice that it should come if it must be so.

Jesus weary at heart.

Jesus, seeing all his friends asleep and all his enemies watchful, commends himself utterly to his Father.

Jesus disregards the enmity of Judas, and sees only in him God's will, which he loves; so much so that he calls him friend.

Jesus tears himself away from his disciples to enter upon his agony: we must tear ourselves away from those who are nearest and dearest to us in order to imitate him.

While Jesus remains in agony and cruellest distress, let us pray longer.

We implore God's mercy, not so that he shall leave us in peace with our vices, but so that he may deliver us from them.

If God gave us masters with his own hand, how gladly we ought to obey them! Necessity and events are infallibly such.

'Take comfort; you would not seek me if you had not found me.'

'I thought of you in my agony: I shed these drops of blood for you.'

'It is tempting me rather than testing yourself to wonder if you would do right in the absence of this or that. I will do it in you if it happens.'

'Let yourself be guided by my rules. See how well I guided the Virgin and the saints who let me work in them.'

'The Father loves all I do.'

'Do you want it always to cost me the blood of my humanity while you do not even shed a tear?'

'My concern is for your conversion; do not be afraid, and pray with confidence as though for me.'

'I am present with you through my word in Scripture, my spirit in the Church, through inspiration, my power in my priests, my prayer among the faithful.'

'Physicians will not heal you, for you will die in the end, but it is I who will heal you and make your body immortal.'

'Endure the chains and bondage of the body. For the present I am delivering you only from spiritual bondage.'

'I am a better friend to you than this man or that, for I have done more for you than they, and they would never endure what I have endured from you, and they would never die for you, while you were being faithless and cruel, as I did, and as I am ready to do, and still do in my elect, and in the Blessed Sacrament.'

'If you knew your sins, you would lose heart.' – 'In that case I shall lose heart, Lord, for I believe in their wickedness on the strength of your assurance.' – 'No, for I who tell you this can heal you, and the fact that I tell you is a sign that I want to heal you. As you expiate them you will come to know them, and you will be told: "Behold thy sins are forgiven thee."'

'Repent then of your secret sins and the hidden evil of those you know.'

'Lord, I give you all.'

'I love you more ardently than you have loved your foulness. *As an unclean beast for the mire.*'[1]

'May mine be the glory, not thine, worm and clay.'

'Acknowledge to your director that in my very words you find an occasion for sin, and for vanity or curiosity.'

Pilate's false justice only causes Jesus Christ to suffer. For he has him scourged by his false justice and then put to death. It would have been better to put him to death at once. The falsely righteous are like that. They do both good works and bad to please the world and show that they are not wholly Christ's, for they are ashamed to be. Finally, when it comes to great temptations and opportunities they put him to death.

I see the depths of my pride, curiosity, concupiscence. There is no link between me and God or Jesus Christ the righteous. But he was made sin for me. All your scourges fell upon him. He is more abominable than I, and, far from loathing me, feels honoured that I go to him and help him. But he healed himself and will heal me all the more surely. I must add my wounds to his, and join myself to him and he will save me in saving himself.

1. Horace, *Ep.*, 1, 2. v. 26.

But none must be added for the future.

Ye shall be as gods, knowing good and evil.[1] We all act like God in passing judgements: 'This is good or evil' and in being too distressed or too delighted by events.

Do small things as if they were great, because of the majesty of Christ, who does them in us and lives our life, and great things as if they were small and easy, because of his almighty power. (553)

920 'We ourselves have received no general maxims. If you look at our *Constitutions* you will hardly recognize us; they make us out to be beggars, kept out of courts, and yet. . . . But this is not infringing them, for the glory of God is everywhere.'

'There are different ways of achieving it. St Ignatius chose certain ones and now we choose others. It was better at first to propose poverty and retreat, later on it was better to choose the rest, for it would have caused alarm to begin at the top of the scale; that is against nature.'

'It is not that the general rule fails to insist on adherence to the *Institutions* [sic], for there would be abuses; you would find few like us, who know how to promote ourselves without vanity.'

Unam sanctam.

The Jansenists will pay the penalty.

Father Saint-Jure. Escobar.

Tanto viro.

Aquaviva 14 Dec. 1621. Tanner q. 2 dub. 5 n. 86.

Clement and Paul V. God visibly protects us.

Against hasty judgements and scruples.

St Teresa 474.

Roman [*de la?*] *Rose.*

Falso crimine.

Subtlety for its own sake.[?]

All the truth on one side; we extend it to both.

Two obstacles: the Gospel, the laws of the state. *From the greater to the lesser.* More recent.

Do not [?] speak of personal vices.

1. Gen. III. 5.

Fine letter of Aquaviva, 18 June 1611.

Against probable opinions.

St Augustine 282.

And for St Thomas, in the places where he specifically dealt with these matters.

Clemens placet. 277.

And novelties.

And it is no excuse for superiors not to have known because they ought to have known. 279–194, 192.

For morality. 283, 288.

The Society is important to the Church. 236.

For good or ill. 156.

Acquoquiez heard the confessions of women. 360.[1]   (957)

921   All conditions of men, even martyrs, have reason to fear, according to Scripture.

The worst punishment of purgatory is being uncertain about judgment.

A God that hidest thyself.   (518)

922   *Concerning miracles.*

As God has made no family more happy, may he also see that none may be found more grateful.   (856)

923   *Concerning confession and absolution without signs of repentance.*

God looks only at what is inward, the Church judges only by what is outward. God absolves as soon as he sees repentance in the heart; the Church, when it sees it in works. God will create an inwardly pure Church, to confound by its inward and completely spiritual holiness the inward impiety of the proud and Pharisees. And the Church will be a gathering of men whose outward conduct is so pure as to confound pagan conduct; if some of them are hypocrites, not so well disguised that it fails to recognize their poison, it endures them. For, although they are not accepted by God, whom they cannot deceive, they are

1. The page references in this and similar fragments intended for the *Provincial Letters* are to the *Historia Jesuitica* of R. Hospinianus, and the letters are from editions of the correspondence of Jesuit Generals. The scraps of Latin include references to these works, to various Jesuit polemics and to papal Bulls.

accepted by men, whom they do deceive. And so the Church is not dishonoured by their conduct, which looks saintly. But you ... you do not want the Church to judge, either from within, because that is for God alone, or from without, because God goes right into what lies within. And thus, leaving it no choice of men, you keep within the Church the most dissolute and those who dishonour it to such an extent that the Jewish synagogues and philosophical sects would have kept them out as unworthy and would have loathed them as impious. (905)

924 It is true that there is something painful in beginning to practise piety, but this pain does not arise from the beginnings of piety within us, but from the impiety that is still there. If our senses were not opposed to penance and our corruption were not opposed to God's purity, there would be nothing painful about it. As for us, we only suffer in so far as our natural vice resists supernatural grace: our heart feels torn between these contrary forces, but it would be very wrong to impute this violence to God, who draws us to him, instead of attributing it to the world which holds us back. It is like a child snatched by its mother from the arms of robbers, who, even while it is suffering pain, should love the loving and lawful violence of its rescuer, and hate only the injurious and tyrannical violence of those who wrongfully hold on to it. The cruellest war that God can wage on men in this life is to leave them without the war he came to bring. 'I came not to send peace but a sword,'[1] he said, and as weapons of this war 'I am come to send on earth fire and sword.'[2] Before his coming the world lived in a false peace. (498)

925 The law has not destroyed nature, but instructed it. Grace has not destroyed the law, but makes it effective.

   Faith received at baptism is the source of all life for Christians and converts. (520)

926 We make an idol of truth itself, for truth apart from charity is not God, but his image and an idol that we must not love or worship. Still less must we love or worship its opposite, which is falsehood.

1. Matt. x. 34. 2. Cf. Luke xii. 49.

I may well love total darkness, but if God plunges me into a state of semi-darkness I am displeased by such darkness as is there, and, because I fail to see in it the same merits as in total darkness, such a state does not please me. This is a fault, and a sign that I am making an idol of darkness, separated from God's order. Now, we should worship only in his order.   (582)

927   What good would it do me?

    Abominable.

    Singlin.

    Anything may be fatal to us, even things intended for our use, as in nature walls, or steps, can cause our death, if we do not walk carefully.

    The slightest movement affects the whole of nature; one stone can alter the whole sea. Likewise, in the realm of grace, the slightest action affects everything because of its consequences; therefore everything matters.

    In every action we must look beyond the action at our present, past, and future state, and that of others affected by it, and see how all these things are connected. Then we shall exercise great restraint.   (505)

928   *External works.* Nothing is so dangerous as what is pleasing to God and men. For states which please both God and men have one element that is pleasing to God and another pleasing to men, like the greatness of St Teresa; what pleases God is her profound humility in her revelations, what pleases men is her enlightenment. So we work ourselves to death to imitate her discourses, under the impression of imitating her state, and thus to love what God loves and put ourselves into a state that God loves.

    It is better not to fast and feel humiliated by it than to fast and be self-satisfied.

    Pharisee, publican.

    What good would it do me to remember, if it is equally liable to do me harm as good, and if everything depends on God's blessing, which he gives only to things done for his sake, according to his rules and his ways?

    Since the way a thing is done matters as much as doing it,

and perhaps more so, since God can bring good out of evil, and
without God we bring evil out of good? (499)

929 'Do not compare yourself to others, but to me. If you do not
find me in those to whom you compare yourself, you are comparing yourself to someone loathsome. If you do find me, compare yourself to them. But whom will you be comparing?
Yourself, or me in you? If it is yourself, it is someone loathsome;
if it is I, you are comparing me to myself. Now I am God in all
things.'

'I often speak to you and give you advice, because your
director is unable to speak to you, for I do not want you to be
without a director.'

'And perhaps I do this at his entreaty, and so he directs you
without you seeing it.'

'You would not seek me if you did not possess me.'

'Therefore be not troubled.'

(Received the sum of 400 livres from Mlle Pascal.) (555)

930 Why has God instituted prayer?

1. To impart to his creatures the dignity of causality.

2. To teach us from whom we derive virtue.

3. To make us earn other virtues by our efforts.

But, in order to preserve his supremacy, he bestows the gift
of prayer on whom he pleases.

Objection: We may think that prayer derives from ourselves.

That is absurd, for even with faith we may not have virtues,
so how could we have faith? Is it not further from lack of faith
to faith than from faith to virtue?

'Worthy': the word is ambiguous.

He was worthy to have a redeemer.[1]

He was worthy to touch such holy limbs.[2]

Worthy to touch such holy limbs.[3]

Lord, I am not worthy.[4] *He that eateth unworthily.*[5]

Thou art worthy to receive glory. . . .[6]

Find me worthy.[7]

1. From Office for Holy Saturday. 2. Office for Good Friday.
3. From hymn *Vexilla regis*. 4. Luke VII. 6. 5. I Cor. XI. 29.
6. Rev. IV. 11. 7. Office of BVM.

God only bestows according to his promises.

He has promised to answer prayers justly.

He never promised prayers except to the children of the promise.

St Augustine formally stated that the righteous will be deprived of strength.

But he said this by chance, for the opportunity of saying it might not have offered. But his principles make it clear that, once the opportunity did offer, it was impossible for him not to say this, or say the opposite. It is therefore rather the case that he was obliged to say this once the opportunity offered than that he said it when the opportunity did offer. One is a matter of necessity, the other of chance, but both together are the most that can be demanded. (513)

931 I love all men as my brothers, because they are all redeemed.

I love poverty because he loved it. I love wealth because it affords me the means of helping the needy. I keep faith with everyone. I do not render evil to those who do evil to me, but wish them a condition like my own, in which one receives neither good nor evil at the hands of men. I try to be just, genuine, sincere and loyal to all men, and I feel special affection for those to whom God has most intimately joined me.

And whether I am alone or in the sight of others, in all my doings I am in the sight of God, who must judge them and to whom I have devoted them all.

These are my feelings.

And all the days of my life I bless my Redeemer, who implanted them in me and who made a man full of weakness, wretchedness, concupiscence, pride and ambition into one free from all these evils, by the power of his grace, to which all glory for this is due, since nothing but wretchedness and error come from me. (550)

932 And will this man scoff at that?

Who should scoff? And yet the one does not scoff at the other, but is sorry for him. (191)

933 Concupiscence of the flesh, concupiscence of the eyes, pride, etc.

There are three orders of things: flesh, mind and will.

The carnal are rich men and kings. Their interest is in the body.

Inquirers and scholars; their interest is in the mind.

The wise; their interest is in what is right.

God should govern everything and everything should be related to him.

Things of the flesh are properly governed by concupiscence.

Things of the mind by curiosity.

Wisdom by pride.

It is not that one cannot glory in wealth or knowledge, but that is not the proper place for pride, for while granting that a man is learned you can still convince him that he is wrong to be proud.

The place for pride is wisdom, for you cannot grant that a man has become wise but that he is wrong to glory in it, for it is right that he should.

Therefore God alone bestows wisdom, and that is why: *He that glorieth, let him glory in the Lord.*[1]   (460)

934   There are perfections in nature to show that she is the image of God and imperfections to show that she is no more than his image.   (580)

935   Since men do not usually create merit but only reward it when they find it in being, they judge God by themselves.   (490)

936   We only understand prophecies when we have seen the events occur, and so the proof of retreat, spiritual direction, silence, etc., is only proof to those who know and believe it already.

St Joseph so inward in a wholly outward law.

Outward penance creates a disposition to inward penance, and humiliations dispose us to be humble, likewise. . . .   (698)

937   When our passions impel us to do something we forget our duty. For example, if we like a book, we read it when we ought to be doing something else. But to remember our duty we need only decide to do something we dislike; we then make the

1. I Cor. I. 31.

excuse of something else to be done, and thus remember our
duty. (104)

938 20 V. The figure used in the Gospel for the state of the soul that
is sick is that of sick bodies. But, because one body cannot be
sick enough to express it properly, there had to be more than
one. Thus we find the deaf man, the dumb man, the blind
man, the paralytic, dead Lazarus, the man possessed of a devil.
All these put together are in the sick soul. (658)

939 'The servant knoweth not what his lord doeth,'[1] because the
lord only tells him what to do and not the purpose of it. That
is why he obeys slavishly and often sins against the purpose.
But Jesus Christ has told us the purpose.
And you destroy that purpose. (897)

940 Jesus did not want to be killed without the forms of justice, for
it is much more ignominious to die at the hands of justice
than in some unjust insurrection. (790)

941 We do not grow bored with eating and sleeping every day, for
we soon feel hungry or sleepy again, otherwise we should grow
bored with it.
Likewise if we do not hunger for spiritual things we find
them boring: 'hunger after righteousness,' eighth beatitude.[2]
(264)

942 Conclusion. Are we safe? Is this principle safe? Let us examine
it. Our own evidence null and void. St Thomas. (941)

943 24 Aa. It seems to me that Jesus only allowed his wounds to be
touched after his resurrection. *Touch me not.*[3] We must only
share in his sufferings.
He gave himself in communion as a mortal man in the Last
Supper, as risen from the dead to the disciples at Emmaus, as
ascended into heaven to the whole Church. (554)

1. John xv. 15.
2. Matt. v. 6, 10: 'Blessed are they who are persecuted for righteousness' sake.'
3. John xx. 17.

944 We must combine outward and inward to obtain anything from God; in other words we must go down on our knees, pray with our lips, etc., so that the proud man who would not submit to God must now submit to his creature. If we expect help from this outward part we are being superstitious, if we refuse to combine it with the inward we are being arrogant. (250)

945 Repentance was the only one of all the mysteries to be plainly declared to the Jews, and by St John the forerunner, and then came the other mysteries, to show that this order should be observed in every man and in the whole world. (601)

946 2. Consider Jesus Christ in every person, and in ourselves. Jesus Christ as father in his father, Jesus Christ as brother in his brothers, Jesus Christ as poor in the poor, Jesus Christ as rich in the rich, Jesus Christ as priest and doctor in priests, Jesus Christ as sovereign in princes, etc. For by his glory he is everything that is great, being God, and by his mortal life he is everything that is wretched and abject. That is why he took on this unhappy conditio.1, so that he could be in every person and a model for every condition of men. (785)

947 25bb. Another reason: that charity considers this as being deprived of the spirit of God and an evil action, because of the suspension or interruption of the spirit of God in him, and repents with much distress.

The righteous man acts by faith in the smallest things. When he reproves his servants he wishes for their conversion by the spirit of God, and prays God to correct them, hoping as much from God as from his own reproofs, and praying God to bless his corrections. Likewise in his other actions. (504)

948 We depart from him only when we depart from charity.

Our prayers and virtues are abominations before God if they are not the prayers and virtues of Jesus Christ. And our sins will never attract God's mercy, but rather his justice, unless they are the sins of Jesus Christ.

He took on our sins and accepted us into covenant with him,

for virtues are proper to him and sins alien; while virtues are alien and sins are proper to us.

Let us change the rule we have hitherto adopted for judging what is good. We took our own will as rule; let us now take the will of God. Anything that he wills is good and right for us, anything he does not will is bad and wrong.

Anything that God does not will is forbidden. Sins are forbidden by God's general statement that he did not will them. Other things which he left without a general prohibition, and which are therefore called permissible, are none the less not always permissible. For when God removes some particular thing from us and it becomes apparent through the event, which is evidence of God's will, that it is not his will that we should have the thing, it is then forbidden as much as sin, since it is God's will that we should not have one any more than the other. The only difference between these two things is that it is certain that God will never will sin, whereas it is not certain that he will never will the other thing. But, while God does not will it, we must regard it as sin, as long as God's will, sole source of good and right, is against it and makes it bad and wrong. (668)

949 That we have treated them as humanely as possible in order to keep a middle course between the love of truth and the duty of charity.

That piety does not consist in never rising up against our brethren. It would be very easy....

It is false piety to preserve peace at the expense of truth.

It is also false zeal to preserve truth at the expense of charity.

Thus they did not complain.

There is a time and a place for their maxims.

Their vanity actually arises from their errors.

Resembling the Fathers [Jews?] through their faults.

And the martyrs through their punishment,

And they will still not deny a single one.

They had only to take the extract and deny it.

They even prepare war against him.[1]

1. Mic. III. 5.

M. Bourseys. At least they cannot deny that they opposed the condemnation. (930)

950 Paul IV, in his Bull *Cum ex apostolatus officio*, published in 1558:
'We ordain, lay down, decree and define that each and every one of those who have been led astray or have fallen into heresy or schism, of whatever rank or condition they may be, laymen, ecclesiastics, priests, bishops, archbishops, patriarchs, primates, cardinals, counts, marquesses, dukes, kings and emperors, in addition to the aforementioned sentence, and penalties, shall *ipso facto*, without service *de jure* or *de facto*, be deprived wholly, completely and perpetually of their orders, bishoprics, benefices, offices, kingdom or empire, nor ever be allowed to resume them. Let us leave their punishment to the discretion of the secular power, granting to those who may in true repentance return from the error of their ways no indulgence save that, through the benevolence and clemency of the Holy See, they may be deemed worthy to be detained within a monastery, there to do perpetual penance on bread and water, but remaining for ever deprived of all dignity, order, prelacy, county, duchy or kingdom. And those who shelter and protect them shall *ipso facto* to be adjudged excommunicated, and disgraced, deprived of every kingdom, duchy, property and possession, which shall fall by right and ownership to whosoever first lays hands on them.'

If they have slain any excommunicated person, we do not consider them guilty of homicide, on the grounds that they happened, burning with zeal for their Catholic mother against the excommunicated, to kill any of them. 23 q.5 of Urban II. (951)

951 When they have really been put through it, you will be sent home.

That is as poor a consolation as appeals by writ of error. For with one major occasion for abuse removed. . . .

Apart from the fact that the majority will not have the means to come up from the depths of Perigord and Anjou to plead before the Parlement in Paris:

Apart from the fact that they will constantly be getting orders in council forbidding these appeals by writ of error.

For though they cannot get what they demanded, by the mere fact of demanding it they none the less show their power, which is all the greater for having led them to demand something so unjust that they would obviously not manage to obtain it.

Therefore this only makes us more aware of their intentions and of the necessity of not registering, and thus authorizing, the Bull, which they want to use as a basis for their new establishment.

This is not just an ordinary Bull but a basis.

Coming out of the law-courts.

121. The Pope forbids the King to marry his children without his permission. 1294.

We wish you to know. 124. 1302.

Childish. . . . (950)

952 *Clemens placentium.*

Our generals were afraid that discredit might result from external occupations. 208, 152, 150, from the Court. 209, 203, 216, 218, from not following the most certain and authoritative views. St Thomas, etc. 215, 218.

Payment against the Constitutions. 218.

Women. 225, 228.

Princes and politics. 227, 168, 177.

Probability. Novelty. 279, 156. Novelty. Truth.

For the sake of pastime and entertainment rather than to help souls. 158.

Lax opinions. 160. Mortal into venial sin. Contrition. 102. Politics. 162. Anticipating. . . . 162.

Amenities of life increase for the Jesuits. 166.

Apparent and false goods that deceive them. 192.

(And it is no excuse for superiors not to have known.)

Father Le Moine. 10,000 crowns outside his province.

'See how little foresight men have. All the things which our first generals feared would be fatal to the Society are just those which have caused it to flourish; the great, infringing our *Constitutions*, large numbers of religious, variety and novelty of opinions, etc.' 182, 157.

Politics. 181.

The original spirit of the Society extinct. 170. 171–4. 183–7. *It is not the same any more.* Vitteleschi. 183. *Other times, other interests.*

Complaints of the generals. None from St Ignatius. None from Laynez. A few from Borgia and Aquaviva. Innumerable from Mutius, etc.

'Have you the right idea about our Society?'

The Church has survived for so long without such questions. Others ask them, but it is not the same.

What comparison do you think there is between 20,000 separated[1] and 200,000,000 united, who will die for one another? An immortal body.

'We support one another to the death.' Lamy.

'We press our enemies.' M. Puys.

Everything depends on probability.

The world has a natural desire for a religion, but an easy one.

I should like to prove it to you by making an unusual assumption. And so I will say to you: 'Even if God did not support us as an act of special providence for the good of his Church, I intend to prove that, even humanly speaking, we cannot perish.

'Grant me this principle and I can prove anything. The fact is that the fortunes of the Society and the Church go together.

'Without these principles nothing can be proved.'

People do not live for long in open impiety, or naturally in great austerity.

An accommodating religion is likely to last.

We try to get them by being easygoing.

For individuals who do not want to rule by force of arms, I do not know whether they could do any better.

Kings, Pope.

3. *Kings.* 246.

6. equity and sincere piety.

(231. Jesuits consulted in everything.)

6. 452. Kings as foster-fathers.

4. Hated for their merits.

1. Probably refers to Jesuits.

University apology. 159. Sorbonne decree.

Kings. 241, 248.

Jesuits hanged. 112.

Religion and knowledge. [?]

A Jesuit is completely human.

Colleges, parents, friends, children to choose.

Constitutions.

253. Poverty, ambition.

257. Mainly princes, great nobles who may do harm or good.

12. Useless, rejected / looking well / wealth, nobility, etc.

What! Were you afraid of failure in accepting them sooner?

27. 47. Give one's property to the Society for the glory of God. *Declarations.*

51, 52. Unanimity of views. *Declarations.* Submit to the Society and thus preserve uniformity. Now today uniformity lies in diversity, for that is what the Society wants.

117. *Constitutions.* Gospel and St Thomas. *Declarations.* Some accommodating theology.

65. Pious scholars rare; our seniors changed their minds.

23. 74. Beg.

19. Do not give to relatives; rely on the advisers given by the superior.

1. Do not practise self-examination. *Declarations.*

2. Absolute poverty; no masses [fees] either for a sermon or in compensatory alms.

4. *Declarations* as much authority as the *Constitutions.*

End. Read the *Constitutions* every month.

149. The *Declarations* ruin everything.

154. Do not encourage the giving of perpetual alms, nor ask for them as rightful, nor alms-box. *Declarations: not as alms.*

200. 4. Advise us of everything.

190. *Constitutions* do not want 'troop'; *Declarations* 'troop' interpreted.

A universal and immortal body.

Great and unscrupulous attachment for the community – dangerous.

Religion would make us all rich but for our *Constitutions*, and so we are poor.

With or without true religion we are strong. (956)

953 [The fragment which follows consists of notes made by Pascal against quotations, in Arnauld's hand, taken from correspondence of Jesuit Generals. Only the page reference is given here]

373. Read the Fathers so as to adapt them to one's fancy instead of forming one's own ideas on those of the Fathers.

390. Modesty.

392. The Mass. I do not know what he is saying.

408. Politics.

409. By misfortune, or rather singular good fortune for the Society, the actions of one are ascribed to all.

410. Strictly obey the bishops. It must not appear that we are taking it on ourselves to stand up to them like St Xavier.

412. Wills, lawsuits.

413. They add to, they even invent false stories.

432. Probability: *A pious man is reliable, he is probable, he does not lack authority.*

433. Failure to punish slanderers.

437. The Society must not be ruined.

441. Disobedience in order to further their reputation.

442. Disobedience, seek support of the great.

443. They do unseemly things, incompatible with the Society and say that great nobles importune them to do so; but it is they who importune the nobles, so that either their enmity must be incurred by refusing them, or the Society is ruined if they get what they want.

443. Chastity.

445. Poverty. Laxity of opinions opposed to truth.

446. Vineyards, etc. (958)

954 Analyse the reason for censure by considering the phenomena and produce a hypothesis consistent with them all.

The habit makes the doctrine.

You have so many penitents who go to confession only once a year.

I thought it was one opinion against another.

When someone is so wicked that he no longer feels the slightest remorse, he is not sinning any more.

So you remorselessly persecute M. Arnauld.

I distrust this doctrine, because it is too kind to me, considering how wicked I am said to be.

Why do you not choose some really gross heresy?

I distrust the agreement between them, considering their individual disagreements.

I will wait for them to agree before taking sides. For one friend I should make too many enemies. I am not learned enough to reply to them.

I certainly used to think that one would be damned for not having the right thoughts, but it is news to me that no one has any.

How does that help? To comfort the righteous and ward off despair? No, for no one can be in a position to believe himself righteous.

M. Chamillard would be a heretic, which is patently false, because he wrote in M. Arnauld's defence.

In 1647 there was grace for all; by 1650 it was rarer.

M. Cornet's grace. . . .

Luther: anything but the truth.

If there had never arisen such occasions within the Church: but I take my parish priest's word for that.

At the slightest inconvenience caused by grace they create other kinds, for they dispose of it as if it were their handiwork.

Only one tells the truth.

A kind of grace for each occasion, for each person; grace for the great, grace for rogues.

In short, M. Chamillard comes so close to it, that if these were steps leading down into nothingness, this sufficient grace comes as close as can be.

Absurd to be a heretic for that.

Everyone was taken by surprise, for such a thing had never been seen in Scripture, in the Fathers, etc.

How long, Father, has this been an article of faith? At the most it is only since the words 'proximate power' came in. And I believe it created this heresy at birth and was born solely to this end.

This censure only forbids us to speak like that of St Peter, and nothing else. – I am much obliged to them.

They are clever people; they were afraid that the letters written to provincials. . . .

It was not worth it for one word.

Childish innocence.

Praised without being known.

Evil creditors.

I think they are sorcerers.

Luther: anything but the truth.

Heretical member.

Unam sanctam.

The *Illuminations* did us harm.

The same proposition is sound in one author and wicked in another. Yes, but there are other unsound propositions.

Some people defer to censure, others to arguments, and all to reason [?]. I am amazed then that you did not choose the general rather than the particular method, or at least did not combine the two.

Multiplicity of graces.

Jansenist translators.

St Augustine has most because his enemies are so divided. Something else to be considered is an unbroken tradition of 12,000 [1,200 years?] popes, councils, etc.

M. Arnauld must have some really wicked ideas to infect those he embraces.

The advantage to them of the censure is that when they are censured they will fight, and say they are imitating the Jansenists.

What a relief! No Frenchman is a good Catholic!

Litanies. Clement VIII, Paul V, censure. God visibly protects us.

Man is truly out of his mind. He cannot create a mite.

Instead of God the grace to go there.   (925)

955   And they are preparing to expel from the Church those who refuse to admit this. Everyone declares that the Propositions are so. M. Arnauld and his friends protest that they condemn them

in themselves, wherever they may be found, and if they are in Jansenius, they condemn them there.

And even if they are not there, if the heretical sense of these Propositions condemned by the Pope can be found in Jansenius, they condemn Jansenius.

But you are not satisfied with these protestations; you want him to assert that these Propositions occur word for word in Jansenius. He has replied that he cannot assert this, because he does not know whether this is the case, but that he has looked for them there, as have countless others, and has never been able to find them. They have asked you and everyone else, to give the page references of where they are, and no one has ever done so. And yet you want to cut him off from the Church for his refusal, although he condemns all that the Church condemns, solely because he will not assert that certain words or a certain sense occur in a book in which he has never found them, and in which no one will point them out to him. Indeed, Father, this pretext is so empty that the Church has perhaps never known such strange, unjust and tyrannical procedure.

The Church can easily oblige.

Clement VIII.

If anyone said....

There is no need to be a theologian to see that their only heresy lies in the fact that they oppose you. I have had the same experience, and the general proof of it can be seen in all those who have attacked you.

The Jansenist clergy of Rouen.

Vow of Caen.

You believe your intentions to be so honourable that you make them the subject of a vow.

Two years ago their heresy was the Bull, last year it was 'inward', six months ago it was 'word for word', now it is 'the sense'.

Is it not obvious that all you want is to make them heretics? Blessed Sacrament.

I attacked you on behalf of others.

You are quite ridiculous to make so much fuss over the Propositions. It is nothing; this must be realized.

Without authors' names; but once your intentions were known, there were seventy against it – Date the decree.

So that the man you had not been able to convict of heresy out of his own mouth, etc.

Who will hold it against me that I showed all this to be in your own authors, even the most dreadful things?

For it all comes out.

Have you nothing else to answer, and no other way of proving it?

He either knows it is or is not, or he is doubtful; either sinner or heretic.

Preface, Villeloin.

Jansenius, Aurelius[1], Arnauld, *Provincial Letters*.

A body of lost souls.

All the alms-boxes of Saint-Merry could be opened without making you any less innocent.

After Pelagius.

So that is not strange. False right. Baronius.

For myself, I would sooner be an impostor than. . . .

What reasons do you give for it? You say I am a Jansenist, that Port Royal maintains the Five Propositions, and that I maintain them: three lies.

Just considering the heathen:

The same light which reveals supernatural truths, reveals them without error, whereas the light. . . .

How could the sense of Jansenius occur in propositions which are not by him?

And please do not come and tell me that it is not you but the bishops who are making all this fuss. I should give you some answers which you, and others, would not like. Spare me that answer.

Either it is in Jansenius or not. If it is there, he is thereby condemned; if it is not, why do you want to have him condemned?

Let us see just one of your Father Escobar's propositions condemned! I will go with Escobar in one hand and the censure in the other, and produce reasoned arguments.

1. Pseudonym of St Cyran.

The Pope has not condemned two things; he only condemned the sense of the Propositions.

Will you say he did not condemn it? 'But it implies the sense of Jansenius,' said the Pope. I see very well that the Pope thought so because of your *word for word*, but he did not say so on pain of excommunication.

Why should he, and the bishops of France, not have believed it? You said *word for word* and they did not know you to be capable of saying so although it was not true.

Impostors: they had not seen my Fifteenth Letter.   (929)

956   *Diana.*

'This is how Diana can be used!

11. "It is permitted not to give benefices without cure of souls to the most worthy," the Council of Trent seems to say the opposite, but this is how he proves it: "For if that were so all prelates would be in a state of damnation, for this is what all of them do."

11. "King and Pope are not obliged to choose the most worthy." If that were so, the Pope and kings would bear a terrible burden.

21. And elsewhere: "If this opinion were not correct, penitents and confessors would have a lot of trouble, and that is why I consider it should be followed in practice."

And in another place where he sets out the conditions necessary for making a sin mortal, he puts in so many circumstantial details that it becomes barely possible to commit mortal sin, and when he has made his point he cries: "How gentle and light is the yoke of the Lord!"

11. And elsewhere: "One is not obliged to give away what is superfluous to one's needs as alms to relieve the ordinary necessities of the poor." If the contrary were true, most of the rich and their confessors would have to be condemned.'

I was becoming impatient with such arguments, when I said to the good Father: 'But who prevents us from saying that they are condemned?'

'He anticipated that as well in this passage,' he answered,

'where after saying (22) "If that were true the richest would be damned," he adds: "To this Arragonius replies that they are so, and Bauny, a Jesuit, adds, what is more, that their confessors are too, but I reply with Valentia, another Jesuit, and other authors, that there are several reasons for excusing the rich and their confessors." '

I was delighted with this argument, when he finished off with this one:

'If this opinion about restitution were correct, what a lot of restitution would have to be made!'

'Oh Father,' I said, 'what an excellent reason!'

'Oh,' said the Father, 'there is a man for you!' – 'Oh Father,' I replied, 'how many people would be damned but for your casuists!' – 'How wrong people are,' he answered, 'not to let us talk about them!' – 'Oh Father, how broad you make the path that leads to heaven! What a lot of people find it! Here is. . . .'   (928)

957 It [the Eucharist] is wholly the body of Christ, in his jargon, but he cannot say that it is the whole body of Christ.

The union of two things without change does not enable us to say that one becomes the other.

Thus the soul united to the body,

And fire to wood without change.

But some change is needed for the form of one to become the form of the other:

Thus the union of the Word with humanity.

Because my body without my soul would not be the body of a man, therefore my soul united with any part of matter will form my body.

He does not distinguish the necessary from the sufficient condition: union is necessary but not sufficient.

The left arm is not the right.

Impenetrability is a property of bodies.

Numerical identity in respect of the same time requires material identity.

Thus, if God united my soul to a body in China, the same body, *numerically identical*, would be in China.

The same river flowing over there is *numerically identical* to that flowing at the same time in China. (512)

958 Part I.L.2.c.1. s. iv.[1]

(Conjecture: there will be no difficulty in taking it another stage down and making it appear ridiculous.)

What is more absurd than to say that inanimate bodies have passions, fears, horrors? That lifeless bodies without feelings, and even incapable of life, have passions which presuppose at least a sentient soul to receive them? Moreover that the object of this horror should be the vacuum? What is there in the vacuum that could make them afraid? What could be baser and more ridiculous?

Nor is this all: That they have within themselves some principle of movement for avoiding a vacuum? Have they arms, legs, muscles, nerves? (75)

959 *If* does not signify indifference.
Malachi.
Isaiah: *If ye be willing*[2]
In the day [that thou eatest thereof]][3] (636)

960 What good has it done you to accuse me of scoffing at sacred things? You will not do any better by accusing me of imposture.

I have not had my say, as you will see.

I am no heretic. I have not maintained the Five Propositions. You say I have, but you do not prove it. I tell you that you said so, and I can prove it.

I have told you that you were impostors, and I can prove it. And that you have the insolence to make no secret of it. Brisacier, Meynier, d'Albi. And that you authorize it: *Annul*.[4]

When you believe M. Puys to be an enemy of the Society he was 'an unworthy pastor of his church, ignorant, heretical, a man of bad faith and morals', since then he has become 'a worthy pastor, a man of excellent faith and morals'.

1. Reference to the uncompleted *Treatise on the Vacuum* (1651).
2. Is. I. 19.   3. Gen. II. 17.
4. i.e. the criticisms of their enemies.

To slander: *this is great blindness of heart*.

To see no harm in it: *this is greater blindness of heart*.

To defend it instead of confessing it: *then the depths of iniquity close over a man*. 230. Prosper.

Great nobles are divided in civil wars,

And so are you in the civil war between men.

I want to tell you so to your face so that it carries more weight.

I am sure of the approval of those who examine the books, but those who only read their titles (and they are the majority) might take you at your word. Regular clergy cannot be impostors; our people have already had their eyes opened by the cogency of quotations, and now the rest must have their eyes opened by *annul*.

By virtue of senatorial decrees and votes of the people. . . .[1]

Ask for similar passages.

I am very glad that you are publishing the same thing as I.

Avoid contentions. St Paul.[2]

He made me the cause.

I cannot help seeing how embarrassed you are, for if you wanted to withdraw, it would be done, but. . . .

The saints go to great lengths to make themselves out to be criminals, and denounce their most virtuous actions, and these men go to great lengths to excuse the most wicked actions.

Do not pretend that this is what happens in debate. If your works were printed in full, and in French, everyone would be able to judge.

A building of equal beauty outside, but on unsound foundations, built by heathen sages; the devil deceives men because of an apparent resemblance, based on quite different foundations.

No one has ever had a cause as good as mine, and no one has ever offered so fine a target as you.

Men of the world do not believe they are on the right path.

The more weakness they discern in my person, the more authority they confer on my cause.

You say I am a heretic. Is that allowed? And if you are not afraid that men will do me justice, are you not afraid that God will?

1. Cf. 507.   2. Titus III. 9.

You will feel the power of truth and yield to it.

I ask people to do me the justice of not taking them at their word any more.

You would have to oblige people to believe you on pain of mortal sin. *Annul.*

It is a sin rashly to believe slanders.

They did not rashly believe the slanderer. St Augustine.

By falling on every side he made me fall, in accordance with the rule about slander.

There is something supernatural about such blindness. *The destiny whereof they were worthy.*[1]

I am alone against 30,000 – Not so. You keep to the Court [?]; you to imposture, I to truth: that is all my strength. If I lose that I am lost, and there will be no lack of people to denounce and punish me. But the truth is on my side, and we shall see who will prevail.

I do not deserve to defend religion, but you do not deserve to defend error. And I hope that God in his mercy, overlooking the evil that is in me and looking at the good that is in you, will graciously grant to us all that the truth will not fail in my hands and lies will not. . . .

You will lie most shamelessly.

230. The extreme sin is to defend it. *Annul.*

340. 23. The fortune of the wicked.

A man shall be commended according to his wisdom.[2]

66. *The work of lying.*

80. Alms.

False piety, double sin.

Annul. Caramuel.

You threaten me.

Since you have only touched on that point, it means approving all the rest. (362, 921)

961 B. You do not know the prophecies unless you know that all this must happen – princes, prophets, pope, and even priests – and yet the Church must survive.

1. Wisdom XIX. 4.
2. Prov. XII. 8.

By the grace of God we have not yet reached that point. Woe unto you priests! But we hope that God will mercifully grant that we shall not be among them.

I Peter II: False prophets of the past, the image of those to come. (888)

962 'It cannot be as certain as all that,' said the Feuillant, 'because where there is dispute there is uncertainty.'

St Athanasius. St Chrysostom.

Morality. Infidels.

The Jesuits have not cast doubt on the truth, but have removed all doubt about their impiety.

Contradictions have always been left to blind the wicked, for anything offensive to truth and charity is wrong. That is the true principle. (902)

963 It is a matter of indifference to the human heart whether it believes there are three or four persons in the Trinity, but not ... And that is why they get so excited about maintaining one but not the other.

It is right to do the one, but the other must not be neglected. The same God who told us. . . .

And so anyone who believes one and not the other, does not believe it because God said so, but because his inclination is not opposed to it, and he is very glad to agree, and thus easily to have a witness to his conscience which. . . .

But it is a false witness. (940)

964 Letter about how the Jesuits have established themselves forcibly everywhere.

Supernatural blindness.

The morality which has at its head a crucified God.

Here are those who have vowed to obey *as though it were Christ*.

Decadence of the Jesuits.

Our religion which is wholly divine.

A casuist. Mirouer.

If you approve of him, that is a good sign.

It is strange that there is no means of giving them any idea of religion.

A crucified God.

They will be punished for taking this punishable affair of the schism separately.

But what an upheaval! In embracing it, the children love the agents of corruption, the enemies loathe them.

We are witnesses.

As regards the mass of casuists, far from throwing blame on the Church, on the contrary it throws the Church into mourning.

And so that we may be above suspicion,

Like the Jews, handing down the books, who are above suspicion in the eyes of the Gentiles, they hand us their *Constitutions*. (953)

965 Consequently, if it is true on the one hand that a few lax religious and a few corrupt casuists, who are not members of the hierarchy, have wallowed in such corruption, it remains true on the other hand that the true pastors of the Church, to whom the divine word has truly been entrusted, have preserved it intact against all the efforts of those who set out to ruin it.

Thus the faithful have no excuse for following the lax doctrines which are only offered to them by the alien hands of these casuists, instead of the sound doctrine which is presented to them by the fatherly hands of their own pastors. Unbelievers and heretics have no reason to adduce these abuses as evidence of a failure of divine providence towards the Church. For, as the Church resides properly speaking in the body of the hierarchy, there is so little to justify us concluding from the present state of affairs that God has abandoned it to corruption, that it has never been more clearly apparent than today that God is obviously defending it from corruption.

For, if a few of these men, who by an exceptional vocation have made it their profession to leave the world and assume the religious habit in order to pursue a state more perfect than that of ordinary Christians, have fallen into aberrations which appal ordinary Christians, becoming among us what the false prophets were among the Jews, then this is a particular and personal misfortune which must indeed be deplored. But this justifies no conclusions against the care God takes for his Church, because all these things have been so clearly foretold and it was announced so long ago that such temptations would be caused by this type of person, that, when we are properly instructed, we can see in this the signs of God's guidance rather than of his forgetting us. (889)

966 Both sides must be given a hearing: that is what I have been careful to do.

When we have heard only one side, we are always biased in its favour, but the opposite side makes us change our mind, whereas in this case the Jesuit confirms it.

Not what they do, but what they say.

All the outcry is directed at me. I do not mind. I know to whom I am accountable.

Jesus was a stone of stumbling.

Open to condemnation, condemned,

Politics.

'We have found two obstacles to our plan of making things easier for men: one, the inward laws of the Gospel, the other the outward laws of religion and the state.'

'We control the first, and this is how we have dealt with the others: *Amplify, restrict, from the greater to the less, more recent.*'

Probable.

They argue like people proving it is night at noon.

If arguments as bad as these are probable, anything may be.

First argument: [the husband] *master of conjugal acts.* Molina.

Second argument: *He cannot be compensated.* Lessius.

Contrast not saintly but abominable maxims.

Bauny burner of barns.[1]

Mascarenhas, Council of Trent on priests in state of mortal sin, *as soon as possible.* (926)

967 In vain has the Church laid down such terms as anathema, heresy, etc. They are used against her. (896)

1. Because he found that circumstances might justify allowing a building to burn down rather than spread the alarm.

968 Difference between dinner and supper.

In God word and intention do not differ, for he is truthful, nor do word and effect, for he is mighty, nor do means and effect, for he is wise. (St Bernard, last sermon on *Missus* [Luke I. 26]).

St Augustine, *City of God*, v. x: This is a general rule. God can do anything, except for those things which, if he were to do them, would make him no longer almighty, like dying, being deceived, lying, etc.

More than one evangelist as confirmation of the truth.

Discrepancy between them useful.

Eucharist after the Last Supper. The truth after the figure.

Ruin of Jerusalem, figure for the ruin of the world.

Forty years after the death of Christ.

Jesus does not know either as man or emissary. (Matt. XXIV. 36)

Jesus condemned by Jews and Gentiles.

Jews and Gentiles prefigured by the two sons. (Augustine, *City of God*, XX. xxix)   (654)

969 'Work out your salvation with fear.'[1]

The poor men of grace.

Ask and it shall be given you.[2] Therefore it is in our power to ask. On the contrary it is not; because obtaining is in our power, praying is not. For, because salvation is not in our power, while obtaining an answer to our prayer is, prayer is not in our power.

The righteous man ought then to put no more hope in God, for he should not hope but try to obtain what he asks for.

Let us therefore conclude that, since man is now unable to use this proximate power, and that it is not God's will that this is what should keep him from estrangement, that it is only an effective power that does stop him from being estranged.

Therefore those who are estranged do not have this power, [by][3] which there is no estrangement from God, and those who are not estranged do have this effective power.

1. Phil. II. 12.   2. Matt. VII. 7.
3. Pascal actually wrote 'without', but the sense is clear.

Thus those, who, after persevering for some time in prayer through this effective power, cease to pray, lack this effective power.

And therefore in this sense God is the first to withdraw. (514)

970 *Concerning Esdras.* Legend: that the books were burned with the temple; disproved by Maccabees [II Macc. II. 1]: 'Jeremiah gave them the law.'

Legend: That he recited it all by heart; Josephus and Esdras note that he read the book.

Baronius, year A.D. 180: *None can be found among the ancient Hebrews who maintains that the books were destroyed, and restored by Esdras, except Esdras, Book IV.*

Legend: That he changed the letters.

Philo, in his *Life of Moses: The language and characters in which the law of old was written remained so until the Seventy.*

Josephus says the law was in Hebrew when it was translated by the Seventy.

Under Antiochus and Vespasian, when there was an attempt to destroy the books and there were no more prophets, this failed, and under the Babylonians, when no persecution took place and there were so many prophets, would they have let them be burnt?

Josephus scoffs at the Greeks who would not suffer. . . .

He [Noah] *could easily have recreated it from memory* [the book of Enoch] *destroyed by the violence of the cataclysm, just as every document of Jewish scripture is agreed to have been restored by Esdras, after the destruction of Jerusalem by the attack of the Babylonians.* (Tertullian, *De Cultu femin.*, I. iii)

He says that Noah could just as easily have reconstructed from memory the book of Enoch, lost in the Flood, as Esdras was able to reconstruct the scriptures lost during the captivity.

During the captivity of the people under Nebuchadnezzar, when the books had been destroyed, God inspired Esdras, the priest of the tribe of Levi, to rehearse all the sayings of the former prophets, and to restore to the people the law given them by Moses. (Eusebius, *Hist.*, Bk V. viii)

He adduces this to prove that there is nothing incredible

in the Seventy having explained the Holy Scriptures with the consistency which we admire, and he took this from Irenaeus, III. XXV.

St Hilary, in his preface to the Psalms, says that Esdras put the Psalms in order.

The origin of this tradition derives from IV Esdras XIV.

God was glorified, and the Scriptures recognized as truly divine, all relating the same thing in the same words and with the same phrases, from beginning to end, so that even the Gentiles present recognized that the Scriptures had been translated by divine inspiration. And that there was nothing strange in God working this in them, since, when the Scriptures had been destroyed during the captivity of the people under Nebuchnadnezzar, and the Jews had gone back seventy years later into their own country in the time of Artaxerxes, king of the Persians, he then inspired Esdras, the priest of the tribe of Levi, to rehearse all the sayings of the former prophets and restore to the people the law given them by Moses.[1]   (632)

971 *Against the story of Esdras.*

II Macc. II.

Josephus, *Antiquities*, II. i. Cyrus released the people on the strength of Isaiah's prophecy. The Jews peacefully owned possessions in Babylon under Cyrus, so they could well have had the law.

Josephus, in the whole of the history of Esdras, says not a word about this reconstruction.

II Kings XVII. 27.   (633)

972 If the story of Esdras is credible, we must then believe that Scripture is Holy Scripture, for this story is based solely on the authority of those who claim that of the Seventy, which proves Scripture to be holy.

Thus if this tale is true, it proves our point, and if it is not, we can prove it in other ways. Those who would like to

---

1. In the English Bible IV Esdras appears as II Esdras. The concluding passage is Pascal's Latin translation of the text of Eusebius of which he had quoted the original Greek conclusion just above. This fragment, and the two following ones, were for some reason only included in the duplicate copy, although the originals survive.

destroy the truth of our religion, based on Moses, in fact establish its truth by the same authority with which they attack it, and so by this dispensation of providence it continues to survive. (634)

973 These are the results of the sins of the people and the Jesuits: the great wanted to be flattered, the Jesuits to be loved by the great. They all deserved to be abandoned to the spirit of lies, some to deceive, others to be deceived. They have been grasping, ambitious, pleasure-loving. *They shall heap unto themselves teachers.*[1] Worthy disciples of such teachers, *they are worthy*, they looked for flatterers and found them. (919)

974 Just as the only object of peace within states is to safeguard people's property, so the only object of peace within the Church is to safeguard the truth, which is its property and the treasure wherein lies its heart. And, just as it would be contrary to the purpose of peace to allow foreigners into a state to pillage it without resistance, for fear of disturbing the peace (because, as peace is only just and useful for safeguarding property, it becomes unjust and pernicious when it permits it to be lost and war, which can defend it, becomes both just and necessary), likewise, in the Church, when truth is injured by enemies of the faith, when attempts are made to uproot it from the hearts of the faithful, and make error reign in its stead, would it be serving or betraying the Church to remain at peace? And is it not obvious that, just as it is a crime to disturb the peace when truth reigns, it is also a crime to remain at peace when the truth is being destroyed? There is therefore a time when peace is just and a time when it is unjust. It is written: 'There is a time for war and a time for peace,'[2] and it is the interests of the truth which distinguish between them. But there is not a time for truth and a time for error, and it is written, on the contrary: 'The truth of the Lord endureth for ever,'[3] and that is why Jesus Christ, who said that he had come to bring peace, said

---

1. II Tim. IV. 3. This and the following fragment are known only through the duplicate copy.
2. Eccl. III. 8.
3. Ps. CXVII. 2.

also that he had come to bring war; but he did not say that he had come to bring both truth and falsehood. Truth is therefore the first rule and ultimate purpose of things. (949)

C. FRAGMENTS FROM OTHER SOURCES

[These survive neither in the original nor in either of the two official copies, but have come down to us from a variety of sources.]

975 Men often take their imagination for their heart, and often believe they are converted as soon as they start thinking of becoming converted. (275)

976 The last thing one discovers in composing a work is what to put first. (19)

977 The most unreasonable things in the world become the most reasonable because men are so unbalanced. What could be less reasonable than to choose as ruler of a state the eldest son of a queen? We do not choose as captain of a ship the most highly born of those aboard. Such a law would be ridiculous and unjust, but because men are, and always will be, as they are, it becomes reasonable and just, for who else could be chosen? The most virtuous and able man? That sets us straight away at daggers drawn, with everyone claiming to be the most virtuous and able. Let us then attach this qualification to something incontrovertible. He is the king's eldest son: that is quite clear, there is no argument about it. Reason cannot do any better, because civil war is the greatest of evils.[1] (320)

Self - love

978 The nature of self-love and of this human self is to love only self and consider only self. But what is it to do? It cannot prevent the object of its love from being full of faults and wretchedness: it wants to be great and sees that it is small; it wants to be happy and sees that it is wretched; it wants to be perfect and sees that it is full of imperfections; it wants to be the object of men's love and esteem and sees that its faults deserve only their

1. This fragment is in fact a version of fragments 30 and 94, edited by Nicole but not published until after his death.

dislike and contempt. The predicament in which it thus finds itself arouses in it the most unjust and criminal passion that could possibly be imagined, for it conceives a deadly hatred for the truth which rebukes it and convinces it of its faults. It would like to do away with this truth, and not being able to destroy it as such, it destroys it, as best it can, in the consciousness of itself and others; that is, it takes every care to hide its faults both from itself and others, and cannot bear to have them pointed out or noticed.

It is no doubt an evil to be full of faults, but it is a still greater evil to be full of them and unwilling to recognize them, since this entails the further evil of deliberate self-delusion. We do not want others to deceive us; we do not think it right for them to want us to esteem them more than they deserve; it is therefore not right either that we should deceive them and want them to esteem us more than we deserve.

Thus, when they merely reveal vices and imperfections which we actually possess, it is obvious that they do us no wrong, since they are not responsible for them, but are really doing us good, by helping us to escape from an evil, namely our ignorance of these imperfections. We ought not to be annoyed that they know them and despise us, because it is right that they should know us for what we are and despise us if we are despicable.

These are the feelings which would spring from a heart full of equity and justice. What then should we say of ours, seeing it quite differently disposed? For is it not true that we hate the truth and those who tell it to us, and we like them to be deceived to our advantage, and want to be esteemed by them as other than we actually are?

Here is a proof of it which appals me. The Catholic religion does not oblige us to reveal our sins indiscriminately to everyone; it allows us to remain hidden from all other men, with one single exception, to whom it bids us reveal our innermost heart and show ourselves for what we are. There is only this one man in the world whom it orders us to disillusion, and it lays on him the obligation of inviolable secrecy, which means that he might as well not possess the knowledge of us that he has. Can anything milder and more charitable be imagined? And yet, such is man's corruption that he finds even this law harsh, and this is one of the main reasons why a large part of Europe has revolted against the Church.

How unjust and unreasonable the heart of man is, that he should resent the obligation to behave towards one man as it would be right, in some ways, to behave towards all! For is it right that we should deceive them?

This aversion for the truth exists in differing degrees, but it may be said that it exists in everyone to some degree, because it is inseparable from self-love. It is this false delicacy which makes those who have to correct others choose so many devious ways and qualifications to avoid giving offence. They must minimize our faults, pretend to excuse them, and combine this with praise and marks of affection and esteem. Even then such medicine still tastes bitter to self-love, which takes as little of it as possible, always with disgust and often even with secret resentment against those administering it.

The result is that anyone who has an interest in winning our affection avoids rendering us a service which he knows to be unwelcome; we are treated as we want to be treated; we hate the truth and it is kept from us; we desire to be flattered and we are flattered; we like being deceived and we are deceived.

This is why each rung of fortune's ladder which brings us up in the world takes us further from the truth, because people are more wary of offending those whose friendship is most useful and enmity most dangerous. A prince can be the laughing-stock of Europe and the only one to know nothing about it. This does not surprise me: telling the truth is useful to the hearer but harmful to those who tell it, because they incur such odium. Now those who live with princes prefer their own interests to that of the prince they serve, and so they have no wish to benefit him by harming themselves.

This misfortune is no doubt greater and more common among those most favoured by fortune, but more modest people are not exempt, because we always have some interest in being popular. Thus human life is nothing but a perpetual illusion; there is nothing but mutual deception and flattery. No one talks about us in our presence as he would in our absence. Human relations are only based on this mutual deception; and few friendships would survive if everyone knew what his friend said about him behind his back, even though he spoke sincerely and dispassionately.

Man is therefore nothing but disguise, falsehood and hypocrisy, both in himself and with regard to others. He does not want to be told the truth. He avoids telling it to others, and all these tendencies, so remote from justice and reason, are naturally rooted in his heart. (100)

979 The day of Judgment.

'So this, Father, is what you call the meaning of Jansenius! So this is what you give the Pope and bishops to understand!'

'If the Jesuits were corrupt and it were true that we were alone, that would be all the more reason for us to stand our ground.'

What war has established, let not a feigned peace remove.

As an angel of the Lord [so is my lord the king] *moved neither by blessing or by cursing.*[1]

They are attacking the greatest of Christian virtues, namely love of truth.

'If this is what the signature means, allow me to explain, so that there is no room for ambiguity; for it must be admitted that many people think that signing signifies consent.'

'If the proper official did not sign, the decree would be invalid; if the Bull were not signed, it would be valid; so it is not. . . .'

'But you might be mistaken.' – 'I swear that I believe that I might be mistaken, but I do not swear that I believe that I am in fact mistaken.'

'No one is guilty for not believing, and they will be guilty for swearing without believing . . . fine questions. . . .'

'I am sorry to be telling you here; I am only giving an account.'

'With Escobar this puts them on top; but they do not take it like that, and showing how much they dislike finding themselves between God and the Pope. . . .'[2] (945)

1. Cf. II Sam. XIV. 17 (Vulgate version).
2. Fragment of Nineteenth *Provincial Letter*.

980 They say the Church says what it does not say and that it does
      not say what it does.   (918b)

981 What would the Jesuits be without probability and probability
      without the Jesuits?

      Take away probability and you cannot please people any
      more, bring in probability and you cannot displease them. It
      used to be difficult to avoid sins, and difficult to expiate them;
      now there are any number of tricks for making it easy to avoid
      them, and it is easy to expiate them.   (918)

982 We have made uniformity out of diversity, for all of us are
      uniform, inasmuch as we have all become uniform.   (918c)

983 M. de Roannez used to say: 'The reasons occur to me after-
      wards, but first of all the thing pleases or shocks me without my
      knowing why, and yet it shocks me for reasons I only discover
      later.' But I do not think that it shocks for reasons we discover
      afterwards, but that we only discover the reasons because it
      does shock.   (276)

984 Only a sudden death is to be feared, and that is why confessors
      live in the homes of the great.   (216)

985 ... now probability is necessary for the other maxims, like
      that of Lamy and the slanderer.

      By their fruits.[1] Judge their faith by their morals.

      Probability does not mean much without corrupt means, and
      the means are nothing without probability.

      It is a pleasure to be confident of being able to do well and
      know how to do well: '*To know and be able.*' Grace and proba-
      bility bring such pleasure, for we can account to God by relying
      on their authors.   (942)

986 We must show the heretics, who exploit Jesuit doctrine, that
      it is not that of the Church ...; and that our divisions do not
      debar us from unity.   (891)

987 If we condemned by delaying, you would be right. Unifor-
      mity without diversity is useless for others, diversity without

      1. Matt. VII. 20.

uniformity disastrous for us. One harmful outside, the other inside. (892)

988 But it is impossible that God should ever be the end if he is not the beginning. We look upwards, but we are standing on sand; and the earth will be dissolved, and we shall fall as we look up at the heavens. (488)

989 *The Jesuits.* The Jesuits have tried to combine God and the world, and have only earned the contempt of God and the world. For, as regards conscience, this is evident, and, as regards the world, they are no good at intrigue. They are powerful, as I have often said, but that is as regards other religious bodies. They enjoy enough credit to get a chapel built or preach a jubilee, but not to secure appointments to bishoprics or governorships. Their position as monks in the world is a very silly one, on their own admission (Father Brisacier, *Benedictines*). Yet you give way beneath those more powerful than yourselves, and use what small credit you enjoy to oppress those who intrigue less than you in the world. (935)

990 If by corrupting the bishops and the Sorbonne they have not succeeded in making their judgment just, they have succeeded in making their judges unjust. And thus, when they are condemned for it in the future, they will say *ad hominem* that the judges are unjust, and so refute their judgment. But that is pointless. For, as they cannot now maintain that the Jansenists have been properly condemned just because they have been condemned, they will then similarly be unable to maintain that they are wrongly condemned themselves because their judges are open to corruption. For their condemnation will be just, not because it is delivered by judges who are always just, but by judges who are just in this respect; and this will be shown by other proofs. (948)

991 As the two chief interests of the Church are preserving the piety of the faithful and converting heretics, we are overcome with grief when we see the factions formed today to introduce those errors most liable to exclude heretics from ever entering into communion with us, and fatally to corrupt the pious Catholics

remaining to us. The operations so openly directed today against the truths of religion, and those most important for salvation, do not merely fill us with distaste, but with alarm and dread, because, apart from what every Christian ought to feel about such disorders, we have the additional obligation of providing the remedy and using the authority given us by God in order to see that the people he has committed to our charge. . . . (952)

992 Annat. He plays the part of the disciple without ignorance and the teacher without presumption. (946b)

993 Their whole society of casuists cannot quieten erring conscience and that is why it is so important to choose good guides.

Thus they will be doubly guilty; for having followed paths they should not have followed, and for listening to doctors to whom they should not have listened. (909)

SAYINGS ATTRIBUTED TO PASCAL

I.   M. Pascal used to say of those authors who always refer to their works as: 'My book, my commentary, my history, etc.', that they sound like solid citizens with a place of their own, always talking about 'my house'. They would do better, this excellent man added, to say: 'Our book, or commentary, our history, etc.', considering that there is usually more of other people's property in it than their own.

II.   I cannot forgive Descartes: in his whole philosophy he would like to do without God; but he could not help allowing him a flick of the fingers to set the world in motion; after that he had no more use for God.

III.   1. People ask if I do not regret having written the *Provincial Letters* – I reply that, far from regretting it, if I had to write them at the present time [1662] I would make them even stronger.

2. People ask why I named the authors from whom I took all the detestable propositions I quoted. – I reply that, if I were in a town where there were twelve fountains, and I knew for certain that one of them was poisoned, I should be obliged to warn everyone not to draw water from that fountain, and, as people might think that it was just my imagination, I should be obliged to name the person who had poisoned it rather than expose a whole town to the risk of being poisoned.

3. People ask why I used a pleasant, ironic, and amusing style. – I reply that, if I had written in a dogmatic style, only scholars would have read it, and they did not need to, because they knew as much about it as I: thus I thought I must write so as to attract women and worldly people to read my letters, so that they should realize the dangers of all these maxims and propositions, which were everywhere current at the time and easily gained acceptance.

4. People ask if I have myself read all the books I quote. – I reply that I have not; it would certainly have meant spending my life reading very bad books; but I read Escobar right through

twice; and, as for the others, I got my friends to read them, but I did not use a single passage without reading it myself in the book quoted, going into the context involved, and reading the passage before and after it, to avoid all risk of quoting an objection as an answer, which would have been reprehensible and unjust.

IV. A fine job for M. Arnauld, working out a system of logic! The needs of the Church demand all his labours.

V. He was often heard to say (in connexion with the education of a prince) that there was nothing to which he would sooner contribute if invited, and he would willingly give up his life for something so important.

VI. When the late M. Pascal wanted to give an example of a fantasy for which obstinacy could win approval, he usually put forward Descartes' opinions on matter and space.

VII. Christian piety destroys the human self, and human civility conceals and suppresses it.

VIII. M. Pascal wrote on the back of his Bible: 'All the false beauties we find in St Augustine have their admirers, and many of them.'

IX. The late M. Pascal called Cartesianism 'the Romance of Nature, something like the story of Don Quixote'.

X. *M. le Maistre. pleas.*

M. Pascal made fun of them and told M. le Maistre that he had however written very well for the bigwigs of the Law Courts who did not understand a word of it.

XI. M. Pascal wanted all forms of poetic diction to be good French; it was fine if they were noble and sustained, but otherwise it was just rubbish.

ADDITIONAL *PENSÉES*

These were discovered by M. Jean Mesnard and first published in *Blaise Pascal, Textes inédits*, Paris, Desclée de Brouwer, 1962.

1. The Jesuits thus oblige people either to accept error or swear that they have done so, force them either into error or perjury and rot either mind or heart.

2. For, although they had taken place some two thousand years before, so few generations had elapsed that they were as new to the men of those times as those which occurred some three hundred years ago are to us today. This is because the earliest men lived so long, so that Shem, who saw Lamech, etc. . . . This proof is sufficient to convince reasonable people of the truth of the Flood and Creation, and it shows the Providence of God; for, seeing that the Creation was beginning to recede into the past, he provided a historian who can be called contemporary and entrusted the care of his book to a whole people. And a further remarkable fact is that this book has been accepted unanimously and unquestioningly not only by the whole Jewish people, but also by all the kings and peoples of the earth, who have received it with quite special respect and veneration.

3. It is a good thing that those persons who have been inwardly renewed by grace should be induced to perform works of piety and penance proportionate to their ability, because both are preserved by the proportion existing between the goodness of the works and the spirit in which they are performed. When someone not yet inwardly renewed is forced to perform extraordinary works of piety and penance, both are spoiled, the man corrupting the works through his wickedness, and the works proving too much for the weakness of the man, who is unable to bear them. It is a bad sign when someone is seen producing outward results as soon as he is converted. The order of charity is to drive roots into the heart before producing good works outside.

4. I feel in myself a certain malice which prevents me from agreeing with Montaigne when he says we grow less lively and resolute with age. I would not wish that to be so. I am envious of myself. My self at twenty is no longer me.

5. Sleep, you say, is the image of death; for my part I say that it is rather the image of life.

6. Aristotle, who wrote a treatise *On the Soul*, only talks, according to Montaigne, about the effects of the soul, which is what everyone knows, and never says anything about its essence, or origin, or nature, which is what people want to know.

7. People go away and hide themselves for eight months in the country so that they can shine for four months at Court.

8. I relish no pleasure, says Montaigne, unless I can share it; a sign of how man esteems man.

9. Scripture sends man to the ant; a clear indication of the corruption of his nature. How splendid it is to see the master of the world sent off to the animals as though to the masters of wisdom!

10. When someone realizes that he has said or done something silly, he always thinks it will be the last time. Far from concluding that he will do many more silly things, he concludes that this one will prevent him from doing so.

11. Philosophers in the Schools talk of virtue and rhetoricians of eloquence without knowing what these things are. Present the former with a truly virtuous but inconspicuous man, and the latter with a speech full of natural beauties but without conceits, and they will make nothing of them.

12. I find nothing easier than to treat all that as a fiction, but nothing harder than to answer it.

13. 'Why does God not show himself?' – 'Are you worthy?' – 'Yes.' – 'You are very presumptuous, and thus unworthy.' – 'No.' – 'Then you are just unworthy.'

14. God is hidden. But he lets those who seek find him. Visible signs of him have always existed throughout the ages. Ours are the prophecies, other ages had other signs. These proofs all hang together: if one is true, the other is. Thus every age, having signs appropriate to itself, has thereby known the others. Those who saw the Flood believed in the Creation, and believed in the Messiah who was to come. Those who saw Moses believed in the Flood and the fulfilment of the prophecies, and we who see the prophecies fulfilled should believe in the Flood and Creation.

FOR THE BEST IN PAPERBACKS, LOOK FOR THE

In every corner of the world, on every subject under the sun, Penguin represents quality and variety – the very best in publishing today.

For complete information about books available from Penguin – including Puffins, Penguin Classics and Arkana – and how to order them, write to us at the appropriate address below. Please note that for copyright reasons the selection of books varies from country to country.

In the United Kingdom: Please write to *Dept E.P., Penguin Books Ltd, Harmondsworth, Middlesex, UB7 0DA.*

If you have any difficulty in obtaining a title, please send your order with the correct money, plus ten per cent for postage and packaging, to *PO Box No 11, West Drayton, Middlesex*

In the United States: Please write to *Dept BA, Penguin, 299 Murray Hill Parkway, East Rutherford, New Jersey 07073*

In Canada: Please write to *Penguin Books Canada Ltd, 2801 John Street, Markham, Ontario L3R 1B4*

In Australia: Please write to the *Marketing Department, Penguin Books Australia Ltd, P.O. Box 257, Ringwood, Victoria 3134*

In New Zealand: Please write to the *Marketing Department, Penguin Books (NZ) Ltd, Private Bag, Takapuna, Auckland 9*

In India: Please write to *Penguin Overseas Ltd, 706 Eros Apartments, 56 Nehru Place, New Delhi, 110019*

In the Netherlands: Please write to *Penguin Books Netherlands B.V., Postbus 195, NL–1380AD Weesp*

In West Germany: Please write to *Penguin Books Ltd, Friedrichstrasse 10–12, D–6000 Frankfurt Main 1*

In Spain: Please write to *Longman Penguin España, Calle San Nicolas 15, E–28013 Madrid*

In Italy: Please write to *Penguin Italia s.r.l., Via Como 4, I-20096 Pioltello (Milano)*

In France: Please write to *Penguin Books Ltd, 39 Rue de Montmorency, F-75003 Paris*

In Japan: Please write to *Longman Penguin Japan Co Ltd, Yamaguchi Building, 2–12–9 Kanda Jimbocho, Chiyoda-Ku, Tokyo 101*

PENGUIN CLASSICS

PENGUIN CLASSICS

Netochka Nezvanova   Fyodor Dostoyevsky

Dostoyevsky's first book tells the story of 'Nameless Nobody' and introduces many of the themes and issues which will dominate his great masterpieces.

Selections from the Carmina Burana   A verse translation by David Parlett

The famous songs from the *Carmina Burana* (made into an oratorio by Carl Orff) tell of lecherous monks and corrupt clerics, drinkers and gamblers, and the fleeting pleasures of youth.

Fear and Trembling   Søren Kierkegaard

A profound meditation on the nature of faith and submission to God's will which examines with startling originality the story of Abraham and Isaac.

Selected Prose   Charles Lamb

Lamb's famous essays (under the strange pseudonym of Elia) on anything and everything have long been celebrated for their apparently innocent charm; this major new edition allows readers to discover the darker and more interesting aspects of Lamb.

The Picture of Dorian Gray   Oscar Wilde

Wilde's superb and macabre novella, one of his supreme works, is reprinted here with a masterly Introduction and valuable Notes by Peter Ackroyd.

A Treatise of Human Nature   David Hume

A universally acknowledged masterpiece by 'the greatest of all British Philosophers' – A. J. Ayer